Constructing Townscapes

LISA C. TOLBERT

Constructing Townscapes

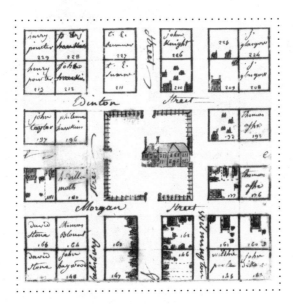

Space and Society
in Antebellum Tennessee

The University of North Carolina Press

Chapel Hill and London

© 1999 The University of North Carolina Press

All rights reserved

Manufactured in the United States of America

This book was set in Monotype Bulmer by Keystone Typesetting, Inc.

Book design by April Leidig-Higgins

The paper in this book meets the guidelines for permanence and
durability of the Committee on Production Guidelines for Book
Longevity of the Council on Library Resources.

Library of Congress Cataloging-in-Publication Data

Tolbert, Lisa C.   Constructing townscapes: space and society in
antebellum Tennessee / by Lisa C. Tolbert.

p. cm. Includes bibliographical references (p.) and index.

ISBN 0-8078-2466-6 (cloth : alk. paper)

ISBN 0-8078-4768-2 (pbk. : alk. paper)

1. Architecture—Tennessee. 2. Architecture, Modern—19th century—
Tennessee. 3. Cities and towns—Tennessee—History—19th century.

4. Vernacular architecture—Tennessee—History—19th century.

5. Architecture and society—Tennessee—History—19th century.

I. Title.

NA730.T4T65   1999   98-27260

307.3′162′09768—dc21   CIP

Portions of this book have appeared in substantially different form in
"Commercial Blocks and Female Colleges: The Small-Town Business
of Educating Ladies," in *Shaping Communities: Perspectives in
Vernacular Architecture VI*, edited by Carter L. Hudgins and Elizabeth
Collins Cromley (Knoxville: University of Tennessee Press, 1997); and
"Murder in Franklin: The Mysteries of Small-Town Slavery,"
Tennessee Historical Quarterly 57, no. 4 (December 1998). They are
reprinted here with permission of the publishers.

03 02 01 00 99   5 4 3 2 1

To my parents

Barbara Ann and E. C. Tolbert

CONTENTS

Contents

ACKNOWLEDGMENTS

This book has been a labor of love. I grew up in Murfreesboro, Tennessee, without really thinking much about the history of the place. There were signs of the past all around—the antebellum courthouse, the imposing residences lining East Main Street, and the modest houses with gingerbread porches along Maney Avenue. But my life revolved around entirely new parts of town—the suburbs and shopping centers, growth rings of small-town space extending outward from the public square. Ironically, studying the history of my hometown has often felt like visiting a foreign country. Some of the landmarks looked familiar, but understanding much of the terrain required an act of historical imagination. Along the way, I have been gratified to encounter many enthusiastic and helpful people who have made important contributions to my work.

The local historians of the county seats I studied have a detailed and refined knowledge that I despair of ever matching. Their generosity and openness have enriched my research immeasurably. I would particularly like to thank the members of the Rutherford County Historical Society, especially Mrs. Mabel Pittard, for sharing her collection of historical photographs. I regret that Jill K. Garrett, who spent her life researching and publishing the history of Columbia and Maury County, died before I completed this book. Her work has been invaluable to me. Thanks also to Paul Cross, Richard Quinn, Lynn Hulan, Tony Aldridge, Shacklett's Photography, Ed DeBoer at Oaklands Historic Site, John Holtzapple at the James K. Polk home, Paula Mitchell at Columbia's Historic Main Street, Canaday Photography, and Mary Pearce at the Heritage Foundation of Franklin.

I depended a great deal on the knowledge of staff members at local libraries and research institutions. Columbia, Franklin, Murfreesboro, and Shelbyville all have carefully tended local history collections. Van West and the Center for Historic Preservation at Middle Tennessee State University served as an important resource for maps, unpublished building surveys, and photographs. I also benefited from the expertise of staff members at the Tennessee State Library and Archives, the Special Collections Department of William R. Perkins Library at Duke University, and the Southern Historical Collection in Wilson Library at the University of North Carolina at Chapel Hill. My research assistants, Gwen Erickson and Pamela Gaddy, helped in the collection of new data during the revision of the book manuscript. I would also like to thank the University of North Carolina at Greensboro for a New Faculty Grant and two Summer Excellence Foundation Research Grants that supported the revision of this book. A summer stipend from the National Endowment for the Humanities provided support for the finishing touches.

Very special thanks go to members of my dissertation group at the University of North Carolina at Chapel Hill: Tom Baker, Tracy K'Meyer, and Kathy Nasstrom. Their careful reading and evaluation of the earliest drafts of these chapters helped me formulate the story during those initial stages of writing when my ideas were only just beginning to come into focus. I have learned to cherish our intellectual community even more since we have gone our separate ways in the profession. Molly Rozum has seen this project develop from dissertation to book, and I have been grateful for our friendship and mutual interest in cultural and architectural history on this long road.

Thanks also to the following colleagues who have read the manuscript in various pieces and stages: Tom Hanchett, John Hepp, Alison Isenberg, Marla Miller, Colleen Kriger, Nan Enstad, John Tolan, Phyllis Hunter, Bill Blair, Bill Link, and Loren Schwininger. All have combined encouragement with useful advice for improving the manuscript. My friend (and former boss) Lynn Holdzkom, archivist extraordinaire, went above and beyond the call by reading the entire manuscript twice.

As members of my dissertation committee, Don Mathews, John Florin, Jacquelyn Hall, and Peter Coclanis always offered constructive criticism. They achieved a rare balance—holding me to the highest standards of scholarship while giving me the academic freedom to take interpretive risks. I am most grateful for their continued support for and contributions to my work.

My work as a historian would have taken a very different form without the direction of John Kasson. He taught me the rich possibilities of cultural history and showed me how to use diverse elements of my training in a meaningful way. His enthusiasm for this project has sustained me through periods of doubt. He has been my teacher, mentor, colleague, and friend.

Finally, my parents, Barbara and E. C. Tolbert, instilled a love of history and architecture and, on a more practical note, provided room and board during the research and fieldwork in Tennessee. The dedication of this book reflects my tremendous gratitude to them.

Constructing Townscapes

Excavating the Foundations

In Search of Small-Town History

Virginia Shelton arrived in Murfreesboro, Tennessee, in 1850—just in time to witness a building boom. It was as if the small town had become a magnet for enterprising migrants. "Persons are moving in from other places & our town is receiving accessions of new citizens every few weeks," Virginia reported.[1] She listed several reasons why so many people were moving to town:

> Many come in for the purpose of educating their children—some purchase property & engage in business, others rent here & carry on their farming in the South. To-day a new couple came to reside in our town & the gentleman engages in merchandise. Every thing [*sic*] around us bears the appearance of a most flourishing community.[2]

Educating children, opening a store, finding a nice place to live—these were some of the attractions of the small towns that grew into "flourishing communities" before the Civil War.

Virginia Shelton's impression of growth and expansion in Murfreesboro was part of a widespread building boom in towns and cities of the Upper South sparked by railroad expansion in the 1850s. By 1860, a local newspaper editor in Columbia, the county seat of Maury County, Tennessee, marveled at the town's recent architectural transformation. "Within the past five years," he observed, "there has been almost a complete renovation of the town. . . . Upon the crumbling foundations of old frame houses, new and beautiful houses have risen, [along with] new and commodious business houses."[3] His observation reveals that not only had the towns been rebuilt but something had gone before—there had been foundations to build on. This evidence of architectural and spatial change suggests that in the years before the Civil War, the small-town South had a much more complex history of social development than we have heretofore understood.

Historians have learned much about the nature of rural and urban life in the antebellum South, but the regional landscape has been drawn largely as a map of contrasting extremes. Widely dispersed plantations and yeoman farmsteads composed the agrarian center,[4] while on the periphery there emerged a few major cities, largely riverine or coastal ports.[5] Small towns appear only incidentally in this landscape, as a backdrop for planter rituals on court days. Elizabeth Fox-Genovese represents the prevailing consensus that even though small towns and villages were "ubiquitous" in the region, "southern towns primarily reflected the countryside."[6]

The small-town South remains obscure, on one hand subsumed by an undifferentiated rural countryside and on the other assumed to be nothing more than an urban microcosm. Nevertheless, Fox-Genovese admits that small towns "constituted the focus of the lives of so many slaveholders, including planters."[7] And James Oakes has acknowledged that small towns were the primary stage for slaveholders' social, legal, political, and religious activity.[8] Despite such recognition of their wide distribution in the region, the assumption has been that nothing of much historical importance happened in small towns until Reconstruction transformed the racial geography of the South. The result is that the antebellum townscape appears changeless—without history—a group of stores and lawyers' offices clustered around a courthouse, a few houses and a church or two rounding out the sleepy village.

The county seats of Middle Tennessee suggest a much more dynamic picture of small-town change and development during the antebellum years. The Nashville Basin was the geographic and economic heart of Middle Tennessee—a region of rolling, fertile farmland named for the largest city on the Cumberland River. Nashville was both a county seat and the state capitol. By 1860 the Basin contained almost 308,000 people, nearly 28 percent of the state's total population, and Nashville itself housed about 17,000 people. Nearly 80 percent of all Middle Tennessee slaves lived in the Basin, where four out of ten people were in bondage.[9]

Introduction

The capital and four county seats in the Nashville Basin of Tennessee.

Few historians have recognized the distinction that fugitive slave Harriet Jacobs was so careful to make: "How often did I rejoice that I lived in a town where all the inhabitants knew each other!" she declared. "If I had been on a remote plantation, or lost among the multitude of a crowded city, I should not be a living woman at this day."[10] Jacobs emphasized the distinctive context of life in the small-town South—the spatial intimacy that imposed restrictions on her abusive master. She placed the small town at the center of her experience as a slave.

This book explores patterns of spatial and architectural change in four county seats of the Nashville Basin during the first half of the nineteenth century. Columbia in Maury County, Franklin in Williamson County, Murfreesboro in Rutherford County, and Shelbyville in Bedford County were the seats of four of the richest counties in the Basin.[11] All were established during the first decade of the nineteenth century, as local leaders worked out the rules for governing and developing the frontier of a new nation. The solutions they conceived directly influenced other American lives when small-town Middle Tennessee lawyers such as Andrew Jackson, James K. Polk, and Thomas Hart Benton, all of whom traveled the court circuits among these four towns, became the architects of a new national political system.

Architectural evidence and spatial experience in Middle Tennessee confirm Harriet Jacob's assertion that the small-town South must be understood on its own terms. The renovations of the 1850s were only the climax of several different building phases before the Civil War. Furthermore, architectural evidence shows that local entrepreneurs actually did much more than simply build bigger, more fashionable houses upon the "crumbling foundations" of the old. Their architectural choices document profound spatial reorganization—the creation of a series of distinctive townscapes, each defined by a different arrangement of buildings and particular uses of space. Such architectural and spatial transformations belie the picture of lethargic and languorous antebellum southern villages whose streets came to life only temporarily, once a month when court was in session. In fact, small county seats served as dynamic forces for cultural change, challenging the configuration of a southern landscape that places the plantation at the center of cultural authority.

Furthermore, analysis of the townscape as a vernacular form shows that although small-town builders were certainly inspired by urban models, they did not simply build urban microcosms. For example, owning and hiring slaves was common practice in Middle Tennessee county seats, where more than 40 percent of the population was unfree. But in stark contrast to southern cities, the free black population in small towns was almost nonexistent. The distinctions went beyond statistics. Slave experience in a small town was considerably different from life in a large city or on remote plantations. These relationships are best understood by focusing on the material world—the architectural fabric—of the small town and by studying the social interactions within that world. Through careful contextual analysis, the small town emerges to play a distinctive role in the southern landscape.

One of the chief obstacles to seeing and appreciating the small town is a problem of vocabulary. The terms "rural" and "urban" have been used interchangeably to describe certain aspects of town life—yet we do not have a comparable adjective that conveniently sums up the characteristics unique to small-town life. Historians have alternately described small towns as "urban" to distinguish them from the countryside and as "rural" to distinguish them from cities.[12] The effect has been to make town status relative, and thus ambiguous.

Darrett Rutman has recently taken a fresh look at the problem of antebellum southern towns, shifting the debate somewhat away from the question of whether towns should be considered more rural or more urban. Rutman argues instead that "the problem is not an urban South apart from the countryside but rather the town, village, and hamlet as integral to the structure of this (or any) agriculturally based society."[13] Rutman's conceptualization of small towns as integral components of a rural landscape, however, still gives us little chance to understand the distinctiveness of small-town life apart from rural experience. The small town remains an abstraction—somewhere on a continuum between rural and urban space.

The problem of vocabulary is reflected by the difficulties historians have experienced in creating a clear-cut quantitative measure of the difference between towns and cities. First is the practical problem that town residents were not consistently identified in the census. It was not that census takers failed to enumerate the people who lived in southern towns. The problem is that they listed inhabitants by county district without clearly noting the boundaries of hamlets or villages within the district. Sometimes the only hint of a change in the landscape comes when a relentless list of farmers gives way to the diversity of merchants, physicians, lawyers, and laborers. Relying exclusively on the census to measure town size can lead to serious underrepresentation of towns in the southern landscape.[14]

There is a second, more fundamental interpretive problem with relying on quantitative measurements of spatial differentiation to distinguish towns from cities. Small towns occupied an ambiguous quantitative position between urban and rural places. Urban historians have focused on cities with thousands of occupants, such as Charleston, South Carolina; Mobile, Alabama; New Orleans, Louisiana. In contrast to these cities, the county seats of Middle Tennessee contained 1,500 to 2,500 residents through most of the antebellum period. One of the largest towns in the region, Columbia, doubled in size during the 1850s to reach a total population of about 5,400 residents by 1860. Towns like Columbia were not precursors to large cities. They developed as small towns not because they were socially or economically stagnant but because they served distinctive roles as small towns.

In order to escape such quantitative ambiguity, the focus needs to move toward a cultural interpretation of small towns that takes account of the distinctive experience of town life. Using the material, architectural evidence of change in antebellum towns can help to overcome the central problem of definition that historians have encountered in previous approaches to the study of small towns. Analyzing spatial and architectural development offers a more reliable method for identifying and understanding the elusive small-town South. Town boundaries were in a sense fluid at the edges. Plantation houses encircled grid-pattern county seats like suburban town homes. Town lots resembled farms with their accompanying outbuildings, animals, and gardens. Towns expanded by subdividing encircling plantations, transforming "big house" into town house and farm into urban grid. Only through a highly visual examination of this dynamic landscape can historians begin to think like the nineteenth-century census takers, who recognized the existence of small towns, yet failed to locate their boundaries clearly in the census. What has often been obscured in the documentary record is prominently displayed in the buildings that shaped town life.

Because of its strategic role in migration and settlement, Middle Tennessee offers particularly fertile ground for developing a cultural definition of small-town experience. Lying between the Appalachian mountain culture of East Tennessee and the cotton culture of West Tennessee, Middle Tennessee represented what one historian has called a "third South," where farms averaged about 100 acres, slaves were numerous, and slaveholders grew a variety of staple crops for export.[15] This pattern places Middle Tennessee within the larger context of the Upland South settlement system produced from a synthesis of characteristics from the Virginia and Pennsylvania culture hearths. Evidence of this synthesis is present in the Pennsylvania street plans residents drew for their county seats and in the Virginian centrality of the courthouse.[16] The territory was divided into land grants to pay former soldiers following the Revolutionary War, and the trickle of westward migration across the Appalachians became a flood. Towns were an integral part of the settlement process of this region from the beginning.[17] County seats, in particular, proved crucial to systematic development of local resources and to further westward expansion. As centers of local government and economy, they were the most influential, if not the only, towns in a county.

The cultural influence of the county seat extended to shaping the most basic ideas about how towns should be designed to perform effectively their most important social and economic functions. County seats with their courthouse squares constituted a distinctive town form. Design choices derived from well-established rules of town planning with European antecedents. Along with their families and property, Tennesseans transported these ideas about acceptable county seat plans. They invariably arranged their streets in a grid design and reserved a square of land at the center, on high ground, for a courthouse and other public structures. Within the structure of the grid, however, there was room for variation at this central courthouse square. Significantly, new patterns began to replace traditional courthouse square designs as migrants crossed the Appalachians to organize the Tennessee frontier.[18] County seat plans in Middle Tennessee document the traditional forms transplanted by settlers, as well as new designs that emerged in the settlement process. Such experimentation demonstrates the important role small towns played as forces of cultural change in the region.

Nineteenth-century county seat residents used completely different language from modern-day historians to define their towns. John Spence and Alfred Hamilton show how town residents focused particularly on physical characteristics. When he sat down to write his *Annals of Rutherford County* in 1870, John Cedric Spence had lived most of his life in the small-town South. Born in 1809, two years before Murfreesboro was platted, Spence became a successful town merchant and manufacturer. His county memoir actually centers on town life. By contrast to John Spence, who was a local "insider," Alfred Hamilton was a temporary resident of Bedford County during the 1850s. Hamilton traveled extensively in the countryside and spent considerable time in Shelbyville. He wrote his father in Lewistown,

Pennsylvania, several letters describing his impressions of the diverse landscape he observed. Despite their different backgrounds, both Spence and Hamilton used similar language to explain the distinctiveness of the small town.

Both the insider and the outsider were primarily interested in what Spence frequently referred to as the town's "appearance"—defined in the broadest possible terms, from the smell of paint to the deportment of its inhabitants. Towns in Bedford County seemed to Hamilton to be the particular habitat of gentlemen: "Gentlemen are pleanty [sic] in the towns," he wrote, reiterating for emphasis, "I notice a great many loafing gentlemen in the towns."[19] For Spence the distinguishing characteristics of a town changed with time and were intimately entwined with the senses. Describing the creation of Murfreesboro, he stated simply that "the smell of paint" was an "indication of a town." Neither observer used population size as the decisive measure of a town's prosperity. Instead they looked for signs of business activity in the bustle of crowds during the day and in the variety of commercial buildings within the town's borders. Even the color of a town could be an indication of affluence, especially during the earliest settlement days when the high cost of pigments made painted town buildings stand out from the countryside. In particular Spence and Hamilton focused on buildings—the types of materials they contained, how tall they were, where they were located.

Taverns, shops, and the hierarchy of building materials, from hewed log, to weatherboard, to brick, gave proof of the complex social structure of a town peopled by innkeepers, merchants, lawyers, and craftsmen. Their life experience was different from a country farmer's. According to Spence, people in towns lived "as one family, what one knew, the whole community knowing and understanding the same thing."[20] As in most families, common knowledge did not entail agreement among all members of the community. Murfreesboro was, after all, part of a region that produced highly competitive political rivalries between Whigs and Democrats, and gave birth to at least two new Protestant groups in the early nineteenth century—the Cumberland Presbyterians and the Christians (as they called themselves) or Campbellites (as they were known by others). These contests were played out on courthouse squares and in town churches, as well as in country neighborhoods throughout Middle Tennessee.

Contemporary observers used architecture as the touchstone for town status. Spence considered construction of new buildings to be momentous events in establishing and legitimizing town institutions. Local newspaper editors shared this standard, cataloging periods of particularly intense building activity and editorializing about structures, such as courthouses, that were imbued with special community significance. Town building was a process that began with the erection of temporary structures. Towns could even be portable. When the county seat was moved from Jefferson to Murfreesboro in 1811, "Col. Joel Dyer, who was keeping entertainment in Jefferson, pulled down his houses, sent them by wagon to this place," and reconstructed them. Similarly Porter & Spence "moved goods, store house and all, rebuilding in town, loosing [sic] little time in the operation."[21] It seems clear that because residents consistently referred to the appearance of buildings to measure town development, studying changes in architecture offers a good starting point for understanding historical change in the small town.

The history that follows examines town space in two basic, interrelated ways. Analysis begins with a physical description of the landscape—what towns looked like and how they were visually distinguished from the surrounding countryside. But understanding a historical landscape—one that was produced to serve historically specific needs—can be achieved only by coming to terms with the social dimensions of town space, what Dell Upton calls the "evanescent qualities" of the historical landscape, particularly "the differences in the ways it was experienced."[22] These two basic ways of studying historical landscapes combine to produce different effects in Parts I and II of this book.

Part I, "Building Towns," describes the overall "appearance" of towns during three chronological phases of development. It chronicles the architectural choices of small-town builders from the first log shanty erected on the public square to the refined commercial blocks and female colleges constructed during the building boom of the 1850s. As they designed and assembled the material fabric that shaped town space, residents collectively created a distinctive sense of the differences that separated their own small-town societies from urban and rural life.

Part II, "Walking the Townscape," dissects the apparently unified communal picture drawn in Part I by examining how town space was used and experienced in different ways by different groups of residents. Instead of an expansive chronology, the temporal dimension of town space explored in this section is measured by the daily rhythms of town life. Although young men, women, and slaves had little power to design and erect buildings, these groups of residents had significant influence on the spatial and architectural arrangement of the small town. Following in the footsteps of these groups as they traveled town streets to perform their daily routines, it becomes clear that each was familiar with a different part of the townscape—from public wells to kitchens, from gardens to counting rooms. These distinctive rhythms of town life shaped the townscape as profoundly as the railroad did; but these experiences also worked against a single interpretation of the townscape. Townscapes evoked multiple meanings based on particular group experiences.

The history of small-town space and society before the Civil War is a complete story in its own right. Subsequent spatial and architectural changes have continued to reshape small-town life. Nevertheless, these changes have been based on social and technological forces—from emancipation to the automobile—that were never envisioned by antebellum town builders. Keeping the focus on the antebellum story, the epilogue explores the remnants of the antebellum townscape in the contemporary world. Most of the historic sites that current residents commemorate are actually elements of the plantation and Civil War past, rather than components of town history. Although much of antebellum town history has been erased, bits and pieces of the antebellum townscape have survived to become incorporated into the life of the community. The epilogue connects the historically specific meanings of town space described in the book to the historical memory of the antebellum townscape embraced by present-day town residents.

Analysis of small-town experience offers a new perspective on the relationship of antebellum southern history to the rest of the United States. Middle Tennessee town builders adapted national urban models to local conditions. Their town plans subsequently proved influential for town development as settlement moved west. In fact, Middle Tennessee town dwellers called themselves westerners rather than southerners until the eve of the Civil War. They designed antebellum townscapes according to national standards of refinement and gentility, not as part of a campaign to build a separate regional identity according to the imperatives of southern nationalism. A different kind of southern landscape emerges through examination of the three distinct phases of architectural development in Columbia, Franklin, Murfreesboro, and Shelbyville. Architectural evidence clearly and dramatically shows profound social and cultural change in the small southern town. Places we have heretofore interpreted as sleepy villages whose stories were incidental to the course of southern history may in the future be understood as distinctive and influential components of antebellum southern culture.

PART ONE

Building Towns

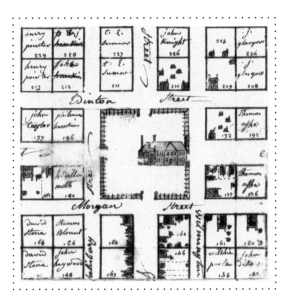

A Square, the courthouse in its grove the center; quadrangular around it, the
stores, two-storey, the offices of the lawyers and doctors . . . each in its ordered place;
the four broad diverging avenues . . . becoming the network of roads and by-roads. . . .
But above all the courthouse: the center, the focus, the hub; sitting looming in the
center of the county's circumference . . . protector of the weak, judiciate and curb
of the passions and lusts, repository and guardian of the aspirations and hopes.

WILLIAM FAULKNER, *Requiem for a Nun*

Actually there was no cultural rift between Murfreesboro and the county whose
seat it was. To call town life bourgeois would not be quite accurate. People had cows
and horses and gardens in town, and the streets were always full, especially on first
Mondays, with teams and wagons, mules, horses, sometimes a flock of turkeys,
animals and fowl brought in for trade or sale. That's what a town was for,
a place for the country to do its business in most easily.

ANDREW LYTLE, *A Wake for the Living*

As the eighteenth century came to a close, town grids were hardly a distinguishing feature of the Middle Tennessee landscape. A half century later, the
countryside was criss-crossed by a network of turnpikes that linked one
county seat to another from Main Street to Main Street. The chapters in this
section explore the history of this architectural and spatial transformation.

To be more precise, there were a series of transformations, for small
towns in the region were not really built in one sustained or continuous
construction effort. Instead, residents engaged in periodic cycles of rebuilding that effectively redefined town space. Furthermore, town development
was not simply a matter of growth and expansion. Although their populations did increase during the first half of the nineteenth century, town
borders expanded slowly. Construction tended to be intensive rather than
extensive. Nevertheless, new building phases did not obliterate buildings
that had been created to suit previous social uses; therefore, chronological
divisions between distinctive periods of development overlap.[1]

During the first two decades of the nineteenth century, residents constructed the first impermanent, "shanty" townscapes, chiefly of hand-hewn
logs. Rapid settlement in the region generated the need for convenient

judicial centers to record the property claims of new migrants. Little architectural evidence remains from this period; however, these residents left an indelible mark in the shape of their grid-patterned town designs. They established the concept of Main Street in their original plats and organized their county seats around central courthouse squares. These core towns are still visible in the central street plans of modern-day townscapes.

Between the 1820s and the 1840s, a more permanent townscape emerged, built of brick, log, and sawn board. Residents used the term "house" as a multipurpose architectural idiom, broadly applied to town buildings of all kinds—courthouses, storehouses, dwelling houses. Such a vocabulary was meaningful in a townscape where commercial and residential regions were indistinct. During this period, enterprising road builders built a town-centered network of turnpikes, and town residents began to assert their own set of goals and attitudes, thereby reshaping the relationship between town and countryside.

The advent of the railroad generated a building boom during the 1850s that effectively redefined the townscape once again. Residents diversified their architectural vocabulary as they replaced "storehouses" with "commercial blocks," and transformed dwelling houses into "cottages" and "villas." They created entirely new regions designed for specialized uses. The public square became a genteel retail center while warehouses were built around railroad depots to collect unrefined agricultural products from the countryside. "Fashionable" residential streets codified social hierarchies but did not develop into segregated, class-based neighborhoods. College campuses for women and a proliferation of separate slave churches simultaneously enlarged and regulated public access to town space.

Each of these three distinctive townscapes—the *shanty townscape*, the *townscape of houses*, and the *renovated townscape*—was composed of a particular arrangement of buildings and regions. Indeed, each was defined as much by changes in how residents used town space as it was by changes in architectural form or style. One of the most striking examples of this process was the transformation of the public square from a mixed-use space combining commercial and residential activities into a genteel business and shopping district.

Because new building phases embodied new uses of town space, the buildings town residents constructed were more than reflections or symbols of social change; they were active agents in shaping change itself.[2] For instance, town residents built new public buildings during the mid-nineteenth century that they in turn incorporated into town-centered rituals. Public ceremonies were central components in the construction of town identities because they helped to sort out differences among town residents by reinforcing hierarchies of status, gender, and race and because they helped to define differences between town and country folk. The interplay between the architectural fabric and the ceremonial uses of town space helped to construct distinctive identities that shaped the border between town and countryside. Thus town building can be fully understood only by studying the interdependence between material and social conditions of town life.

The distinctive phases of town building show that creating a county seat was a complicated and dynamic process—much more than a matter of simply setting a courthouse at a convenient crossroads. Linked by an expanding market economy to a world far beyond their local communities, Middle Tennesseans self-consciously selected urban models and adapted them to suit small-town needs and resources. As residents reorganized town space, they altered the context of town life. Thus, the history of architectural change is also the history of change in small-town society. The process began with the felling of the first tree on a newly platted public square.

From Landscape to Townscape, 1790–1825

When the American Revolution ended, Nashville was a lonely shanty town, little more than a stockade, on the Cumberland River surrounded by fertile farm land. Tennessee was still the western frontier of North Carolina. In 1796 the territory achieved statehood, and as a new century opened, Middle Tennesseans became avid town builders. Most prominent among them were powerful politicians and land speculators, ambitious farmers and merchants. But they could not have succeeded without industrious women, orphaned apprentices, and lowly slaves. Together they built the courthouse squares, dry goods stores and taverns, townhouses and kitchens that composed the scaffolding for town life—and they started from scratch. Before there were towns there were contesting landowners vying to become town fathers.

Gatherings

On a balmy spring afternoon in 1812, the citizens of Rutherford County gathered in a thick grove on the farm of William Lytle, "where a table was spread with provisions, beside a good supply of liquors on hand."[1] The people had come together for more than entertainment—there was important community business at hand. Before the day ended, they would decide where to locate their county seat. Actually seven men, town commissioners appointed by the state legislature, had the ultimate power to make the decision. But they put their choices before the community as if it were an election campaign and each site a surrogate candidate.

William Lytle, who owned one of the sites under consideration, was in no hurry to bring the matter to a vote. Instead, he waited for the good food and liquor to work their persuasion. "Toward the turn of the day, the tongues of the men had become sufficiently loosened," and advocates for each site took the stage to promote their "candidates." "Good humoredly they commenced drinking toasts and sentiments," listing the qualities of their property. Lytle caused a noisy stir in the crowd when he stood to declaim the merits of his site. Seizing his opportunity, Lytle went beyond hyperbole to make a concrete offer. He would give the sixty acres of land required by the legislature for establishing the town, with the privilege of retaining, free of charge, the lot of his choice. Whether due to his liquor or his offer or the merits of his site, Lytle carried the day by a narrow margin. Four of the seven commissioners voted for the Lytle land. The opinion of the gathered citizens may have been less divided. According to observers, the Lytle site "appeared to be the choice of the people as a more central location."[2]

It took the imagination of an optimist to envision a town on the site they had chosen. Only a small portion of William Lytle's grant was cleared. The rest of the aborning town was heavily wooded, with a matted undergrowth of cane, brush, and grapevine. Undaunted by the prospect, Hugh Robinson— one of the original commissioners, a Lytle ally, and a surveyor—confidently imposed a geometric order on the land with his rectangular town plan. Common sense intersected ambition, and the surveyor's grid contained a modest seventy half-acre lots. County commissioners envisioned a small town, not a great city. William Lytle chose a lot on the southeast corner of the public square, where his son had already built a log dwelling and planted a small plot of corn.[3]

Whether they intended to build a town or clear farm land, Middle Tennessee settlers encountered the same challenges from the land. Caroline Nicholson, whose family settled at Bear Creek in Maury County in the early 1800s, recalled that as they sat around the evening fire, her mother "would tell us children of how our father cleared the cane, as high as the house, in order to build" their first dwelling.[4] The speed with which Middle Tennesseans platted their county seats during the first decade of the nineteenth century documented a rapid and relentless migration that had transformed the

land by midcentury, but it belied the labor required to perform that transformation. It was one thing to draw neat rectangular lines on paper and quite
another to translate that idea on the ground. Before town builders could
erect their courthouses, they faced the heavy work of clearing the land.

About the same time as Rutherford County citizens came together to
select a site for their county seat, Maury County residents gathered on the
newly cleared public square in Columbia. Nathan Vaught recalled the scene
vividly because it was the day when he and his brother were "taken to a
shanty of a Court House on the east side of the Public Squar[e]" to be
bound out as apprentices. Unlike the elite men who had toasted the development prospects of their land at the gathering on Lytle's farm, Nathan
Vaught had only his labor to offer the people who collected on the new
public square in Columbia. As he remembered it, they found themselves,

> in the midst of what might be called a new ground clearing[,] large
> trees cut down and lying loose all about and the brush scattered in
> every direction all over the Square and the new brick Court House was
> in progress of being built. . . . There was but 2 small houses on the
> Square and they built of logs and covered with oak boards and fitted in
> very plain manner for dry goods.[5]

It had been about two years since the initial sale of lots, and the logs were
still strewn about the square. Some of them had been split in half and used
to build the "shanty" courthouse while the more permanent brick structure
was under construction. A cabinetmaker purchased Vaught's indenture, but
the orphaned apprentice was not destined to learn the furniture trade. Since
local consumers were in greater need of shelter than furniture, Vaught's
employer took up carpentering and Vaught learned to make houses rather
than chairs.

The boisterous event at Lytle's farm and the recently cleared square in
Columbia were signs of the new towns that gathered themselves all over
Middle Tennessee in the first two decades of the nineteenth century. The
creation of each new county set in motion a process of construction that
ultimately produced a town from scratch. Landowners eagerly competed for
town locations because of the enriching potential of town lot sales and the
longer term promise of roads that would connect farms to markets. But town
building also required the labor of the propertyless—orphaned apprentices,
like Nathan Vaught, and slaves.

Country residents, too, played an important role in town building. Their settlement decisions determined the population clusters, and thus the general locations of county seats intended to serve as government centers. Already, in the sociability of communal picnicking, liberal toasting, stump speeches, and voting, the crowd on Lytle's farm had enacted some of the fundamental rituals that would become more formalized with the articulation of town space. This story of town building was downplayed by popular myths about frontiering in the trans-Appalachian West, with their emphasis on the lone, independent pioneer and the search for elbow room. Nevertheless, Murfreesboro and Columbia were part of a larger process of town building that collectively occupied migrants to the trans-Appalachian West.

For Governmental Convenience: Creating Counties and County Seats

Middle Tennessee settlers migrated chiefly from North Carolina and Virginia in increasingly large numbers by the end of the eighteenth century. They departed a region that had been transformed during the second half of the century by the emergence of backcountry towns. During the initial stages of settlement, the southern colonies had been slow to develop towns, instead creating a decentralized plantation system spread out along the rivers. This settlement system was less influential on the southern frontier, where small towns played dynamic roles in political and economic organization of the backcountry.[6] In the Shenandoah Valley, where the plantation economy of the tidewater region failed to take hold, the role of small towns evolved gradually over the course of the eighteenth century.[7]

When westward-bound migrants crossed the Cumberland Gap into Middle Tennessee in ever increasing numbers at the turn of the century, they established their towns during the initial stages of county formation. The settlement landscape of Middle Tennessee was thus an extension of the town-country settlement system developed in the southern backcountry during the late eighteenth century. In contrast to the slow development of towns in the eighteenth-century backcountry, however, towns were an integral part of the settlement process in Middle Tennessee. Franklin, Tennessee, was established in 1799, about ten years after the first permanent settlers reached the Harpeth River and three years after statehood. By the end of the next decade Columbia, Shelbyville, and Murfreesboro had all been platted. It was a landscape composed of a small-town hierarchy in which county seats played the central governmental and marketing role.

Town development and county formation went hand in hand in Middle Tennessee. Historians have long known that the county was the most important political division in the rural South.[8] Examining the process of county formation, however, shows how the placement of towns was a driving force in county development. County seats were planned towns rather than preexisting communities. They did not develop gradually and organically as marketplaces; instead they were ordered into existence by the state legislature. The formula typically required that towns be placed near the center of the county as the boundaries of each new county were drawn. But the county seat was far from a formulaic afterthought in the legislative process. The need for new counties was determined by the need for new towns.

The creation of Rutherford County and the failure of its first county seat illustrates how town planning was central to the process of county development. The gathering that convened at William Lytle's farm in 1812 was necessary because the first seat of government for Rutherford County had failed to serve its purpose.

Rutherford County was formed in 1803 when a group of citizens living in Davidson and Williamson Counties petitioned the Tennessee General Assembly for a more accessible town. They complained that "the vast extent of said counties renders it inconvenient for your petitioners to attend Courts, General Musters, Elections, etc. at the Towns of Nashville and Franklin," the county seats of Davidson and Williamson Counties, respectively. "We your petitioners therefore pray that you will consider our situation and grant us a new county."[9] They had asked the legislators for a new county, but what the petitioners really wanted was a new town. The Assembly responded to the petition by forming Rutherford County and, according to custom, appointed a committee of five local citizens to choose a central site for the seat of government.

Meanwhile, in an effort to cash in on the sale of town lots in the new county seat, real estate speculators Robert Weakley and Robert Bedford platted a town they called Jefferson in honor of the president. As a cousin of Griffith Rutherford (the Revolutionary War hero for whom the county was named) and former president of the first Tennessee territorial legislature, Weakley was in a strong position to promote his site.[10] Indeed, Weakley and Bedford appear to have had no competitors in their bid to secure the county seat. The five commissioners chose Jefferson, already laid out on the west bank of a fork in Stones River, as the county seat.[11]

The river was navigable by flatboat, at least to the fork, for most of the year, and Jefferson appeared to have a future as a prosperous port town. Flatboats loaded and unloaded at wharves along the riverfront, while commissioners used the proceeds from the sale of town lots to build a brick courthouse, signifying the intended permanence of the town. Hopeful businessmen built several taverns and dry goods stores in Jefferson in the first seven years of development after the town was platted. But the Stones River became shallower every year, as the springs that fed it dried up. More important than the decline in water traffic, which was always confined to flatboats even when the water was at its deepest, the population center of Rutherford County shifted south. In fact, although Jefferson was officially recognized as the county seat in 1805, the court wandered from house to house to accommodate citizens in the southern region, who complained that Jefferson was too remote for convenience.

The accessibility of town was once again the central issue when citizens petitioned the General Assembly in 1811 to establish a more convenient county seat:

> the present place of holding Court in the County of Rutherford at the town of Jefferson, is not near the center of said County and said town being laid out, and the lots sold, before the county was established in consequence of which the greatest part of the citizens thereof, are put to great inconvenience attending said place, when compelled to do so by law.[12]

The petitioners argued that Jefferson was a failure because it had been laid out by real estate speculators before the county boundaries were drawn. The location of the town had not solved their original problem—an accessible courthouse. The failure of Jefferson shows the importance of town formation as a critical issue in the creation of new counties. Furthermore, the inability of an influential landowner like Weakley to insure the success of Jefferson suggests that though they had a clear advantage, powerful politicians and land speculators did not control the process completely. Jefferson withered as merchants and lawyers abandoned the town for the new county seat.

In contrast to the uncontested selection of Jefferson as the first seat of Rutherford County, the second selection process (which culminated with the barbecue at William Lytle's farm) generated intense interest and vigorous competition among landowners, who aggressively wooed the newly appointed seven-member town commission. The commissioners spent several months studying five different locations, and two sites emerged as the leading contenders. In addition to Lytle's farm, the other favored site was six miles south of Jefferson on a good road in a well-settled portion of the county. Charles Ready, a landowner in the vicinity, promoted the latter site with a barbecue of his own—but he was outmaneuvered by Lytle, who managed to schedule his barbecue on the day of the vote. The commissioners split their votes, three for Ready and four for Lytle. Acrimonious in defeat, the three Ready supporters refused to sign deeds for town lots in the new county seat and resigned their town commissions. The zealous competition suggests there was more at stake than simply the location of a convenient courthouse.

County seats began as places of local government where county residents gathered to attend courts, musters, and elections.[13] The central locations that made government more convenient also gave the county seats an advantage in local commerce as residents built new roads to connect the countryside to the town. By the mid-nineteenth century, Middle Tennesseans had created a network of county seats, each town within thirty or forty miles of another and connected, Main Street to Main Street, by a system of turnpikes. Thus, county seat and county grew together as a political, economic, and cultural system for organizing and developing local resources. Ultimately, it was the location of towns that propelled the system.[14]

Grids: The Oldest Artifact of Small-Town Life

More durable than the courthouses and law offices, stores and houses that gave them form and definition in space, the street patterns laid out by the first town planners have survived to form the core of the modern county seat. Though Middle Tennesseans emphasized the governmental functions of the county seat in their petitions for new towns, their town plans revealed a more diverse set of social and commercial ambitions. The search for larger meanings of town life begins on the ground, with the oldest surviving artifact of town development—street plans.

In stark contrast to the meandering lines of county boundaries, which often followed the natural course of rivers or streams, Middle Tennessee surveyors used pure geometry to lay out their seats of government. During the nineteenth century, these small towns grew intensively rather than extensively. County seats did spread beyond their original boundaries long before the end of the nineteenth century, but town residents typically rebuilt existing townscapes faster than they annexed additional territory.[15] Therefore, much of the architectural evidence from these early towns has been obliterated. But for a handful of exceptional examples, the buildings constructed by the first settlers have disappeared or been altered beyond recognition. Ironically, what endured were the square lines that surveyors sketched on paper and settlers translated on the ground as they carved streets and town lots out of canebrakes and forests. Like parchments scraped and reused many times by ancient scribes, town grids have provided the foundation for each generation of town builders to draw and redraw their townscapes.[16]

Although choosing a site for a county seat could spawn acrimonious debate, as it did in Murfreesboro, the written record of town formation in Middle Tennessee reveals no argument among town founders about the shape their county seats should take. Town plans were rarely even discussed, much less disputed. Nevertheless, the street maps they produced speak volumes about conventional ideas concerning the appropriate organization of small-town space. The Assembly followed customary routine when, in 1807, it directed commissioners for the town of Columbia to purchase 100 acres near the center of Maury County, "on which they shall cause a town to be laid off." According to standard practice, the legislature instructed town commissioners to reserve about two acres "as near the center [of town] as may be [possible], on which the court house, prison and stocks shall be erected."[17] The instructions for designing the new county seat were simple, but they left much to local interpretation. The town should be composed of the "necessary streets and alleys, neither of which streets shall be less than one hundred feet wide."[18] Except for its order that two acres at the center of town be reserved for a public square, the Assembly did not impose any specific requirements. It did not spell out how many or what kind of streets it considered to be "necessary," nor did it explicitly order commissioners to use any particular street pattern. But by the early nineteenth century, the concept of the central courthouse was enough to convey expectations of the grid.

Surveyors and town commissioners in Middle Tennessee almost invariably placed the courthouse in the middle of the public square at the center of a grid. But if the location of the courthouse and public square were automatic, the street pattern that would articulate the town grid was not. By the early nineteenth century, American county seats employed a variety of central courthouse square plans, and local commissioners were granted a great deal of autonomy in designing the particular street pattern that would shape each new town.[19] One of the oldest and most influential grid-patterned plans derived from William Penn's 1682 design for Philadelphia.[20]

Throughout the first half of the nineteenth century, Philadelphia served as a kind of cultural capital in the development of Middle Tennessee's county seats.[21] Town merchants traveled every year to the Pennsylvania marketplace to buy merchandise for their stores. But it was not necessary to visit Philadelphia in person to be familiar with the city's central square design. The towns of the Shenandoah Valley were closely tied to Pennsylvania, particularly to Philadelphia, where backcountry merchants routinely bought the goods they sold to their customers in backcountry towns like Winchester, Virginia.[22] Pittsboro, North Carolina, had been laid out on the Philadelphia plan, with a courthouse on the central square, by 1785. The state capital, Raleigh (Fig. 1.1), a town familiar to many settlers of Middle Tennessee, was laid out in 1792 according to the Philadelphia plan. Designed as an urban capital, Raleigh incorporated the garden squares of Penn's original plan. But small-town surveyors from countless grid-patterned towns west of the Appalachians paid particular attention to the street pattern that defined Philadelphia's central square. In the 1790s, Abram Maury used it for Franklin, Tennessee, named for Philadelphia's most famous resident.[23] Maury laid out sixteen rectangular blocks, each containing twelve lots, with a central square for the courthouse at the intersection of Main and Main Cross Streets (Fig. 1.2). As the nexus of the major intersection in town, Columbia's central square (Fig. 1.3), platted in 1807, also shows the influence of the Philadelphia plan.

Philadelphia may have been the most influential model for early county seat designs, but Middle Tennesseans employed a surprising variety of alternatives for arranging the central square within the grid. In fact, the variety of town plans in the region suggest that Middle Tennessee was an area of significant cultural experimentation, where surveyors played with the idea of the grid and created new designs in the process.[24] Indeed, they were among the first to design new county seats that took the grid to its logical conclusion. Shelbyville (Fig. 1.4) was laid out in 1810 in an early and very influential example of the central or block square plan.[25] By 1812, Fayetteville, Pulaski, and Winchester, all county seats south of Shelbyville, had also used the central square plan. According to this design, the central square

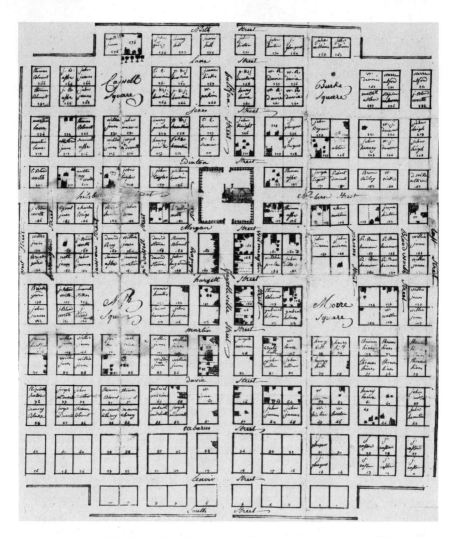

FIGURE 1.1. Raleigh, North Carolina, designed in 1792 according to the Philadelphia plan. The central square was formed by the intersection of two major streets, and four more public squares defined the quadrants of the city. The street pattern that bifurcated the rows of blocks leading to the central square, however, differed slightly from the Philadelphia model, which more closely resembled the street plan of Franklin, Tennessee, where town blocks were of equal size. (Courtesy of Southern Historical Collection, Wilson Library, University of North Carolina at Chapel Hill)

FIGURE 1.2. (*Facing page*) Franklin, Tennessee, platted in 1799 according to the Philadelphia plan. (From the Canaday Files, Franklin, Tennessee)

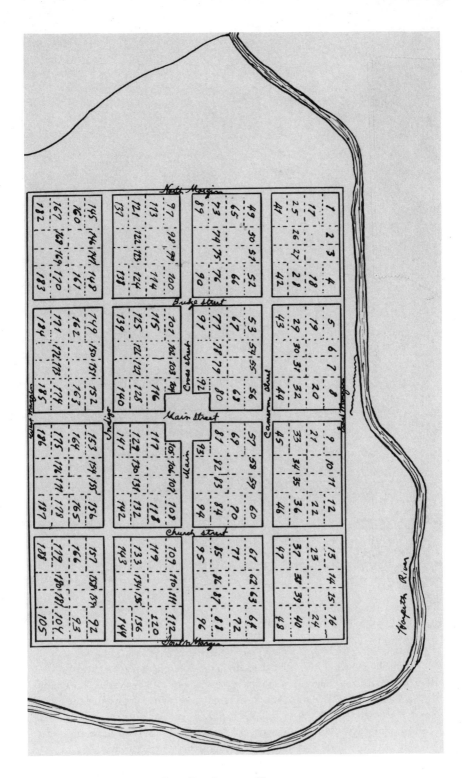

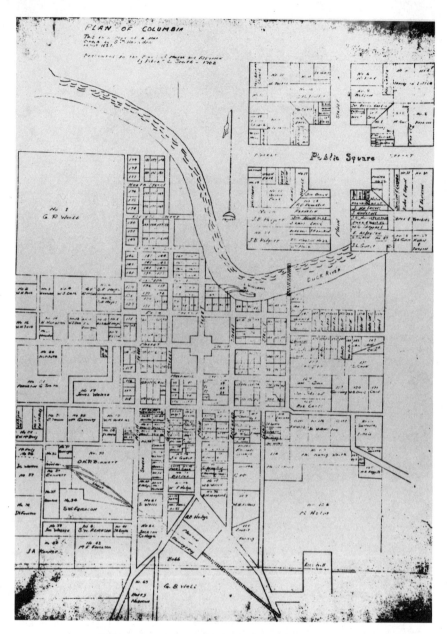

FIGURE 1.3. This map of Columbia, Tennessee, is a 1902 copy of a town plan originally drawn in 1852. The diagram of the public square (inset, top right) documents the 1807 central square street pattern, which followed the Philadelphia plan. The overall view shows both the original town plan, composed of the blocks contiguous to the public square, and the haphazard antebellum development, which did not fully extend the grid pattern established by the town's original planners. (Courtesy of Tennessee State Library and Archives)

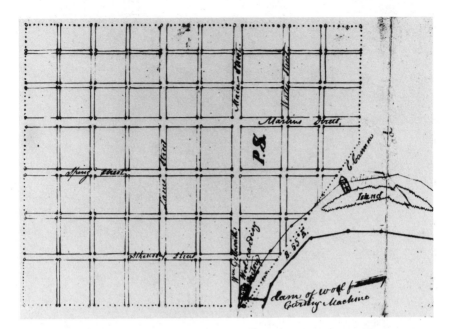

FIGURE 1.4. Shelbyville, Tennessee, laid out in 1810. The Duck River cuts across the southeastern corner of the grid. (Courtesy of Tennessee State Library and Archives)

occupied a full block of the town without altering the basic grid street pattern. It was simpler and easier to lay out than the Philadelphia plan, and the block square became the most frequently used county seat plan in new counties of the South and Midwest. Seventy-two percent of courthouse squares created on the Georgia Piedmont between 1811 and 1830 were of this type.[26]

Murfreesboro (Fig. 1.5) was designed in 1811 according to what may have been a hybrid of the block square and the Philadelphia square.[27] Surveyor Hugh Robinson drew three narrow rectangles at the center of the standard grid. His arrangement retained the visual impact of the Philadelphia plan with its mid-street location of the central square. At the same time, Robinson incorporated elements of the block square—instead of merely setting the courthouse into an open space cut out at the intersection of two major streets, he created a well-defined central block.

All of the variations on the central square plan affected the visual impact of the public square and the courthouse—heightening the drama of the approach by placing the square at the center of a major intersection or diminishing its effect by integrating the central square seamlessly into the

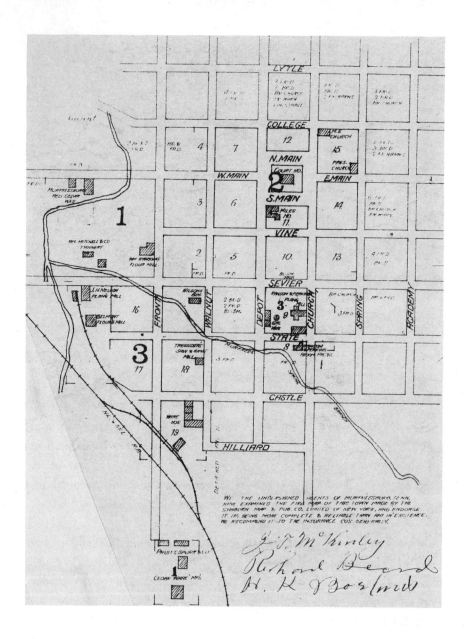

FIGURE 1.5. Murfreesboro, Tennessee, designed in 1811, combines elements of the block square and the Philadelphia square plans. This insurance map from the late nineteenth century documents the original town plan in the blocks bordered by Lytle, Academy, Sevier, and Front Streets. (Sanborn Map & Publishing Co., July 1887)

overall grid. Their varied approaches to street patterns only served to emphasize the unchanging importance of two primary concepts for county seat
design—the ideas of the public square and main street. County seats were
consistently built around a central block, designated as "public" space; and
from the beginning of town development, "Main Street" was designed to be
set apart from other town streets by its width and its role as the primary
route to the central square. Even in Shelbyville, with its simple block arrangement, Main Street formed the eastern side of the public square, running along an axis from north to south. In Murfreesboro, Main Street led
dramatically to the center of the public square, where the courthouse stood
impressively as if in the middle of the street. Town residents ultimately
extended their Main Streets into the countryside as turnpikes, often plotted
in straight lines that connected one county seat to another.

The generalized, even automatic, creation of central courthouse squares
had significant implications for the intended role of county seats in the life of
the community. The courthouse square was the center of a town, which was
as "near the center" of the county as possible. The placement of courthouse
and stocks in the middle of the county seat emphasized its role as the seat of
justice, not merely for the town but also for the surrounding countryside. By
consistently building their county seats around central courthouse squares,
Middle Tennesseans acknowledged the permanent connections between
town and country. Shelbyville commissioners put it more explicitly when
they invited "tradesmen and merchants" in particular to attend the sale of
lots in 1811, assuring them that "the county town of Bedford" was "elegantly
situated on the banks of Duck river, and surrounded by a very rich body of
land, on which a number of wealthy farmers have already settled."[28] Central
squares were essentially "hybrid" ground, where town tradesmen and merchants did business with prosperous farmers.

From the start, the public square also signaled the distinction between
town and country, creating opportunities for nucleated settlement and a
readily identifiable town center. In Shelbyville, where the central block plan
made no visible differentiation between the central square and other squares
in the grid, lots around the public square were deeper than other town lots,
turned so that the short side of the rectangle faced the courthouse. Such an
orientation made it possible for street frontage to be divided among the
maximum number of owners. In general, the value of town land was based
on its proximity to the central square. Lots on the public square in Shelbyville sold for more than forty times the price of lots on the outer margins of

town. Lot number 55, for example, on the north side of the square sold for three hundred dollars in 1810; one year later lot 114, in the northwest corner of town, sold for seven dollars.[29] By design, the square would become the most densely settled heart at the center of town. Created to serve the political and governmental needs of the countryside, county seat plans also suggest the outlines of towns set apart from the countryside by densely settled commercial centers. The public square, however, was only one segment of a larger townscape. As we shall see, much of the social and ceremonial life of the county seat was *not* centered on the courthouse.

Tree Stumps and Hewed Logs: Temporary Townscapes

As town lots began to be sold off, the first rickety townscapes rose amid the tree stumps that outlined the street grid. In his *Annals of Rutherford County*, John Spence described a townscape composed of hastily constructed, one-story log buildings, most containing only one room—a townscape that residents would be working to replace almost as soon as it emerged. Few of the buildings from these temporary townscapes have survived. The descriptions and memories of town residents represent the most vivid documents of these early stages of town development.

Two residents in particular—John Spence and Nathan Vaught—grew to maturity with the county seats of the early nineteenth century, and both chronicled town development. Nathan Vaught became a house carpenter in Columbia, and John Spence, whose family had opened one of the first stores on the public square, was a merchant in Murfreesboro. Vaught and Spence both wrote their memoirs during the 1870s, when the towns they had known as young men were being rapidly rebuilt and profoundly reorganized. Spence recorded that the first brick residence built in Murfreesboro, a two-story building "finished in the finest art of the time" with cherry paneled doors, was still standing in 1870, though "in a decayed condition" and "used as a negro tenement."[30] By the end of the century, the early pattern of town development that Spence and Vaught described had become submerged within subsequent development phases, which were based on completely different dynamics. Their accounts therefore contain vital evidence of the earliest town forms, which survive piecemeal at best in the present-day townscape. Although the two men never knew each other, and each grew up in very different economic and social circumstances, they described remarkably similar architectural processes at work during the early nineteenth century.

John Cedric Spence was born in 1809, the same year that his parents, John Spence of Ireland and Mary Chism of Virginia, moved to Middle Tennessee. Spence's father and his uncle Marmon became wealthy and influential businessmen in Murfreesboro. Marmon Spence was the town's mayor from 1834 to 1835 and accumulated much property on the public square. John Cedric Spence spent at least part of his adult life outside Murfreesboro. From 1832 to 1847 he owned a store in Sommerville, Tennessee, then moved to Memphis and operated a store there until 1849, when he returned to Murfreesboro permanently.

When Spence wrote his *Annals of Rutherford County* in 1873, he intended the two volumes as "ground work for a better written history of the County in future time." It is clear that Spence had access to town records long since vanished. He quotes from a set of aldermen's minutes "found in a store house since burned."[31] In addition to written sources, Spence attempted to preserve much of the oral tradition of town life, gathering information from the "oldest inhabitant" and recording stories he had no doubt heard countless times before from friends and neighbors.[32]

Nathan Vaught prospered on a different level of town society from that of John Spence. Born in Shenandoah County, Virginia, in 1799, the son of Patsy and Abraham Vaught, Nathan migrated with his family to Rutherford County, Tennessee, about 1804, settling near Jefferson, then the county seat. Vaught's mother died soon after their arrival in Tennessee, and Nathan and his two brothers were orphaned by the death of their father in 1807. The youngest child, an infant, was sent to live with an uncle in Kentucky, but neighbors in Tennessee, a childless, older couple named Radford, assumed responsibility for the care of the two older boys. In 1808, soon after the sale of town lots in Columbia, the Radfords moved to the new seat of Maury County, where Mrs. Radford had the dubious distinction of being the second person buried in the town cemetery. The Vaught boys were "thrown on the charities of the town" by Mr. Radford, who left Columbia soon after his wife's death.[33]

From 1810 to 1820, Vaught was a carpenter's apprentice. He enjoyed his most productive years as a house carpenter in Columbia with the building boom of the 1850s. But even during the economic hard times of the late 1830s, Vaught achieved enough standing in the community to become a member of the Masonic Fraternity.[34] Throughout his fifty-year career he received commissions from county as well as town residents. In 1871, he wrote what he called "a diary" beginning "from the time [he] was old enough to labor" and continuing the story through 1861 when he sold the tools of his trade. But his *Youth and Old Age* was less a personal memoir about Vaught's family and career than it was a catalog of architectural change in Columbia. Vaught described the buildings he helped construct and ranged more broadly to discuss his memories of town and county development.[35]

Spence and Vaught revealed that the first job of town building was clearing the land. Vaught's vivid memories of logs strewn about the public square in Columbia are very similar to Spence's description of Murfreesboro. Except for John Lytle's cornfield, the streets and the public square were "generally thickly set with stumps and other obstructions after removing the timber."[36] Lytle's hewed log dwelling was soon joined by others, as a "temporary" town of log buildings began to define the public square and grid-patterned streets. Clearing was more than the responsibility of individual property owners; it was a communal obligation, particularly the clearing of common areas like town streets. Town and country residents followed similar procedures—"warning hands living in town to work the streets, as they do on public roads."[37] Many of the "hands" that carved out the towns streets and public roads belonged to slaves who were part of the town-building process from the beginning.

Town building meant hard work and big business for carpenters, who beat a path to new county seats as soon as the announcements for lot sales were published. John Spence recorded what Murfreesboro's early residents remembered about the labor it took to create the first town amid rotting tree stumps.

> All carpenters conducting shops had apprentice boys bound to them. . . . The planing, tounging [tonguing], grooving all by hand. This was boys work. Weatherboarding, window framing, all sizes of mouldings for cornice, all this requiring a great deal of sawing and planing. Great quantities of this material packed over various parts of town on the shoulders of men and boys from the shops. No other conveyance used. Every thing done by hard labor. Little time to loose [*sic*] from morning till night. It was either planing, nailing or carrying lumber to some building in some parts of the town.[38]

With this kind of time-consuming (not to mention back-breaking) labor, it is not surprising that businessmen took shortcuts to establish their shops.

When the county seat was moved from Jefferson to Murfreesboro, Joel Dyer dismantled his two-story tavern in Jefferson and moved the logs and other construction materials by wagon to the new county seat. Dyer soon reconstructed his tavern on the south side of the public square, not far from where Porter & Spence reconstructed their dry goods store, another two-story, cedar log building that had recently stood on the public square in Jefferson.

Several sawmills had been built along the Stones River before Murfreesboro was established; thus, sawn lumber was available for town builders, who moved quickly to cover log buildings with weatherboarding. In addition to the mills, one of the first industries in Murfreesboro was a nail factory, owned by Joshua Harrison. Located on the Square, in a small, one-story, cedar log shop of about eighteen by twenty-five feet, "blank nails were cut from pieces of iron. . . . Each nail taken separately, placed in a vise, [and] a head hammered on them." Harrison & Company sold their locally produced nails at twenty-five cents a pound, but were soon driven out of business by merchant competitors who could afford to sell their imported nails at fifteen cents per pound.[39]

Wood was not the only building material in the temporary townscape. The first brick structures in Columbia appeared two or three years after the original sale of town lots. Among the earliest of these was the courthouse, which was under construction when Nathan Vaught first came to Columbia in 1809. As a carpenter, Vaught emphasized the wood buildings that were his bread and butter when he enumerated the houses that composed Columbia's first townscape. But he also worked closely with the brickmason Levi Ketchum, providing the woodwork to finish many of Ketchum's building projects. Most of the brick buildings Vaught identified stood on or near the Square and included the jail, seven dry goods stores, and a law office. He mentioned only one brick dwelling completed during this initial development phase, and it was located just over one mile south of town.

Nathan Vaught and John Spence both agreed that about six years after the original sale of lots in Columbia and Murfreesboro, recognizable towns had emerged. Vaught specifically identified eighteen log, nine frame, and eleven brick buildings, all constructed in Columbia by 1815. In Murfreesboro, "houses were dotted over the place," chiefly built of rough-hewn cedar logs, occasionally covered by sawn boards.[40]

John Lytle's house on the southeast corner of Murfreesboro's Square was typical of the first town dwellings. The one-and-a-half-story log house consisted of two rooms, separated by an open passage, with chimneys of wood and clay. Lytle's house in town resembled countless dwellings rising throughout the countryside. Caroline Nicholson remembered the houses in the neighborhood of her childhood home on Bear Creek in Maury County. "Our chimneys . . . were remarkable as the only stone ones we knew," she explained. "They were in other places built of logs, as were the houses, daubed with clay, and provided with large flat stones set upright at back and sides of fireplace."[41]

In fact architectural historians have found that the double-pen (or two-room) house with a dog trot (or breezeway) dividing the two rooms was typical throughout the Upland South region. Peter Voorhies built another archetypal Upland South house about 1809—a "large heavy double log house 2 stories high with 2 rooms below and 2 rooms above and 2 halls one above and one below"—on Free Street in Columbia. This type of house— one room deep and two rooms wide, often two-stories tall—was the one most commonly built in the Upland South region throughout the nineteenth century.[42] Peter Voorhies's house in Columbia could have been found on country roads throughout Maury County.[43]

The ratio of building materials would shift by midcentury, when brick and frame construction predominated, but amateur and professional house carpenters alike continued to use logs as a significant structural material, in town as well as in the countryside, in the years leading up to the Civil War. Town and countryside became increasingly distinct however, in the selective use of building materials and technologies, according to the intended purpose of particular structures. In the beginning, town builders used logs indiscriminately for commercial buildings and dwellings. By the time of the Civil War, commercial buildings on the Square were built almost exclusively of brick. During the first town-building decade, however, residents used interchangeable floor plans and similar materials in the construction of town houses and country houses.[44]

If the materials and types of dwellings were the same, what was it then, that distinguished town from countryside during this early phase of town building? Residents pointed most often to experiential factors—competition between neighbors to improve the appearance of town property, and the sense of smell, for example—to express the distinctions they felt.

John Spence suggested that the impetus for architectural improvement was especially strong in town. Some "lots [were] fenced in," he noted "all giving a general appearance of [a] growing town and making the people feel they were comfortably situated in town."[45] Also, Spence and Vaught both

FIGURE 1.6. Gideon Blackburn house, built around 1810 in Franklin, Tennessee. The original log house has been obscured by subsequent additions. (Photograph by author)

noticed the speed with which town dwellers covered their log dwellings with sawn boards. Few of the wooden buildings constructed during the earliest years of town development remain, and none endures unaltered. A rare survival of this period, the residence of Presbyterian minister Gideon Blackburn in Franklin, built around 1810, was constructed in stages that suggest the rapid architectural improvements described by Vaught and Spence (Fig. 1.6). The oldest part of the house consists of hewn logs, but the minister quickly covered the logs with sawn clapboard. The brick chimneys of the Blackburn house distinguished it from other structures with chimneys of wood and clay. It appears that each small-town homebuilder who improved his property provided incentive for his neighbors to do likewise. Such incentives were less apparent in the countryside, where neighbors had to travel greater distances to compare architectural improvements.

When Murfreesboro was about six years old, residents recalled that "the finer portions of houses were having the smell of paint." Indeed, John Spence emphasized that "this was another indication of a town, the smell of paint." Businesses on the Square received a coat of "either yellow ochre or venetian red." White lead was expensive to import, Spence explained, so "the standard article of paints for common use was yellow ochre and Spanish brown or red." John Tilford's one-story storeroom on the Square in Murfreesboro was "known a long time as the red house" because of the memorable embellishment of its weatherboarded facade. Some residents went to greater lengths to make a green paint "when a more fancy finish was desired. This was made by grinding on a stone the crude verdigris, usually a tedious article to prepare. Only used in painting window shutters and similar articles." More often, however, "when painting houses over, the shingles usually received a coat or two of brown paint." These brown and red towns would eventually be supplanted by the more familiar whitewashed towns of the mid- and late-nineteenth century.[46] But in the first town-building decade, the smell of freshly painted shutters (not to mention the sound of hammering) was an indication to eager country customers that they were nearing a rising town.

Above all, towns set themselves apart from the countryside by the density and arrangement of buildings. When he wrote that "houses were dotted over the place" in early Murfreesboro, Spence seemed to suggest that buildings were scattered indiscriminately on cleared lots. However, new residents began to define particular town regions almost from the beginning. Much of the building, in fact, was initially concentrated on the public square, which swiftly became the business center. Nathan Vaught remembered that by about 1815 Columbia had "a good many one story houses built around the Square for offices and shops of different kinds. Now and then a one story wood house for dry good stores and drinking places."[47] In fact, dry goods stores and taverns became the commercial backbone of the first townscape. "In a new town," John Spence declared, taverns were "about one of the first wants of the people."[48] Churches were conspicuously absent from the temporary townscape.[49]

Six years after the sale of town lots, John Spence claimed that the Square alone contained more than thirty buildings.[50] Among the businesses surrounding the courthouse were at least fifteen "storehouses," at least three taverns, three law offices, and several small businesses, including a hatter's shop and a saddler's shop. These buildings ranged along the sides of the Square in no particular order. On the west side, a row of "three small one story rooms, used as shops" stood beside "a two story brick house, [containing] two store rooms each, occupied by merchants Trott & McBroom, Jones & Organ."[51] A total of seven brick buildings—all two stories tall and identified as "storehouses"—were scattered along the four sides of the public square, interspersed with single-story shops and two-story taverns of log and sawn board.

Despite the concentration of business on the Square, town regions were still imprecise. "A frame dwelling and out houses" stood in the middle of the north side of the Square in Murfreesboro, and the families of shopkeepers and merchants often lived in the upper floors and back rooms of storehouses.

According to Spence, the public square quickly became the busiest, most prominent part of the county seat; after all, he wrote, "the town was small." But it was not the number or size of the buildings that distinguished the spot. The diminutive proportions of the town could not restrain commercial ambitions, and businessmen boldly announced their desires

> with large sign boards of tradesmen and occupations . . . conspic-
> uously lettered with gold leaf, and placed over the doors. These large
> shining signs, dotted round the public square, gave things a lively
> cheerful and business appearance. Tavern keepers with swinging signs
> on posts, at the corner of streets, with the name of the house and man.
> Travelers coming on the public square would know where they wish to
> stay without enquiring.[52]

From one grid-patterned county seat to the next, travelers knew how to follow Main Street to the public square. Once at the center of town, business signs made the territory as familiar to a stranger as it was to a local resident.

Merchants, too, decorated the Square with colorful and creative emblems of their occupation. "Beside the name over the door, a store was known by a piece of red flannel three or four yards stretched across two projecting slats in the door side, a long string [of] tin cups, coffee pots, a fiew [sic] other articles. This is the sign [that] dry goods and all other articles [are] for sale."[53] Thus, the public square presented a mosaic of small-town aspirations. The sides of the Square were composed of the widest imaginable variation of buildings constructed in the temporary townscape. The smell of paint, signs embellishing stores, the rapid pace of improvement in the houses, the emergence of identifiable town regions—these were the distinguishing markers of the first, ramshackle townscapes. But the center square was soon filled with the structure that would embody the long-term prosperity and stability sought by residents of town and county alike.

Town residents swiftly and crudely assembled "shanty" log courthouses until they could erect more substantial brick ones. They wasted no time. Typically, courthouses were among the first brick structures built in a new county.[54] Williamson, Rutherford, Maury, and Bedford Counties each constructed brick courthouses within the first few years after establishing their county seats.[55] Standing amidst the temporary log taverns and stores with their wood and mud chimneys, the first brick courthouses were set apart by the materials and technologies employed in constructing them. Though built during the earliest stages of town development, these brick courthouses pointed toward a different, more permanent townscape.

In November 1812, less than a year after Murfreesboro was platted, the town's commissioners published an announcement in the *Nashville Whig*, seeking a builder for the new courthouse. According to the advertised specifications, the building was to be two stories tall and forty feet square. The foundation was to be of stone, "sunk two feet under ground, and raised two feet above, the stone above ground to be neatly dressed," its brick walls, two feet thick with ten windows below and thirteen in the second story. Interior walls were to be wainscoted "as high as the window-sill, and plaistered [*sic*] and whitewashed above to the ceilings," made of poplar "neatly planed and beeded." Exterior and interior doors were to be paneled, "with sufficient locks and hinges." The roof of yellow poplar shingles was to be "nailed on with good and suitable nails" and painted red.[56] Rutherford County citizens ultimately invested $4,000 to build this courthouse at the center of Murfreesboro.

The Murfreesboro courthouse was not unusual. It followed the same principals of design used in the construction of other courthouses in the region. As in the selection of town plans, there seems to have been no debate about the form or appearance these important community buildings should take. Published specifications suggest that building committees from county seat to county seat followed the same basic courthouse pattern (Fig. 1.7).[57] In fact, the Rutherford County building committee inspected the six-year-old courthouse in neighboring Franklin and ordered that work on the Murfreesboro courthouse be completed "in the same manner as the court-house in Franklin."[58] Even before county seats were connected by turnpikes, their residents were already learning from each other how towns should look.

Generally about forty feet square, the first brick courthouses stood two

FIGURE 1.7. Courthouse built in Charlotte, Tennessee, between 1806 and 1812. The present building was reconstructed on the original foundation after a tornado destroyed the first courthouse in 1830. Wings were added in 1930, but the central block of the building was left essentially intact. This original core, capped by a cupola, was typical of the brick courthouses that replaced log shanties in county seats throughout Middle Tennessee during the 1820s and 1830s. (Photograph by author)

stories tall, usually on stone foundations. Embellishments varied from wain-scoting "painted a marble color" in the Shelbyville courthouse to arched windows and doors on the courthouse in Franklin. Invariably, the brick boxes were capped by a hipped roof, "drawn from each square [side] to the centre," usually with a cupola in the middle.[59] The Murfreesboro court-house incorporated the symbols of the new American republic. A fourteen-foot cupola, surmounted, in proper patriotic fashion, by "a steeple of 15 feet long, with an eagle" accentuated the height and significance of the build-ing.[60] In keeping with the town color scheme described so vividly by John Spence, the shingles were often painted red or brown.

Courthouses required a sophisticated level of technology. In Murfrees-boro the building was distinguished by heavy masonry construction, not only in the dressed stone of the foundation but also in the rock sills of the windows. Embellishments as simple as smoothly planed flooring, beaded ceiling boards, or paneling were no small accomplishment for a town where tree stumps still outnumbered houses. Typically located on high ground, the two-story brick courthouses built at the center of the public square were often visible well beyond the town limits. Courthouses played an integral part in the lives of county and town residents alike, who gathered there to attend concerts, dances, and church services, as well as courts. Without a doubt courthouses stood out in the temporary townscape.

Despite its symbolic placement and accessibility, the courthouse was neither the largest nor the finest building in town. In Franklin, for example, the Masonic fraternity built a three-story lodge that towered over the courthouse in the 1820s. In the emerging townscape, it became one of several important town buildings. Ultimately the power and meaning of the courthouse derived from its relationship to other town spaces. Roads converged not at the courthouse, but at the public square, an equally powerful symbol of centralization. In Middle Tennessee, the courthouse was not the isolated marker of a country crossroads, it was one element of a larger, changing townscape.[61]

For this reason, courthouses have been among the most disposable buildings in Middle Tennessee towns. Most counties built two or three different courthouses before the Civil War, and statewide only seven antebellum courthouses survive.[62] At once symbolic and utilitarian, courthouses were replaced because they were expected to embody a complex array of ever-changing meanings—expanding social and governmental functions, changing standards of taste and comfort. The brick boxes built in the early stages of town development became obsolete in the townscapes that emerged by the mid-nineteenth century.

Log shelters constructed in haste would gradually be replaced by more substantial brick and clapboard houses or somehow altered (typically by covering the logs with sawn boards) during the first forty years or so of town development. This process was by no means orderly. Building technologies were employed unevenly; brick structures appeared within the first six years of construction, while dwellings continued to be built of cedar logs well into the 1840s.[63] Patrols in Murfreesboro dodged tree stumps in the middle of town streets during the panic over news of Nat Turner's rebellion, twenty years after the original sale of lots.[64] The brick courthouses, which appeared to be so permanent when surrounded by the first shanty townscapes, were eventually overshadowed by new architectural improvements.

Ostensibly established as county seats with a narrowly defined governmental role during the first decade of the nineteenth century, by 1819 Columbia, Franklin, Murfreesboro, and Shelbyville had all become incorporated towns.[65] Incorporation, empowered towns to elect mayor and aldermen, levy taxes, and enact ordinances without petitioning the state legislature. Anchored by their brick courthouses, county seats began to shed their makeshift appearance. In the years following incorporation, residents rebuilt the temporary townscape, creating a distinctive arrangement of town space. John Spence declared that by 1827 Murfreesboro was "appearantly [*sic*] completed. No new buildings going up."[66] In one sense, he was right. With their central courthouse square town plans, residents had established a spatial pattern that would hold sway for generations to come. But his conclusion that the townscape was essentially "completed," would prove to be premature.

CHAPTER TWO

A Townscape of Houses, 1819–1849

During the early years of town building, county seats in the region competed aggressively to become the political and commercial center of the state. Murfreesboro served as state capital from 1818 to 1826, while Columbia threatened to redirect trade away from Nashville by building a railroad directly to the Tennessee River.[1] Ultimately, Nashville prevailed as the state capital and commercial center of Middle Tennessee.

But small-town residents also looked beyond Nashville for urban models as they became integrated into the national economic and political landscape. Philadelphia in particular continued to be an important cultural influence. The central basin, in turn, put its own mark on the new nation, sending to Washington two presidents who had practiced law in the county seats of Middle Tennessee. Indeed, small towns asserted a far greater influence than their diminutive proportions might indicate.

From the 1820s through the 1840s, town residents constructed full-scale permanent townscapes composed of a variety of dwellings and public buildings. From day to day, however, a stranger to town might not be able to measure the evidence of architectural progress. Relics of the earliest shanty towns lay strewn about the emerging sturdier townscape. Towns grew incrementally, in fits and starts, in the decades immediately following incorporation. This building process created an uneven appearance—a patchwork of muddy lots, log shanties, modest clapboard houses, and substantial brick buildings designed in the latest architectural styles.[2]

Though progress was intermittent, the distinctions between town and countryside became ever clearer. As town residents borrowed from rural and urban models to construct their townscapes, they created a distinctive pastiche. It was a landscape particularly expressive of social conditions unique to small-town life. Selective imitation meant that small towns sometimes reflected the countryside and sometimes appeared to operate like urban microcosms. Taken alone, however, these interpretations offer only a partial understanding of small-town life as a distinctive experience.[3] The combination of rural and urban elements made towns unique—more than a farm neighborhood, but not quite a city.

Nineteenth-century southern culture is usually interpreted as an overwhelmingly rural, family-centered, folk culture. With town sizes that ranged from about 1,000 to 1,500 residents, it is easy to see how these tiny places might be overlooked.[4] In fact, however, the small-town context of the Jacksonian era shows how people in the Upper South linked themselves to a national political and commercial culture. Despite their diminutive proportions, these county seats adopted spatial and social patterns common to much larger cities of the era. In the process, small-town residents began to construct a town-centered identity that set them apart from their rural neighbors. We begin this evaluation of the second phase of town development with one town builder's inventory of a changing countryside.

Town "Houses"

Local residents measured progress by dramatic changes in the landscape, and in turn the changing environmental context of their lives helped to shape their identity as a community. In 1834, John Shofner, who lived just outside Shelbyville in Bedford County, barely contained his enthusiasm as he recounted in evocative detail the material changes that had transformed the landscape of Middle Tennessee. "I murst go back to former days when father first mooved to bedford county," Shofner began his vivid tale, displaying spelling skills that were as creative as the story he composed. About twenty-seven years earlier, he wrote, his fifty-year-old father had "settled here in a thick forrest of heavy timber and the powerfullest cain brake that was eaver saw." In a single generation, the family had constructed an entirely new landscape. "We now have large farms open," Shofner proudly declared, "and our lands are productive."[5] Clearing land for a farm, however, was only the beginning.

The Shofners were town builders too. At first there was "no plase of market," John continued, "only as we cold sell cattle to the drovers[,] or hogs." But by 1834, Shelbyville had weathered more than its share of misfortunes to become a market town of 600 inhabitants. Shofner recorded with amazement that when his family first reached Bedford County "we had no mills and now we have plenty and in some plases whare they haint got the warter power they bild mills to go by steam."[6] In keeping with its role of serving an agricultural community, Shelbyville boasted a combination of grist mills, saw mills, and cotton gins in the town and vicinity.[7]

The first sign that county seats were beginning to form an identity independent of the countryside came soon after the original shanty townscapes had supplanted the canebrakes. In 1817, the state legislature prohibited the town commissioners of Shelbyville from taxing "any citizen or citizens of the county of Bedford, who may wish to trade or sell in said town, their produce, or goods and wares of domestic manufacture."[8] At the same time, the legislature upheld the right of town authorities to suppress any "disorderly conduct or behaviour" within town limits. Such legislation suggests the emergence of competing interests between the aborning market town and its country customers and suppliers. The competition reached a boiling point one busy afternoon in 1822. There was "quite a crowd" in Franklin shopping and doing business when a fight broke out on the streets. The "mele" pitted "the town boys against the country boys," and a local businessman seemed pleased that "the town boys got the advantage of the country boys greatly in the fight."[9] Town residents ultimately sought more than the authority to manage disorderly conduct on the streets—and more constructive ways to express their civic pride than besting the country boys in a street brawl.

When they became incorporated towns in the second decade of the nineteenth century, county seats gained an advantage in the power struggle over regulation of the local market. Town aldermen, empowered with an authority that was independent of the county government, passed laws to regulate the use of town space, restricted the behavior of residents and visitors, and imposed taxes to be spent for the benefit of the town as a whole. Achieving incorporation gave small-town residents the tools to begin constructing their own distinct communal identities in contrast to the larger county. Small-town reputations would be based more concretely however on the physical appearance of the townscapes they built.

Whereas the "shanties" that formed temporary townscapes sprang up seemingly overnight, the buildings that would compose a more permanent townscape took time and money. There was plenty of the former, but the latter was often in short supply during the early nineteenth century. John Shofner's proud recital of changes in the landscape suggested steady growth from the time of the family's arrival. Actually however, from about 1815 to the late 1840s, building activity ebbed and flowed in Middle Tennessee's county seats with the booms and busts of a volatile national economy.[10] Town residents recovered from the Panic of 1819 only to be plunged into the banking crisis of the late 1830s and a depression that lingered into the mid-1840s. John Spence noted that in 1823 there was just enough work to keep a few carpenters employed, "the town having ceased to improve much in the way of buildings." At the time, Murfreesboro consisted of seventy-two town lots in various stages of improvement, inhabited by about 955 residents.[11] Spence concluded that the town had "virtually received the first growth, [and was] content to remain at a stand, waiting for something to give a new impetus."[12]

Likewise, Nathan Vaught remembered that the 1820s and the 1840s were particularly lean decades for building. About the year 1824, he found himself mostly at loose ends. "I employed myself for a short time in building a shanty for a shop to work in and keep my tools in," Vaught wrote, "and to keep from being idle I would employ myself in regulating and fixing up any tools hoping to have work to do after a while."[13] By 1830, frustrated ambitions drove him briefly to storekeeping, which he found even less remunerative than housebuilding. Vaught returned to his hammer in time to receive some large contracts during the 1830s, including several substantial houses, a school, the state bank, and the Methodist Episcopal Church. Once again, around 1840, "work in the building line was getting quite slack," he remembered. "But I kep[t] hammering away[.] Got a little to do now and then."[14] Thus the physical townscape emerged gradually, in fits and starts, in the period that followed incorporation.

Nevertheless, by 1834 when Eastin Morris published his descriptions in the first *Tennessee Gazetteer*, the motley assortment of taverns and shops huddled among tree stumps during the first decade of the century had become "flourishing," "thriving," "handsome" towns.[15] Morris counted 1,000 residents in Murfreesboro. Columbia and Franklin were larger, with about 1,500 residents. Unfortunately for Shelbyville, however, publication of the *Gazetteer* could not have come at a more inopportune moment. The town had recently suffered a double misfortune that reduced the population to about 600. First, a devastating tornado had "almost entirely demolished" the county seat, leaving four dead "and above forty wounded." The beleaguered inhabitants had only just begun to pick up the pieces when they were struck with a cholera epidemic that "raged with great malignancy, . . . about one tenth of the population fell victims to the scourge."[16] For years after publication of this widely circulated account, Shelbyville was forced to defend itself against rumors that it was "a 'sickly' and 'unfortunate' town."[17] *Gazetteer* readers tended to overlook Morris's assertion that since the storm, "most of the buildings have been rebuilt which gives the village a very thriving and handsome appearance."[18]

The judgment that small towns were thriving and handsome was based on an inventory of particular buildings. Each county seat, including the beleaguered Shelbyville, had a printing office, three or more schools, three or four churches, at least ten and as many as twenty stores, and "a number of grist mills, saw mills, cotton gins, &c. in the town and vicinity."[19] Morris's inventory of buildings documented considerable progress in the efforts to replace the first shanty towns with more permanent structures. But to fully understand the relationships among town buildings and the uses of town space, one must dig deeper than the *Gazetteer*. Morris left it up to the imagination of his readers to picture how buildings were arranged within the grid and what made these towns look so "handsome."

Notably absent from the inventories of town buildings listed in the *Gazetteer* were the courthouses that stood at town center. Perhaps these buildings were identified as much with the county as they were with the towns that encircled them. In any case, it is instructive to begin the tour of the townscape of houses on the powerfully symbolic central square. The courthouse was designed to serve the needs of lawyers and judges, yet residents consistently used it for a wide variety of purposes. The Methodist circuit rider, Isaac Conger, preached at the Shelbyville courthouse in 1813 and received dinner invitations from Baptist and Presbyterian families who attended the services. "Had some Imbarresments [*sic*]," he confided to his diary, "as some of the people were diverted with a young fellow that came to the side of the house playing of the juice harp & was stoned away."[20] In 1848, one of the workers laying telegraph line through Williamson County entertained the locals with a "burlesque" lecture on phrenology at the courthouse in Franklin.[21] One year later, a quartet called "The Alleghanians" sang at the courthouse in Columbia.[22]

The variety of ways residents found to use these buildings offers clues to their larger conceptions of town space. Courthouses were multipurpose structures, used for church services, community meetings, and a wide variety of public entertainments. Residents applied a similar principle to their conception of space in the larger townscape.

Though they built in fits and starts throughout the mid-nineteenth century, county seat residents nevertheless conceived their townscapes according to a consistent spatial pattern—the idea of multiple and interchangeable use. In particular, town residents made few distinctions between commercial buildings and family dwellings, either in placement or in appearance. In such small places this kind of spatial use might be considered predictable and unremarkable. Nevertheless, it was consistent with the mixed use of space in larger preindustrial cities. In the county seat, commerce centered on the public square, but the area did not become exclusively defined as a business district. Instead, commercial and residential space intertwined. Shops and stores around the public square served also as residences for the families who managed them. Taverns housed transients and long-term residents alike. As late as 1850, dwellings with their accompanying outbuildings still stood on the streets surrounding the courthouse. Virginia Shelton informed her aunt and uncle the first day she arrived in town that "the very finest house in Murfreesboro [was] a splendid brick edifice on the square & next door to Lytle's Hotel." The Sheltons, a respectable middle-class family, boarded at the hotel while they looked for permanent quarters. It was not considered unfashionable or inconvenient to live in the busiest part of town. On the contrary, Virginia emphasized the social position of her hostess. "Mrs. Spence, a widow[,] is very wealthy & lives in very handsome style," she wrote.[23]

Though town residents did not discriminate between working and living areas, they did begin to sort out certain occupational regions that had long-term influence on town development. The design of the grid, with its central square, played a decisive role. Public squares, where stores and lawyers' offices encircled the courthouse, were the professional and commercial heart of town. It soon became apparent, however, that not all blocks in the grid were created equal. Certain districts acquired early reputations for the character of their entertainments. A ferry house at the Duck River on the northeast margin of Columbia was known as "a very rough place indeed."[24] And by 1826 in Murfreesboro the section of Vine Street extending from the southeast corner of the public square acquired a name because of "several small houses occupied as grocerys [sic], or more generally know[n as], 'Dogerys.'" Long-term town residents remembered this as "a popular neighborhood . . . for meetings by the thirsty from the surrounding country, spending their time, imbibing spirits and boasting of manhood."[25]

Geography was another important factor in the development of small-town neighborhoods. Shallow rivers like the Duck and the Stones may not have been navigable trade routes, but they did provide important sources of power. Mills, warehouses, and factories clustered near the waterfronts. Wealthier town residents built their homes on high ground, rather than near the flood prone "bottoms."

Throughout the mid-nineteenth century, however, these regions remained indistinct. Class differences and considerations of specialized usage played a limited role in the overall arrangement of town space during the 1830s and 1840s. In general, residents did not separate work and residence, and next-door neighbors were likely to display various economic circumstances. As we shall see, this organizing principle of town space would be radically redefined during the 1850s in the third town-building phase.

Significantly, the architectural vocabulary of town residents during the 1830s and 1840s mirrored their generalized organization of space. Town dwellers referred indiscriminately to their buildings as "houses."[26] They built courthouses, storehouses, dwelling houses, and outhouses. Builders chose their materials according to their pocketbooks—brick if they could afford it, clapboard or logs if they could not. Materials and often floor plans were interchangeable, whether the building was intended for commercial or residential purposes. Just as the incorporated town contained few specialized regions, there were also few specialized building forms.

Three surviving buildings in Columbia and Franklin—two residences and a business—suggest the appearance of this townscape of houses. In 1816, while his son James was attending the University of North Carolina in Chapel Hill, Samuel Polk began to build one of the first brick houses in Columbia and moved the rest of his family into town from their farm, which was several miles north of the young county seat. The new Polk home (Fig. 2.1) was on Market Street, three blocks from the public square. (James K. Polk would make a triumphal return to this Columbia home after being

FIGURE 2.1. Polk home in Columbia, Tennessee. (Courtesy of James K. Polk Home)

elected president of the United States in 1844.)[27] Meanwhile, in Franklin, a comparable house (Fig. 2.2) was under construction by 1818 at the corner of Main Street and Cameron, one block from the public square.[28]

Begun within two years of each other, both houses are cut from the same architectural mold, though they were built in different towns by different builders.[29] At a glance, the houses clearly share the same decorative elements, with their three bay facades, off-center arched doorways outlined by fanlights and side lights—all characteristic of the classical revival, or Federal style, sweeping the new nation. The builders saved their most elegant embellishments for the front doorways, which clearly signal their owners' attempts at urban refinement in raw conditions of the newly incorporated towns.[30] Franklin has the best collection of surviving brick dwellings from this period and they all tend to share stylistic and construction characteristics—from their limestone foundations and Flemish bond masonry to their classical door and window designs.

Viewed in the context of a larger townscape, however, the similarities among these dwellings are more than a matter of style. The concept of a townscape of houses is based primarily on the overall arrangement of build-

FIGURE 2.2. Federal house in Franklin, Tennessee. (Photograph by Carroll Van West)

ings and their uses within town space rather than on isolated examples of architectural style and embellishments. A clearer view of these larger relationships among town buildings emerges when the typical residential buildings are compared with a commercial structure from the same period.

In 1818, the same year construction began on the Federal-style house at the corner of Main Street and Cameron, two brickmasons, named Maberry and Faircloth, were paid about $1,100 to build a two-story bank on the northwest corner of the public square in Franklin (Fig. 2.3).[31] This bank building stands today as the oldest commercial building in Franklin and one of the oldest surviving commercial structures in Middle Tennessee. Maberry and Faircloth built the bank to be free-standing. No wall of storefronts encircled the mid-nineteenth-century square. Plate glass windows added later in the nineteenth century significantly altered the appearance of the ground floor. Undoubtedly, the entry was simpler than the elegant doorways of the Eaton and Polk homes. Nevertheless, the commercial building did share many of the visual characteristics of the town's private dwellings. Like the Polk and Eaton houses, it had a three-bay facade, although its narrow orientation to the street made the bank one room wide rather than two. A brick chimney at the north end supplied heat to both the upstairs and the

FIGURE 2.3. The building on the right with the sloping roof is the bank built on the public square in Franklin, Tennessee, in 1818; the bank on the left was built in 1901. Together, the two buildings document a century of change in commercial architecture on the public square. (From the Canaday Files, Franklin, Tennessee)

downstairs rooms. Families of storekeepers often lived upstairs or in back rooms of such business houses on the public square, combining commercial and residential space.

The most popular form of house by far was what Nathan Vaught called the "double house"—one room deep and two rooms wide, divided by a central hall (Fig. 2.4).[32] If the building had a second story, rooms were arranged identically upstairs. Built of log, frame, or brick, "double houses" were common both in town and throughout the countryside. In fact, this type of balanced spatial arrangement was so universal that Virginia Shelton's toddler son, David, mastered the double house form almost before he learned to walk. His mother proudly watched as the aspiring young architect constructed houses on the parlor floor. "He has a set of little blocks not two inches square & I am amused at the mathematical figures, the fine houses &

FIGURE 2.4. This "double house" in Murfreesboro is typical of the form frequently constructed by Nathan Vaught and other Middle Tennessee builders. It is a close cousin to the "I-house," a type of domestic building defined by vernacular architecture historians as one room deep, two rooms wide, and two stories tall with a central hall. (Photograph by author)

porticoes & temples & amphitheatres &c. which he constructs." David Shelton already had a keen eye for style, but regardless of embellishment, the child always arranged his floor plans in the same way. "Everything he makes is perfectly regular," his mother noticed. "Sometimes he has quite a castle with a dozen rooms, but there is always the same number [of rooms] & of the same size on the opposite sides."[33] David may have been an imaginative young builder, but he learned the interchangeable applications of symmetry by observing the "double houses" of Murfreesboro.

Young David clearly grasped the same spatial principle that Nathan Vaught used to build houses—a wide range of styles and uses could be applied to the same balanced floor plan. Just as David used the same principle for his miniature dwellings, temples, and amphitheaters, John Spence's descriptions of stores on the Square in Murfreesboro suggest that the double-house form was also commonly used for commercial buildings. One store on the north side of the Square had two "store rooms each occupied by merchants" on the ground floor, while one of the second story

FIGURE 2.5. Originally detached, the service buildings of this house on Margin Street in Franklin have been incorporated into the main body of the house to form a rear ell. (Photograph by author)

rooms was used by the Masons. Another large two-story brick building housed two stores on the west side of the Square.[34] Thus the double house was adapted to both residential and commercial uses in the townscape of houses.

Architectural embellishments became more elaborate as new sawmills improved building technology, and local builders chose from an increasing variety of decorative possibilities. By 1831, John Gadsey even advertised himself not simply as a builder or house carpenter, but as an "architect and joiner." Signaling a new level of industry in the local building trades, he established a lumberyard in Franklin, where he erected a "substantial kiln, for drying plank," and promised to "constantly keep on hand a good assortment of well seasoned timber," including poplar, cedar, and walnut.[35] Emphasis shifted from the elegant doorways of the Federal style to the imposing porticoes of the Greek Revival; yet, regardless of style, the first generation of town builders continued to conceive their buildings indiscriminately as "houses."

With its widely scattered collection of "double houses" there was little to

FIGURE 2.6. This rear view of the Spence house in Murfreesboro shows the service region of the dwelling. Often apparent wings or ells of town houses were originally detached service buildings like those commonly found on rural farmsteads. (Photograph by author)

physically or architecturally distinguish town from countryside during the mid-nineteenth century. For example, in 1845, John W. Childress advertised his mother's house for rent. In addition to the dwelling itself, the property also offered "a large Garden, with a variety of Fruit trees, a well of Water on the premises, and a large horse lot, with all necessary out buildings."[36] Such a description might apply to countless farms throughout the countryside except for the fact that Childress indicated that the property was located "in the East end" of Murfreesboro.

Thus, in many respects, town lots resembled farm yards. Dwellings stood back from the street on large, unsubdivided blocks, accompanied by the same kinds of outbuildings necessary to operate country households—smokehouses, kitchens, barns (Figs. 2.5 and 2.6). Moving from the center of town to the margins, residences became increasingly dispersed until the townscape of houses merged with the countryside.

Nevertheless, Mary Polk quickly learned that local residents perceived a great deal of difference between town and countryside when she took up residence in Columbia as the new bride of William Polk. Among her first

visitors were Mr. and Mrs. Andrew Polk, "as they are considered the aristocracy of the neighborhood, suppose I ought to feel flattered," Mary allowed
begrudgingly. The visit left a residue of ill will for the new town dweller.
"Mrs. Andrew informed me that it was considered *more aristocratic to live
out of the town.*"[37] Apparently, they hadn't read the newspaper during the
election campaign of 1844 when the local editor had declared that selfish
aristocrats predominated in town while the countryside was the stronghold
of honest yeomen. Architectural evidence suggests that the truth was somewhere between these two extremes. Aristocrats could be found at home in
both town and country, intermingled with humbler homeowners.

Certainly many of the finest dwellings were built several miles from town
on country plantations. Mary Polk herself attended a dinner party at Gideon
Pillow's plantation, five miles west of town. Columbia builder Nathan
Vaught had done "the carpenter's work" on the Pillow residence, which
impressed him as "a very fine large brick dwelling house containing 12
rooms and 2 large halls."[38] But small towns contained a diverse population
that included residents of considerable wealth as well as the middling and
lower sort.

Besides architecture, town residents used a variety of other tools for
making social distinctions.[39] In particular, status markers tended to be portable and personal—carriages, clothing, speech patterns. According to John
Spence the owners of carriages "were considered the first class" because
they made such an elaborate public show of their status, "usually putting on
considerable style," using their carriages "whenever the roads would permit
travelling."[40] Since only a very few families owned carriages, clothing and
education served as a more widespread markers of social status and distinctions between town and country folk.[41] Duncan Brown Frierson, a merchant
in Columbia, had great disdain for his country customers. He complained
bitterly that he spent "every day of his life measuring calicoes and Lasses[,]
weighing nails and copperas, and talking to old women as old as Methusilah
[*sic*], and as ugly as a Jackass, or quarelling with some fellow about his
account, who couldn't take two from five and tell how many remained, or
trying to fit some Gall from the nobs in a pair of shoes, the sight of whose
foot would make a Bull bellow, or some other menial office of which a
picture is a shadow to the reality."[42] Such attitudes also suggest why country
residents might consider town dwellers pretentious and aristocratic.

Thus the border between town and country was defined by attitudes as
much as it was apparent in the landscape. The architectural boundary

between town and country remained obscure in the townscape of houses, particularly at the margins where town lots resembled farm lots. Moreover, architecture played a secondary role in distinguishing social ranks in town and beyond. But Middle Tennesseans increasingly recognized a distinction between town and country during the mid-nineteenth century.

The relationship between town and country changed significantly as the townscape of houses took shape during the early nineteenth century. When Shelbyville became an incorporated town in 1819, it had only recently lost a struggle to impose taxes on farmers who sold their produce within town limits. By the 1840s, Middle Tennesseans could not agree on whether the town or the countryside was more aristocratic. During the intervening years, towns had developed into thriving communities. Thus, changing attitudes toward town life were produced in large part by the appearance of a substantial and prosperous townscape of houses.

But the changes were not confined to town space. At the same time that residents were building the townscape of houses, they also extended Main Street into the countryside. By the 1840s, improved roads made the county seat accessible to an ever-widening circle of country residents. When Mary Polk arrived in Columbia just after her marriage to William Polk, one of her first jobs was to get acquainted with the neighborhood. She found that her circle of acquaintances extended well beyond town limits. "This has been quite a 'reception week,'" she declared, "every body has called within six miles."[43] Perhaps not everyone who lived within six miles of Columbia came to town to welcome Mary, but it was no exaggeration that towns drew their steady customers from a six-mile radius by the 1840s. Mary herself had traveled five miles outside of town for a fashionable dinner at the Pillow plantation. In order to fully understand the relationship between town and country during this period, it is necessary to look more closely at the ways that road building affected the extension of town influence and the construction of distinctive town identities.

Main Streets and Turnpikes:
The Construction of Town Networks

The transportation and market revolutions that stimulated urban growth in the Northeast also had a profound impact on the relationship between town and countryside in the Upland South. Middle Tennessee's county seats expanded their role from small government center to diversified service and retail center for the surrounding farming communities. The key to progress and prosperity was transportation. John Shofner could barely contain his amazement at the ongoing revolution in space and time. His father had arrived in Bedford County when flatboats supplied the chief means of river traffic. "It was then a trip of three month to go from nashvill to New Orleans and back," he remembered. The new steamboat had changed those days forever. "Now they purform a trip in 12 or 15 days to and from[,] lode and unlode[,] and carrey a burden of four or five hundred thousand [pounds?]." Unfortunately, the steamboat had only limited impact on daily travel conditions for Bedford County residents. "Our rodes are muddey in the winter time so that it is harde to get to market," he complained. But not for long. "To remmidey this evil the legeslater chartered a rode from Shelbyvill to Nashvill by way of Murpheesburrow."[44] With this simple statement, John Shofner announced the arrival of the turnpike era—one of the most significant mid-nineteenth-century projects of spatial transformation in Middle Tennessee.

Turnpikes were not the first roads to be built in the region. Between 1799 and 1802, laborers had hacked a wagon road up to fifteen feet wide through the forest from the mountains of East Tennessee to Nashville.[45] In 1821, the Tennessee legislature classified three different grades of roads in the state—stage roads (the Main Streets of the countryside) about twenty or thirty feet wide; wagon roads about twelve feet wide; and a third class of roads wide enough only for horse and rider.[46] Five years before the turnpike was completed from Nashville to Shelbyville, a four-horse stage already traveled three times a week between Murfreesboro and Shelbyville.[47] But whether they were wide enough for a stage or mere paths for horse and rider, Middle Tennessee roads were often impassable.

John Spence made no notice of the different grades of roads, saying simply that "the usual travel was on common roads, with great labor, wear and tear of wagon and teams."[48] In 1834, one Nashville newspaper editor bemoaned the condition of the road between Franklin and Columbia, a distance of about twenty-seven miles:

> With a heavy load of cotton a strong team cannot travel more than 10 or 15 miles a day. The mud is from 6 to 18 inches deep, the ruts are frequent and dangerous quagmires, which occur "ever and anon," are bridged over with logs that are often broken or decayed. . . . The driver

60   BUILDING TOWNS

whips and swears and sweats—the horses pull and plunge—the gears break—some of the cotton bales are tossed off in the *melee*—and, thus, at last, after three or four days of toil and labour, by mending the gears with *hickory withes*, and propping the wheels with *fence rails* and probably losing part of his cargo by the way side, the tired driver and jaded horses reach Franklin, with a load of six or eight bales of cotton.[49]

Once they reached Franklin, however, the "tired driver and jaded horses" could complete their journey to Nashville with relative ease, unloading what was left of their cargo at the Cumberland River. The muddy quagmire from Columbia to Franklin gave way to a newly paved, eighteen-mile turnpike that connected Franklin to Nashville. Historians have chiefly defined turnpikes in economic terms, as toll roads built by private stock companies, chartered by state governments. But contemporaries like John Spence and the Nashville newspaper editor were more impressed by the practical differences between mud and macadam. Macadamized roads were paved with several compacted layers of sized gravel. Larger stones provided a solid roadbed and smaller gravel was compacted on the top layer for a smooth road surface.[50] In many ways the construction of macadamized roads created two worlds in nineteenth-century Middle Tennessee. One world centered on towns, including about a six-mile radius of surrounding countryside, connected by paved turnpikes. Another, more isolated and geographically expansive world depended on unpaved country roads that could become impassable after a soaking rain.[51] The residents of this deep countryside might make a trip to town once a year to trade homemade jeans for store-bought cups and saucers.[52]

In 1834, the year John Shofner described the transformation of Bedford County to his brother, the turnpike from Nashville to Franklin was the only macadamized road in Middle Tennessee. By 1841, a system of macadamized roads radiated outward from Nashville to surrounding county seats, including Franklin, Columbia, Murfreesboro, and Shelbyville.[53] Shofner himself bought a share in the Shelbyville Turnpike, for which he had already "pade 70 dollars and owed 30 dollars." He did not actually attempt to spell the word, but he did explain how macadamization was applied to the new fifty-five-mile turnpike that ran south from Nashville, through Murfreesboro, to Shelbyville. "This rode is to bee throd up leavel thirty feete wide . . . and then graveld over twenty feete wide and the gravel to bee nine inches thick," he wrote. Local residents expected great returns for their investment. "It is thought then that a teem can pull from 5 to 6 thousand pounds."[54] But in 1853, Virginia Shelton still found traveling from Murfreesboro to Shelbyville fatiguing, "even on that fine smooth turnpike."[55]

The paved turnpike Virginia Shelton traveled linked Murfreesboro and Shelbyville from public square to public square. Known as Church Street in town, it became the Shelbyville Turnpike as it left Murfreesboro. Likewise, Main Street in Murfreesboro led out of town to the east as the Woodbury Turnpike. Three of the primary streets leading from the public square in Murfreesboro became major turnpikes at the outskirts of town. In fact, macadamized turnpikes became essentially extensions of macadamized town streets, connecting one public square to another, often along a straight line through the countryside. Main Street may have passed almost imperceptibly into a macadamized turnpike, but these roads did not simply connect a town to its contiguous countryside. From a broader perspective, turnpikes also linked county seat to county seat, creating a whole network of towns clearly differentiated from the countryside.

This town network offered a whole series of social and commercial possibilities unlike any rural experience. In 1845, Fannie Blount O'Brien told her sister she had been "to every store in Franklin," looking for just the right piece of velvet to make a new dress. Unfortunately, none of the Franklin stores had what she sought, but Fannie told her sister with complete confidence, "I expect you can get some in Murfreesboro." If the merchandise could not be found anywhere in the town, all roads led to Nashville, the largest city in Middle Tennessee. Indeed, Fannie sent a store clerk from Franklin "all over Nashville," in pursuit of a particular sample of fringe.[56] Alas, the coveted fringe was not discovered anywhere within the broad limits of the city.

County seats carefully cultivated their economic position as market centers, building public squares and Main Streets that were increasingly emblematic of commercial prosperity. Macadamized turnpikes radiated through the countryside but gathered rural commerce to the center of the county as they converged on the public square. There the townscape differentiated itself most clearly from the countryside. By 1844, in Franklin "all of the paved sidewalks in town were on Main Cross Street & Main Street."[57] Small-town ambitions could be frustrating, as Fannie O'Brien learned in her futile search for the perfect fringe. But residents increasingly aimed to set the fashion standard and rarely confined themselves to the commercial limitations of Nashville. In fact, from the initial stages of development, town businessmen established connections to an urban network that extended far beyond regional boundaries.

Public Buildings and Urban Aspirations

From the 1820s to the 1840s, residents added a series of public buildings that signaled the commercial opportunities of town life. The *Columbia Observer* noted, in 1838, that a joint stock company "with a capital of $20,000" had been formed to build a "new and commodious" hotel. According to the newspaper, this building would join "the various and important public structures that are now going up in our town."[58] From 1835 to 1839, Nathan Vaught found himself very busy providing framing, flooring, and finish work on many of these projects, including a female college, a Methodist church, a new brick jail and market house, and the state bank.[59] Such public structures differentiated the communal life of the town from the dispersed households of the countryside. The public buildings that emerged in the townscape of houses clearly demonstrated town residents' identification and familiarity with architectural developments in distant cities. Few banks or Masonic halls graced the countryside, and town dwellers self-consciously selected specific urban models to design appropriate public buildings.

From the initial stages of development, the townscape of houses reflected prevailing concepts of urban design. Cities of the eighteenth and early nineteenth centuries displayed the same patterns of spatial organization that small towns employed. Work space and residential space intertwined in the preindustrial city and the early-nineteenth-century county seat alike. Social classes lived in close proximity on the same streets, instead of forming class-based neighborhoods. Town and urban dwellers attached similar value to property. Town lots were most valuable around the public square in the same way that land concentrated near the urban center was more expensive than property at its fringes.[60] Town and urban dwellers spoke the same architectural language. They lived, worked, and played in store houses, market houses, and coffee houses. These similarities were not coincidental. During the earliest stages of town building, county seat residents aligned themselves with urban interests that set them apart from their rural neighbors.

As soon as the first dry goods store opened on the square—long before the first turnpike was macadamized—merchants established a commercial circuit that took them regularly to urban centers far beyond Middle Tennessee. Every year they traveled down to New Orleans or up to Philadelphia to purchase goods for their stores. In 1818, a year before the town was incorporated, Shelbyville merchants announced the results of their business trips one after another. Roberts and Green declared that their brick storehouse on the east side of the public square was bursting with "a new & elegant assortment of Goods" recently selected "at Philadelphia, by an experienced hand and good judge of merchandize."[61] William Wightman was opening a new store where "a large, elegant & fashionable assortment of merchandize" had "just arrived from Philadelphia and Baltimore."[62] James Brittain bought groceries in Baltimore: green coffee, teas, pepper, allspice, brimstone, indigo, madder, Spanish Brown, ginger, sugar.[63] John A. Marrs opened a general store "in his new frame house" on the northeast corner of the public square. He purchased his "new and well selected assortment of dry goods, hardware," and groceries in Philadelphia, Baltimore, and New Orleans.[64]

Dry goods and groceries were not the only things town dwellers were importing from distant cities. Philadelphia in particular set the architectural standard for public building in the townscape of houses. Merchants who traveled there yearly to select merchandise from urban wholesalers, also witnessed the latest architectural developments. As town dwellers added public buildings—churches, banks, Masonic halls—they often selected specific urban models and modified them to suit small-town budgets. Middle Tennesseans seemed especially fond of buildings designed by the fashionable young Philadelphia architect William Strickland. In fact, Strickland actually ended his career in Nashville as architect of the state capitol and was buried on the grounds in 1854, before the building could be completed.[65] But versions of Strickland's buildings were already familiar features of county seat townscapes long before the architect himself set foot in Tennessee in 1845.

While town commissioners were laying out streets in Middle Tennessee county seats, Strickland was beginning his career in Philadelphia. He would ultimately become widely recognized for his Greek Revival buildings, but his first independent commission was a Gothic structure. In 1808, Strickland designed the Masonic hall in Philadelphia. Gothic windows and battlements distinguished the two-story brick building, which was crowned by a 180-foot steeple (Fig. 2.7). Philadelphia Masons dedicated their new hall in 1811. The steeple burned in 1819 and was not replaced. Four years later, the

FIGURE 2.7. William Strickland designed the Masonic hall in Philadelphia in 1808. (Courtesy of Historical Society of Pennsylvania)

Masons in Franklin, Tennessee, completed their own lodge, clearly inspired by Strickland's Philadelphia design.[66]

One block from the public square, with its streets laid out on the Philadelphia plan, the Masonic lodge rose an impressive three stories to become the tallest building in Franklin.[67] The unknown designer modified Strickland's Gothic composition, but retained the essential configuration of the Philadelphia facade (Fig. 2.8). Both buildings were symmetrically divided into three parts by shallow pilasters, capped with pinnacles that punctuated a crenellated roofline. The arched windows were accentuated by masonry

FIGURE 2.8. Facade of Masonic hall built in Franklin, Tennessee, around 1823.
(Photograph by Carroll Van West)

BUILDING TOWNS

FIGURE 2.9. Side view of Masonic hall, Franklin. (Photograph by author)

stringcourses. Viewed from the front, the Masonic hall in Franklin had all
the stylistic features of its urban counterpart. Viewed from the side, however, the small-town lodge revealed its humbler circumstances (Fig. 2.9).
The body of the building was an unembellished brick box disguised behind
the three-story facade that extended beyond its walls.

The Masonic hall stood out in the Franklin townscape not only because it
was the tallest building but also because it was one of the few Gothic
structures in town. The style was a logical choice given the purpose of the
building. Architecture and experience converged in the small-town Masonic
hall. "The new lodge is very handsome," Joanna Rucker told her aunt,
Sarah Polk, after attending "a Masonic 'Levee'" in Murfreesboro in 1849.
"The whole effect was heightened by the regalia," she continued, suggesting
the symbolic connections between the building itself and the "ecclesiastical"
rituals practiced by the Masons. "The royal high masons had their robes
and caps on," she explained the ceremony. "I was escorted in by the high
priest & you know I must have enjoyed it as I have a leaning toward the
Catholics."[68] The building Rucker knew no longer stands, but the ceremony
she witnessed was practiced in Masonic halls throughout Middle Tennessee
and beyond. Such buildings, and the rituals that enlivened them, aligned the
town with social forms of the city in contrast to the countryside.

FIGURE 2.10. United States Bank in Philadelphia, designed by William Strickland in 1818. (Courtesy of Library of Congress, Prints and Photographs Division, HABS PA, 51-Phila 223-5)

While Masonic halls were surrounded by highly civilized associations of ancient ritual, banks declared small-town dreams of financial power and urban prosperity.[69] On west Main Street in Columbia, residents constructed their branch of the state bank, and they found architectural inspiration in Philadelphia. There, in 1818, the board of directors for the Second Bank of the United States sought competitors to design their new building. The directors specified that they were "desirous of exhibiting a chase [*sic*] imitation of Grecian Architecture, in its simplest and least expensive form."[70] The winning architect, William Strickland, took his inspiration from the ancient Parthenon, striving "to preserve all the characteristics of a Grecian temple" yet adapt the design to the modern commercial interests of a bank, "requiring a peculiar internal arrangement and distribution of space and light."[71] The architect resolved this dilemma by designing Doric porticoes at the front and rear of the building, while eliminating the surrounding colonnade (Fig. 2.10). Strickland explained that the "flanking columns of a Grecian building" were "decidedly beautiful," but "they cannot be applied with

FIGURE 2.11. Bank of the State of Tennessee, built in Columbia by Nathan Vaught around 1839. (Photograph by Carroll Van West)

their proper effect to places of business, without a sacrifice of those principles which have a constant application to internal uses and economy."[72]

Strickland's temple of commerce became an influential model of the proper Philadelphia banking house, widely imitated in Tennessee. In his *Gazetteer*, Eastin Morris remarked that the Union Bank of the State of Tennessee, under construction in Nashville in 1833, was "a splendid house on the style of the United States Bank at Philadelphia."[73] Knoxville boasted its own version of the bank by 1836, and in 1839 Nathan Vaught was hard at work on Columbia's own rendition (Fig. 2.11). Vaught did not design the building himself, and his experience illuminates the role vernacular builders played in rendering small-town versions of urban models.

In sharp contrast to the classically trained architect William Strickland, the small-town builder Nathan Vaught received his only formal education in a country school, where he spent ten or twelve months acquiring "some knowledge of figures and the use of the pen to a very limited extent."[74] Vaught typically used classical embellishments requested by his fashionable clients, but he never employed academic terminology in matters of style. While Strickland puzzled over the salient characteristics of ancient Grecian temples, Vaught consistently described his own buildings in terms of size and materials.[75] In 1838, Vaught constructed an impressive two-story Ionic portico for Gideon Pillow's country house but described the building simply as "a very fine large brick dwelling house containing 12 rooms and 2 large halls."[76] One year later, construction of the state bank at Columbia brought together the academic architectural design of William Strickland and the vernacular building practice of Nathan Vaught. Vaught betrayed no knowledge of the Greek Revival architect in his memoir and probably worked from architectural plans provided by the bank's directors.[77] Nevertheless, the bank itself revealed Strickland's influence. A modest Doric portico framed the entrance, but it was the composition of the side walls that displayed the most direct connection to the Philadelphia temple of commerce. Though the Columbia bank was smaller and had fewer windows, the fenestration pattern followed Strickland's own compromise for a bank "requiring a peculiar internal arrangement and distribution of space and light" (compare Figs. 2.10 and 2.11).[78]

The Masonic hall and the state bank were designed to serve specialized social and commercial functions, yet these communal buildings fit easily within the townscape of "houses." Neither building signaled a significant reorganization of town space. Masonic halls, like courthouses, hosted a wide variety of public events. Before they built their own church, Episcopalians in Franklin began meeting at the Masonic Hall in 1827, and Andrew Jackson negotiated the Chickasaw Treaty of 1830 there, rather than at the courthouse. In Columbia, the community attended concerts, and church ladies held fairs and suppers at the Masonic Hall.[79] As for the Columbia bank, Nathan Vaught's contract specified that he construct, in addition to the bank itself, "all the family apartments connected with the same[.] Also all the outbuilding[,] driveways[,] ectera. All these improvements built of brick and covered with tin."[80] Bank directors did not conceive of their town lot as a purely commercial space. Instead, residential space mingled with business space in the pattern of mixed-use that defined the townscape of "houses."

Although town dwellers often selected specific urban models for their public buildings and organized town space within an urban grid, towns were not simple urban microcosms. Lodged on a spatial continuum somewhere between the city and the country, small towns offered a distinctive lifestyle. Joanna Rucker personally experienced the difference. She spent time with her aunt and uncle, Sarah and James K. Polk, at the White House in Washington. When she returned to her family in Murfreesboro, town residents found it difficult to believe that she could be content with the decidedly slower social routine. "I am often asked if I do not find the town *intolerably* dull after living in a place so gay as Washington," she told her aunt.

> My reply is that I was prepared to find Murfreesboro just as I left it or rather as it is & I would not alter it if I could. I amuse myself by laughing & talking. I have as many & more books of interest to read than I can get through with. I sometimes walk down to grandma's and back. And every few days I am cheered with a letter or a bundle of newspapers, & sometimes a novel from some of my friends in Washington.[81]

Rucker found small pleasures in town life that compensated for the faster pace of the city. Conversation, reading, walking—these were her satisfying small-town amusements. She felt far from isolated, within a few days' news of her friends in Washington. Nevertheless, when her sister, Sarah, was planning to visit the Polks at the White House, Joanna advised her not to have any dresses made in Murfreesboro, "as they will look odd and old fashioned in Washington."[82] Measured by eastern standards, Middle Tennessee county seats seemed out-of-date, but they were far from backcountry towns by the 1840s.

At the same time that the Rucker sisters were comparing the relative merits of town and city life, Elizabeth Bowman, who had migrated west, wrote to her old friend in Franklin, wistfully seeking the latest fashion news from her old home.

> Martha Ann I must ask you a very *important* question so considered in these parts as I have been living so secluded and so far from the "cross roads" for some time past—so you must not laugh at me as I ask more for the benefit of others than myself.—What is the fashion for making sleeves now to all kinds of summer dresses? . . . if I was up at Home I would have to be *remodeled before* I could make my appearance in *Franklin* as I am *old timey*—though *quite fashionable* looking by some of the people in the country here.[83]

Bowman's choice of words was not accidental. From her perspective, Middle Tennessee towns truly occupied a "cross roads"—the median between the western edge of the frontier and the eastern standard of fashion. Bowman's regional identity was also largely based on the distinctive position of small towns in the spatial continuum between city and countryside.

The Ceremonial Townscape:
Constructing a Distinctive Town-centered Identity

From the 1820s through the 1840s, towns increasingly stood out from the countryside. New public buildings, patterned after examples in distant cities—churches, courthouses, Masonic lodges—provided landmarks of town space. This townscape of houses was the stage for a rich ceremonial culture enacted in political contests, local fairs, and civic celebrations.[84] The rituals of small-town life, however, did not necessarily mirror the forms and meanings of urban ones. Town residents used new public buildings in gatherings and ceremonies that helped to construct distinct town identities.[85]

At first glance, the parades, orations, picnics, and fairs that composed the ceremonial townscape appear to flow seamlessly into one another—one parade looking very much like the next. Upon closer inspection, however, these separate elements of the ceremonial townscape may actually be organized into two different types of celebrations. One set encompassed countywide events like the mass political meetings of the period. In contrast to the countywide mass meetings that brought thousands of people to town during the 1840s, a second set of much smaller town-centered celebrations primarily involved town residents as the chief participants. Small-town streets and public buildings had the capacity to contain these crowds, and as a result the action of these public ceremonies took place primarily within town borders. Town-centered ceremonies shaped small-town identities by distinguishing town from countryside and by sorting out town residents according to race, gender, and status.

The ceremonial townscape was constructed almost exclusively by white town residents. This is not to say that black residents were absent from public ceremonies, rather their roles were unofficial and thus largely undocumented.[86] Nevertheless, scattered references make it clear that black residents participated at least as spectators and occasionally played more prominent roles. For example, during a hazardous celebration in Columbia "two Negro men" were wounded when the town cannon misfired due to "carelessness in *swabing* [*sic*]."[87] Apparently, they had been helping to reload the weapon, which served a ceremonial rather than a defensive purpose, to fire another round when it went off. Beyond such occasional references it is also logical to assume that slaves played important behind-the-scenes roles—as cooks for picnics, as polishers and menders of parade regalia—that made public celebrations successful.[88]

BUILDING TOWNS

In addition to its racial configuration, the ceremonial townscape was also gendered. Men and women played distinctive roles and organized distinctive types of rituals. As organizers of public fairs and suppers, genteel white women in particular played an important role in the construction of this ceremonial townscape. For example, the Masonic hall in Columbia was the site of a "Ladies' Fair" on the Fourth of July in 1834. Although plenty of country folk were probably in town to celebrate the popular national holiday, the advertisement for the fair emphasized that items on display had been "tastefully and dilligently prepared by the Ladies of Columbia." They did more than put their homemade wares on public display. They sold the goods, "combining all the varieties of utility and ornament, for the use of both Ladies and Gentlemen," at "moderate" prices. In addition to the exhibition and sale, the fair concluded with "a supper, also, furnished and served by the Ladies . . . spread at candle-lighting."[89] In this instance there is no indication of how the ladies intended to spend the proceeds from their fair—whether as personal income, or for a good civic cause. The latter seems more likely.

Ladies' fairs and ladies' suppers, organized by genteel town women and housed in prominent public buildings like the Masonic hall seem to have been designed as charity events for important town causes. The women of the Methodist Episcopal Church in Columbia held a "Ladies Supper" at the Masonic hall in 1834. They intended specifically to raise money "to aid their Brethren in the liquidation of the heavy debt (by which they are now severely oppressed) incurred by them in the erection of the splendid new church in this place."[90] The announcement is a rare piece of evidence suggesting the role town women played in the construction of buildings.

More often than this direct participation of Methodist women as fund-raisers for a specific building in Columbia, women played a broader social role in the construction of town identities. The contrasts between the Ladies' Fair at the Masonic hall in Columbia and an agricultural fair at the courthouse in Shelbyville suggest the competition between town and country women that helped to shape the ceremonial townscape. According to John Shofner, the women of Shelbyville displayed their "industry and inginuity" in the courthouse to a large and appreciative audience. "Counter-pins[,] jenes[,] linsey[,] sowing silk and even socks ware exhibited and the best of each parsel got the premiumb." Clearly if Shofner had been the judge each craftswoman would have received a prize. "I can say with truth that I neaver have saw such a parsel of counterpins for beauty," he declared. Based on the display of female skill and refinement that day at the courthouse, Shofner concluded enthusiastically, "the sosiety bids fare to improve our cuntrey."[91]

Though he expected women to play a significant role in a generalized social improvement, the women themselves seem to have had more individualized achievements in mind. Shofner could not help but notice that "thare was a gratual of interest among the brite eyes to know which shold excell the other." These female participants were far from passive spectators in the judging process. The emphasis was on skill and the competitive spirit among the women was conspicuous. It is tempting to speculate, given this evidence of palpable competition in Shelbyville, how the genteel ladies of Columbia competed to see who could sell the first utilitarian or ornamental handiwork, who could earn the most money or public praise for their skill. More importantly, it is interesting to note the timing of the Ladies' Fair, with its items "tastefully and dilligently prepared" specifically by genteel town ladies, on the Fourth of July—a day when rural women would be in town to witness their exhibit. Perhaps there was an element of competition in the event as town women sought to differentiate their refined skills and fashionable designs from the old-fashioned jeans and counterpanes produced by their rural counterparts.

Of course, not all town women were considered "ladies" and it is unclear who actually attended these seemingly public events. Though the Ladies' Fair in Columbia was announced in the local newspaper, the advertisement noted that "Ladies and Gentlemen are generally and respectfully invited to attend." Whether this was simply a polite way of inviting everybody in town or understood by readers as a message of exclusion, the appellation of "Lady" seems to have had broader application in the 1830s and 1840s than it would have in the 1850s.

In contrast to the potentially selective audience of the Ladies Fairs, discreetly contained within a public building, it was almost impossible to avoid masculine celebrations in the small town. When the Odd Fellows dedicated their new lodge in Murfreesboro with "a great parade and dinner," Joanna Rucker may not have heard the orations, but as the next-door neighbor she was a reluctant member of the audience. "The noise and confusion was so great that the day appeared a week long to me," she complained.[92]

The most elaborate and conspicuous roles in the ceremonial townscape were played by men who organized themselves into militia companies (the Franklin Independent Blues, the Franklin Guards, the Columbia Guards) and civic groups (the Odd Fellows, the Freemasons and the Sons of Temperance). Regardless of the group or the occasion, masculine ceremonies were composed from a particular set of activities. They rarely stopped with a single event, instead combining parades, orations, and picnics into entire days devoted to public celebration. The 1831 Fourth of July celebration in Franklin began in typical fashion with a parade. "At 10 o'clock in the morning, the two volunteer companies, the Franklin Independent Blues, and Franklin Guards, were paraded in handsome uniform and equipment, on the public square. After being carried through a routine of military exercises by their officers, they marched to the Methodist Church, where they were met by a numerous assemblage of ladies and gentlemen."[93] Orations at the church were followed by a public picnic.[94]

Processions tended to be hierarchical but inclusive. For example, the following order of procession at a Fourth of July parade in Columbia was announced in advance in the local newspaper:

> Cavalry, with Orator, in front. Music. President and Vice President. The Clergy. The Columbia Guards. The Artilery. The Citizens in General.[95]

The procession reserved prominent positions for participants from Columbia—ministers, town militia, President Polk. Thus the parade reinforced the rank and status of powerful town leaders, but in proper Jacksonian style it also included "the citizens in general."

Unfortunately, the newspaper did not publish the parade route on that Fourth of July in Columbia. Nevertheless it is clear that town space shaped these events in significant ways. Announced in local newspapers, such celebrations seem to have been broadly attended by a wide range of town residents. While the public square usually served as the starting point for parades, public buildings—churches, Odd Fellows and Masonic halls—places capable of accommodating an audience, were the destination of paraders. The parade route through town streets offered a virtually unrestricted audience. By contrast, the scene for orations and ladies' fairs worked to restrict the audience to the advertised "ladies and gentlemen." These events tended to be housed in churches or Masonic halls, where seating was limited and some town residents might have understood themselves to be excluded.

The public buildings that contained town-centered ceremonies were certainly no match for the mass meetings of Jacksonian era politics. In particular, the election campaign that sent James K. Polk to the White House in 1844 was the most exciting event Middle Tennesseans had ever witnessed. "I must commence on polliticks as our state neever was in such a commotion," John Shofner wrote his brother from Shelbyville. "We are living here at the home of Jackson and Poke[.] You may gess that everything is at the hiest pitch. Thare is mass meeting after mass meeting."[96] The campaign truly did bring out masses of Middle Tennesseans in unprecedented numbers—and they streamed into town. Shelbyville, Murfreesboro, and Columbia (Polk's hometown)—one after another, county seats all over Middle Tennessee played host to mass meetings.[97]

James K. Polk came of age in the small towns of Middle Tennessee. He started his political career as a clerk in the state senate when Murfreesboro was the capital. There he met Sarah Childress, and they were married in her father's home on Main Street. They took up residence in Columbia, where several generations of the Polk family presided among the wealthiest plantation owners and town residents.

Though Polk was from Columbia, he was not necessarily a local hero. His opponent, Henry Clay, found ardent supporters among Whigs like John Shofner from Shelbyville. In a two-day mass meeting there in November 1844, the Whigs tried their best to outdo the Democrats, who had recently concluded a meeting in town. According to Shofner's eyewitness account, they must have given the Democrats a run for their money.

On normal days Shelbyville was home to less than a thousand people. If Shofner's estimates were accurate, the town's population increased twenty times overnight. "I think thare must have been over 20 thousent person and they ware all intertaind free of cost two days and nites." Shofner was consistent in his estimates of the crowd's size. At the public dinner on the second day of the rally "thare was 20 tables each 80 yards long." Shofner calculated that "ten thousand cold eate at a time."[98] Multiple seatings at the dinner tables showed that most of the people who had arrived in town for the parade on Wednesday stayed to picnic on Thursday. Whatever the actual number of participants, the small town clearly strained at the seams.

The impressive crowds that gathered in Shelbyville on that November week in 1844 may have been unprecedented in the town's history, but they were actually participating in a widespread American phenomenon. The 1830s and 1840s were the heyday of public ceremonies in American cities. Parades in particular developed as a way of sorting competing constituencies in a pluralistic urban society.[99] Participants in urban parades represented all ranks of society, but actual paraders were almost exclusively male. John Shofner's vivid description of the Whig rally in Shelbyville demonstrates that small-town and rural southerners also were enthusiastic paraders. Nevertheless, small-town ceremonies had a dynamic all their own. As the Whig rally in Shelbyville unfolded, the ceremonies presented some interesting contrasts with the pattern of urban parades from the same period— particularly regarding the participation of women.

Town and country residents combined their resources to make the meeting a success. "Thare was a grateeal of corn and fodder halled in," Shofner boasted, "and abundence of meete and bread besides that," he added. Normally, the public square was the exclusive territory of signs, but this week visitors found the whole town swathed with banners. "Every whighouse in town was throde wide open and a sine hange at every dore withe the motto [']welcome here[.']"[100] But even if every Whig household in Shelbyville had taken in a visiting family, the crowd must have spilled out into camps around town.

With all the chaotic hustle and bustle, it must have been difficult to organize these Whigs into meaningful political ritual. But somehow they did achieve a ceremonial order, spending most of the first day with a highly entertaining parade. Festivities began on a Wednesday about two o'clock in the afternoon when "the uniform compenies came poring in from the surrounding counteys." They kept coming all afternoon "till the town was filled with people," Shofner exclaimed. A motley assortment of uniformed militia companies, "drest in thare difrent garbs," lined up to march through town. Their costumes suggested that the Whig Party attracted supporters from the middling and lower ranks of rural society as well as from the elite:

> some with muskits and bayonets[,] some with hemp stalks with a bunsh of hackled hemp at the top[,] some armed with lances[,] some with broad axes made out of seeder wood[,] some armed with booyea knives made of steel and almost all kinde of wepens that cold bee invented[.][101]

Just as bands of artisans carried emblems of their work in holiday parades through the streets of New York and Philadelphia, yeomen farmers marched with the tools of their trade down Main Street in Shelbyville.

After the militia companies came a group of marchers carrying homemade banners. "Henry Clays likeness on a good many," Shofner explained. There could be no confusion on that part of bystanders that this was a Whig rally. But paraders declared more than party loyalty; they celebrated a high tide of nationalist feeling as the marchers continued. "And then banners ripresenting the 26 United States[.] The men had twenty six large ones for the states." Shofner estimated that altogether, "I suppose thare was near one hundred banners of the large kind then thare was a grate maney small ones."

It was at this point that the small-town parade took a unique turn compared to urban parades of the same period, for the small banners were carried primarily by women:

> then thare was twenty six small ones [banners] that 26 young ladys careed and they was all drest in uniform that was about as nise a site as men ginerley seese 26 handsome young ladys all drest in uniform marching and each carriing a banner[.][102]

The presence of women marching in the parade rather than simply observing from the sidelines reveals a considerably higher degree of public participation than historians have generally found for urban women of the period.[103] In major cities, women were excluded as parade participants, though their presence as spectators took on increasingly symbolic importance during the mid-nineteenth century. Perhaps small towns—where the population was homogeneous and where residents knew each other very well—were considered a safer, more acceptable stage than city streets for female participation in public roles. Shofner's description also suggests that most of the female paraders in Shelbyville were young and single. Their politics did not challenge the small-town gender hierarchy. Shofner noted approvingly one of the messages emblazoned on the banners, "Thare was one kind the young ladys carried the inscription was [']whig or no husband.' "[104]

Weapons and banners and uniforms presented a lively visual display. But what would a parade be without a band? Musicians enlivened the crowd all along the parade route, Shofner reported:

> then thare was musick[,] the nisest band of musick that I ever herde[.] Besides that the drum and fife[.] Some cumpeneys had horns[.] All of thame a large bell drawn on a waggon it kept toling[.][105]

The loyal Democrat's only escape from the sights and sounds of the Whig parade was to leave town.

On the second day of the rally, the Shofners arrived to find that "All was bussel forming to march out to the stand whare thare was to bee speaking." Once again women played an active public role in the mass meeting, marching out to the grandstand in the front of the procession. Shofner was impressed with their performance, to say the least: "I cant give you a description of thare marching but if nepolion Boneyparte had been thare with his army he cold not have beete thare marching." Shofner did not specifically describe the parade route, but his account implies that the crowd gathered at the public square and lined up to walk out to a speaker's stand set up at the margin of town. Unlike the smaller, town-centered rituals of Freemasons and Odd Fellows, there was no public building large enough in town to accommodate the crowd. The entertaining parades, public dinner, and speeches (including one from James C. Jones, the governor of the state) combined to make the Shelbyville mass meeting a huge success. Shofner felt confident that the Whigs had done their work effectively to mobilize Henry Clay supporters. "I was fearfull a while that poke [Polk] wold get the state but I have no fears now[.] The Whigs have all got roused up and will vote."[106]

Shofner's renewed confidence in a Whig triumph was imperfectly repaid. In the wake of Polk's victory, Democrats in Columbia enacted a ritual that could only have been accomplished in town space. By day, the Whigs had swathed Shelbyville houses in banners to show their allegiance to the party; by night the Democrats of Columbia illuminated the skies with firelight. A sympathetic Columbia newspaper editor favorably judged the results. "At night our town was beautifully illuminated in consequence of the glorious victory the Democracy have recently won—and in consequence of the promotion to the first office in the Republic, of our own distinguished fellow-citizen." Whig residents of Columbia were decidedly less complimentary of the illumination, declaring irritably that "in town generally, lights, like intelligence in the party, were precious dim, and scattered, as thin as hen's teeth."[107]

Given the election returns in town, the Whigs may have been more accurate in their evaluation of Columbia's illumination than the Democrats—at least where the scattered lights were concerned. Gleefully, vindictively, the local Whig newspaper chided, "Look at the Columbia precinct, (the 9th,) where Col. Polk resides and is best known, and see how his neighbors licked him."[108] Though Maury County had gone for Polk, his own hometown neighbors in Columbia had voted for the opposition party! The split of voters in Maury County suggests that the interests of town and country did not mesh seamlessly with one another by the 1840s.

Columbia Democrats spelled out what they saw as the essential difference between town and country: "We do not expect to gain much in towns and villages where aristocracy and selfishness reign predominant, but our gains and our strong holds are generally to be found, as in old Maury, among honest yeomenry—the independent denizens of an intelligent and honest community."[109] As we have seen, not everyone agreed that towns were the exclusive domain of aristocrats. Nevertheless, the rhetoric and rituals of party politics in Middle Tennessee revealed the increasing distinctions between town and countryside thirty years or so after county seats were established in the area.[110]

On one hand, the rituals of party politics knit town and country together more closely than ever, as rural residents paraded through the streets with their small-town neighbors. County seats, of course, had been created specifically to serve the governmental needs of the surrounding countryside, so it is not surprising that Whigs and Democrats found the courthouse towns to be the ideal stage for attracting and mobilizing party supporters. The chaos of the mass meeting in Shelbyville found order at the public square where marchers gathered to parade down Main Street to the grandstand. But the town was too small to contain the crowds, so much of the rally had to take place where buildings gave way to groves at the outskirts of town. Differences between town and country residents were visible for all to see, however, as yeomen farmers paraded with homemade hemp stalk "muskits" in their respective militia companies.

The highly visible performances of town and country residents parading down Main Street in broad daylight took a back seat to the undeniable physicality of town buildings, as illuminated windows drew a line in the darkness between town space and rural space. Town and country did not melt seamlessly into one another. Indeed, such displays would hardly have been meaningful for Whigs and Democrats who lived in scattered farmhouses. The illuminations that demonstrated party victories also threw the small town into relief—a patch of light in the darkened landscape.

By the 1840s a full-scale townscape had emerged, both physically on the landscape and symbolically in the ceremonies through which town residents differentiated themselves from the farmers who lived in rural neighborhoods outside of town. The architectural fabric and the ceremonial uses of town space, were indispensable partners in town building during the mid-nineteenth century. New public buildings provided the context for a variety of gatherings and rituals that drew participants from town and county alike. At the same time, turnpikes connected one small-town Main Street to another, forming networks that linked town residents to each other and not simply to the countryside that sustained them.

Farm families routinely came to town for fairs and political rallies, but by the 1840s town residents, despite their limited numbers, had formed their own set of civic groups and ceremonies. Because many ceremonies were composed of the same elements—parades, orations, picnics—the subtle distinctions between countywide events and town-centered events have been overlooked. Town-centered celebrations focused on town issues, and the chief participants were town residents. More specifically, these events helped to sort out differences among town residents by reinforcing hierarchies of status, gender, and race. Thus, public ceremonies were integral to the construction of town-centered identities because they made distinctions among town residents and because they helped to differentiate town from country folk.

By the 1840s, John Spence might properly have declared the townscape to be "completed."[111] Substantial public buildings joined numerous town "houses" to separate town space from the countryside, and the county seat had become the ceremonial center of the county. Nevertheless, Middle Tennessee county seats were on the verge of another architectural transformation. New commercial opportunities and changing standards of fashion would prompt dramatic spatial reorganization during the next decade. By the time of the Civil War, residents had built a considerably different townscape—one that reflected new divisions between residential and business space and a social geography that emphasized privacy, refinement, and more rigid class distinctions.

CHAPTER THREE

Complete Renovation, 1850–1861

Celebrating Architecture: A Communal Rite of Passage

On a "beautiful, clear and calm" day in June 1849, an "immense" crowd gathered in the refreshing shade of an oak grove at the edge of Murfreesboro, about a half mile east of the courthouse (six blocks from the public square).[1] John Spence, recently returned to Murfreesboro after seventeen years of storekeeping in West Tennessee, probably stood among the people "from town and the surrounding country" who waited "patiently" together for the ceremonies to begin. Spence later recalled ensuing events with the detail of an eyewitness. All eyes turned toward Main Street, with an air of mingled solemnity and festivity, to watch the approaching orderly procession of fraternal orders "decked in full regalia." The Masons led the parade, displaying various "ensigns of the order" and accompanied by "a band of music." Next came the Independent Order of Odd Fellows, "bearing their appropriate banner; then the Sons of Temperance, decked in the[ir] peculiar style of regalia, bearing a banner, symbolical of the order." The Appollonian Order, "a society formed by the students" of Union University, brought up the rear. Altogether, they made "a grand display and imposing appearance," Spence declared.[2]

These fraternal organizations had marched ceremoniously down Main

Street many times during the last twenty years or so—celebrating the triumphal victories of conquering heroes like Andrew Jackson and James K. Polk and commemorating national holidays and local events. What was different about this public ceremony was not the parade itself but the cause for communal celebration. Town residents had gathered to lay the cornerstone at Union University. In years past, the community had laid the cornerstones of churches and courthouses, but this particular cornerstone-laying ceremony marked the small town's coming of age in two ways. First, the college was a new type of town institution that signaled an enlarged cultural and economic role for the town. And second, the cornerstone laying at Union University was an architectural event that opened a decade of rebuilding on so massive a scale that by the time Union soldiers marched down the same streets eleven years later, the townscape had been utterly transformed.

On this sunny June day in 1849, the paraders and their audience could not have known that they stood on the verge of such a complete architectural transformation; nevertheless, they clearly believed the day marked a turning point in town life. The procession of fraternal orders marched purposefully from the square to the site of a new building going up at the edge of town. The building would be set back from the town's principal street, surrounded by eight acres sodded with bluegrass and shaded by scattered oaks "and other timber." A speaker's stand had been erected in the shade for the delivery of "an eloquent oration befitting the time." Among the orators was the new college president, Rev. J. H. Eaton, who spoke of "the great benefits arising from institutions of this kind in the country, and his hope of the future success of the one now in prospect." The university for young men would attract students from far beyond the local community. They would contribute to the local economy and advertise the reputation of the town as a good place to live and work. College leaders insisted that the school would be built "by the people, for the general good of the community." Therefore, the school's Baptist managers had deliberately chosen the name "Union University" in "a spirit of liberality," to encourage all denominations to participate broadly "in the general working of the institution." The success of the university and the progress of the town would be inextricably linked.

The speeches emphasized communal unity and cooperation. They characterized the university as a sign of progress for the entire town, rather than as the exclusive privilege of an educated elite. Yet the rituals that accompanied the rhetoric revealed that the town's maturing identity was based not only on presenting a united promotion of shared communal interests but also on maintaining a highly stratified society. There were actually two different ceremonies to commemorate the building of Union University—the official cornerstone-laying ritual, led by the Freemasons and young men who would attend the school, and a workers' torchlight parade and barbecue to celebrate the completion of the building. John Spence described the cornerstone laying, the actual construction, and the worker's parade as if they were each different phases of one continuous public celebration.

Spence emphasized the mystery and formality of Masonic ritual as the Freemasons took charge of the ceremonies at the conclusion of the speeches. They encircled the freshly laid foundation, and the crowd that had assembled in the shade moved closer to get a good look at the formal cornerstone-laying ceremony they were about to perform. Attention turned to the exposed foundation, where the men dressed in the formal regalia of the organization were "proceeding to apply the emblems peculiar to the craft, to the corner stone, . . . finding the work all correct."[3] When the foundation was judged to be level and firm, each fraternity approached in marching order to fill the compartment. One by one they inserted copies of their constitutions, by-laws, and lists of charter members, a Bible, several newspapers, an account of how the college was organized, a list of the faculty, some coins, and "a few volunteer relicts added by individuals." Literacy, formalized contractual agreements, general biblical rather than particular denominational affiliations, brotherhood—the documents and emblems placed within the cornerstone represented the essential instruments for successful competition in the masculine world. Then the stone was sealed.

But as one performance ended, another began in a burst of activity. As the crowd dispersed, action shifted from the ornately attired Society of Freemasons to "a society of practical 'Masons,'" the workers who had been "standing in the back ground . . . witnessing the ceremonies of the mystical building." The knowledge and expertise of the artisans provided a sharp contrast to those emphasized in the cornerstone-laying ceremony. Rather than the ornate regalia of the Freemasons, the workers were "all wearing aprons, and badges of mortar, and ensign, the field inscriptive of a mule, and water dray." They moved forward, "bearing in their hands, the implements peculiar to their art, trowels, plummets, and lines, squares and levels." The master builder, who had remained "in the background during the mystic ceremonies," now took charge. The tools they used and the work they performed required the mastery of skills that were as mysterious to most of the spectators as the cabalistic rituals of the Freemasons. Spence's particular fascination was for the physicality and cacophony of the display. The "corps of brick and mortar men" surrounded the foundation and sprang into action as the order was given. "'Up cotton' calls here and there, m-o-r-t-h-a-r-e? h-a-r-d-b-r-i-c-k! Hurry along, you bats al-l r-i-g-h-t!" The boisterous scene presented quite a contrast to the hushed placement of documents into the cornerstone. "The trowels ringing with merry peels, along the lines, at intervals the mystic cry 'up cotton.' This sound and motion continued till the close of day, which time the corner stone, lying deeply bedded in brick and mortar, there to remain, speaking to future generations of things done to day, as things of the past." Thus ended the first day of construction.

Though the crowds has dispersed, Spence wrote that the sounds of construction at the edge of town reminded the inhabitants of the cornerstone-laying ceremonies "day after day," until the last brick was laid in the "massive body," at which time "the ringing trowel-notes are heard no more," and a shout went up—"We celebrate the day!"

The master builder, William Sommerhill, "a large fleshy man" who weighed about 300 pounds, was considered to be "eccentric in his manner, having a fund of wits, and many quaint sayings." Sommerhill had promised his hands they would celebrate "the day the last brick was laid on the wall of the College building" with a barbecue. But these "practical" masons—over thirty workers in all—did more than sit down to supper on the day the building was finished. Led by Sommerhill, "all hands, both white and sooty" took up lanterns and torches to light the evening streets, "mounted on horses and mules," and paraded in a circuitous route through town, "all singing merry songs." As promised, the parading workers concluded their ceremonies with a "sumptuous supper, which had been prepared for the occaision [sic]. . . . all eating and drinking to hearts content."

Judging by members of the Summerhill household listed in the census taken one year after Union University was built, these paraders were likely more "sooty" than white. Summerhill's twenty-five slaves made him one of the largest slaveowners in Murfreesboro.[4] All but one of these slaves were men, who ranged in age from nine to fifty. In addition to the master mason himself, the Summerhill household also included five white brickmasons, two of whom were Summerhill's sons.

The various celebrations surrounding Union University represent a communal rite of passage—an architectural event that marked a transition in the life of the community.[5] The building itself was unlike preceding town struc-

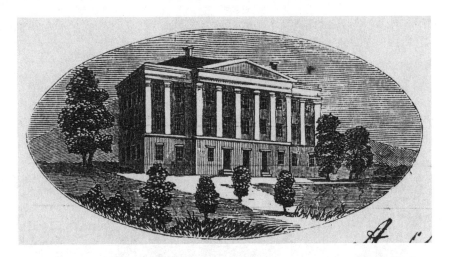

FIGURE 3.1. This view of Union University was printed on stationery Virginia Shelton used in 1856. The engraving suggests there is a Doric portico along the front of the building, but the photograph (Fig. 3.2) shows clearly that instead of a free-standing colonnade, pilasters were used to ornament the facade. (Courtesy of Rare Book, Manuscript, and Special Collections Library, Duke University)

tures. It was not the first school to be built in town, but it was the first university, and one of the most impressive buildings ever to rise above the streets of Murfreesboro.[6] Union University stood three stories high, and its massive size—80 feet wide and 110 feet long—rivaled the two-story courthouse at town center (Figs. 3.1 and 3.2). Built at the opposite end of Main Street, the new university established an architectural boundary between town and countryside—the easternmost edge of the townscape. By the end of the 1850s, the architectural perimeter of town would be more clearly defined than ever before and the townscape itself dramatically reorganized.

The architectural transformation of the 1850s would be broadly participatory, involving town residents across the lines of race and class. It was fitting that John Spence emphasized widespread community participation in support of the university. Town residents gathered with country folk, as if to underscore the "union" principle Eaton had so carefully outlined in his speech. The celebrants represented a cross-section of town and county, mechanics and merchants, slave and free. The regalia and "mystical" expertise of "practical" masons was commensurate with the elaborate rituals of Freemasons and Odd Fellows. The community felt common cause in celebration of town architecture.

FIGURE 3.2. Union University, built in Murfreesboro in 1849, closed in 1873.
This photograph of the building was taken sometime after the Civil War.
(Courtesy of Mrs. Mabel Pittard)

But Spence's tale also revealed significant social stratification. The
cornerstone-laying ceremony initiated a ritual of construction that ended
months later with the workers' parade and barbecue. The decorum of the
Masonic ceremony, with its strict hierarchical order of elite white male
paraders, following a planned parade route and delivering solemn orations,
was the antithesis of the "white and sooty" workers who wandered bois-
terously through lantern-lit streets singing "merry songs." It was not only a
matter of parade styles; different modes of celebration demonstrated different uses of the streets, different attitudes toward, and experiences of,
town space. One group celebrated the building before its completion as a
symbol of town progress and prosperity; the other group performed the
work and celebrated the building as the product of their labor.

The architectural transformation of the 1850s required the work of an
entire community—slave artisans, merchant investors, industrious house-
wives. But broad participation did not entail democratic results. In the
renovated townscape, residents used architecture in new ways to define
communal hierarchies and to make distinctions among town residents. As
county seats came of age in the 1850s, more than ever before town residents
aspired to city ways.

The 1850s commenced with a burst of optimism and energy on the heels of an economic depression that had stifled town growth well into the 1840s. Prosperity daily attracted new town residents. Virginia Shelton and her husband William, a teacher at Union University, were among the new arrivals to Murfreesboro in 1850. By 1851, William informed Virginia's family that the University was "in a very flourishing condition. During the present session the number of students is much larger than it has ever been before. More than 160 have already entered and others are almost continually arriving."[7] The university was one of several new assets that promoted town growth. Four years after her arrival in Murfreesboro, Virginia surveyed the rapidly changing townscape with the eye of a practiced inhabitant and described for her uncle what drew people to town:

> Persons are moving in from other places & our town is receiving accessions of new citizens every few weeks. Many come in for the purpose of educating their children—some purchase property & engage in business, others rent here & carry on their farming in the South. To-day a new couple came to reside in our town & the gentleman engages in merchandise. Every thing around us bears the appearance of a most flourishing community.[8]

Families and businessmen joined the students to create a steady stream of incoming residents. What Virginia failed to identify was the spark that had ignited the local economy. These new people were arriving, not by turnpike as the Sheltons had come, but by train.

A few months after moving to Murfreesboro, William Shelton revealed that "the railroad from Nashville through this place to Chattanooga is rapidly advancing. It is already finished ten or twelve miles from Nashville, and the cars are running for that distance. It is believed that the entire road from here to Nashville will be completed by the first of July."[9] His prediction proved entirely accurate. The first train steamed its way from Nashville into Murfreesboro on the Fourth of July in 1851. People turned out from miles around for a lavish barbecue: "five hundred feet of table, well filled from end to end with the barbecued meats and bread. And another table, one hundred and twenty five feet long . . . covered with meats, bread and confectionaries, and handsomely decorated." Hungry citizens and invited guests from Nashville listened while the mayor of Murfreesboro heralded the railroad as "another step bringing cities and towns in reach of each other, condensing the country as it were in a small space."[10] On that Fourth of July, the mayor was struck as much by the spatial impact of the train as he was by its commercial possibilities. All tracks led to Nashville, the largest city in the region, and extended outward, drawing Murfreesboro closer to cities outside the region as well. But the train not only brought cities and towns closer, it changed the relationship between town and countryside. The town became the gateway that linked county residents to the wider world, in effect "condensing" the surrounding countryside within small-town space. With unbounded enthusiasm the mayor declared that Murfreesboro "is, and shall be, a city."[11]

Months after the grand celebration, the railroad was still a local attraction. As if on a sightseeing expedition, Virginia Shelton and her Aunt Lavinia visited the depot one day in September. "Just as we reached there the cars arrived from Nashville," Virginia told her uncle. "Every person & every thing seemed busy & bustling & we had a fine view of them going off at rapid speed towards the south, for they run 18 miles beyond our town now."[12] The pace of town life seemed already to be more vigorous.

By the end of the year, train passage was part of the local routine. Virginia and William planned a trip to Nashville to buy a piano. "We will be from home but a few hours," Virginia explained, "as there are now two trains of cars running & a person may go there & return the same day & accomplish much shopping."[13] The train was creating eager consumers like Virginia Shelton, who no longer had to confine their shopping habits to the public square when an urban emporium was only hours away. Clearly, small-town shopkeepers faced a new challenge to keep local customers at home.

Though the train carried off some small-town shoppers, it was far from an economic drain on the local economy. Edmund Cooper, small-town lawyer and budding industrialist, had recently invested in a weaving factory in Shelbyville. For him, the spatial and economic impact of the railroad were inextricably linked. He boasted to his father that Shelbyville had already attained newfound importance as a commercial center:

during the year we have shipped from the Depot at this place 150,000 bushels wheat—10,000 head of fat hogs—3750 hogsheads of bacon— besides an amount of corn since November, almost fabulous—and at a pork establishment in town, they have slaughtered this winter over 10,000 head of hogs—the bacon & lard to be shipped during the year, and at least $120,000 paid to our farmers. At this glance of our village, and its operations you can at once see, how rapidly commercial prosperity is gathering capital around it as a common center.[14]

Edmund Cooper and Virginia Shelton identified two emerging commercial realms thrown into sharp relief by the advent of the railroad. Shelton inhabited an increasingly refined sphere of retail trade, while Cooper rushed eagerly to expand the profitable agricultural market. During the 1850s, town residents physically divided these two branches of commerce into separate town regions. Thus the railroad became one of the most powerful forces for architectural renovation. In fact, railroad construction was generating a building boom all over the Upland South.[15]

Clearly, the railroad quickened local commerce, enhancing the importance of county seats as market centers and drawing small-town shoppers and businessmen into the expansive possibilities of urban trade. A pervasive spirit of improvement led to greater public expenditures for schools, gas lighting, and paved roads, in addition to widespread private spending on commercial and residential building stock.[16]

But there was no easy economic cause and effect between the prosperity generated by the railroad and the building boom that redefined the townscape. Murfreesboro residents celebrated their new university well before the train brought new business to town. Franklin did not charter its first railroad until 1852, and the tracks linking Nashville to Columbia were not completed until 1859.[17] By then, the building boom was already well under way.

Long before any profits had been collected from the first train shipments, anticipation of the railroad inspired residents to reevaluate the appearance of their towns. In 1850, the editor of the *Shelbyville Expositor* ominously warned his readers, "It will not do to wait till the Rail Road gets here, and then commence building—'In times of peace prepare for war.'" His argument suggests some of the reasons why architectural renovation preceded the railroad:

> remember that the Rail Road with its thundering cars will soon be rolling through our *city*—we should build up, add every thing possible to the looks and comfort of our town that will tend in the least to make it still more attractive, so that every man looking for a home would direct his course *towards Shelbyville* [in] the first place. . . . Every man who has town property should remember that by improveing [*sic*] it, he adds not only to his *individual* interests, but also to the interest of his town, and the community.[18]

The train might just as easily transport people away from Shelbyville as it would attract them to it. In that light, the town's appearance and comfort were essential for progress and prosperity. The successful rebuilding campaign should be regarded as a kind of total warfare, targeting every town lot. Property owners bore particular responsibility for promoting the public good. Perhaps the editor remembered how difficult it had been twenty years earlier to overcome the unflattering impression Easton Morris's description of Shelbyville had given readers of his *Gazetteer*. In any case, his logic was clear—appearances constituted a vital component of the small-town economy. Architectural change was more than a matter of comfort and convenience; it was perceived as an essential component of local progress. Renovation was serious business.

The editor's crusading language and sense of urgency was not unusual by mid-nineteenth-century standards. "The example of one good house is sometimes followed by an improvement in the style and taste of a whole village," declared the authors of a popular architectural pattern book.[19] It was in fact an era of national architectural reform, during which Americans launched "a broad crusade to replace what they saw as the older eighteenth-century ideal of home and family with a set of new standards for domestic architecture and social behavior."[20] Businesses too, from refined hotel parlors and luxurious department stores to machine-filled factory floors, were built to accommodate profound changes in patterns of consumption and the division of labor. The renovated townscape demonstrated not so much the originality of Middle Tennesseans as their grasp of new national standards of domesticity and modes of consumption.

Small towns did succeed in attracting new residents in the 1850s. Virginia Shelton could not help but notice that Murfreesboro was growing by leaps and bounds. "Persons are moving in from other places & our town is receiving accessions of new citizens every few weeks," she told her uncle.[21] Such population growth fueled the building boom. Anticipating that the railroad would bring dramatic expansion, Murfreesboro annexed so much land to the north and east that the size of the corporation nearly doubled in 1850. This was not the first extension of town limits. Middle Tennessee county seats had begun to outgrow their original boundaries during the early stages of development. In 1819, four years after Franklin was incorporated, Alabama land speculator Hincha Petway ambitiously subdivided land he had bought just west of the original town to create fifty-nine lots. [Fig. 3.3]

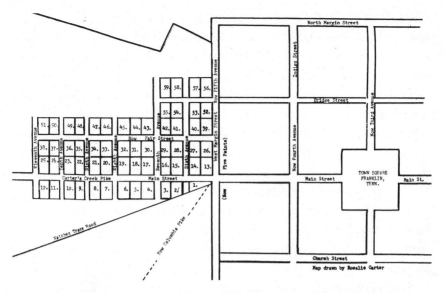

FIGURE 3.3. Map showing the Hincheyville suburb of Franklin, a six-block area between Main Street and Fair Street, just west of West Margin Street. The haphazard development of Columbia (Fig. 1.3) was more typical of antebellum town growth than was the planned, grid-patterned Hincheyville tract. Though the suburb was platted about 1819, most of the houses in Hincheyville were built after the Civil War. (From the Canaday Files, Franklin, Tennessee)

However, the overwhelming majority of these "Hincheyville" lots remained empty until the 1850s.[22]

By midcentury, the rate of population growth and town expansion had increased considerably. In 1848, Columbia extended its city limits to include the suburb of Nazareth—a move that was hotly debated in the local news-papers.[23] Suburban residents complained that annexation would saddle them with a tax burden for which they would receive few additional benefits beyond what they already enjoyed for free. Those living within preestab-lished corporation limits argued that suburban residents were liable for support of town services they received. The corporation prevailed, and Nazareth was annexed. In 1850, census takers counted 2,455 town residents. By 1860, one Columbia newspaper estimated that "including the suburbs, its population is about five thousand," and city officials began to argue once again for expansion of the city limits.[24]

Alfred Hamilton, an entrepreneur from Pennsylvania, was one of the new residents attracted to Shelbyville during the 1850s. The description of the town he sent to his father back in Lewistown, Pennsylvania, documents the progress of renovation. "Shelbyville contains 4,000 inhabitants and the houses are scattered over an area of two miles square," he explained. What stood out for Hamilton were the cottages and commercial establishments. He identified two basic town regions, residential and commercial, each arranged according to different spatial principles. "Excepting the business houses," Hamilton explained, "there is only one dwelling on each lot of 120 feet front."[25] The dispersed placement of dwellings at the center of large lots was the key distinction between residential space compared to the increasing density of small-town commercial space. While houses were separated from the street by landscaped yards and gardens, new stores built at town center covered every square inch of their commercial lots, rising from the very edge of the sidewalk.

Overall, Hamilton was impressed with the prosperity of Shelbyville residents. "The people are generally rich and aristocratic," he declared. Nevertheless, Hamilton described a townscape composed primarily of modest houses. "The buildings are mostly frame one and two story, cottage style," he wrote, adding that they were "painted white and they look beautiful."[26] Hamilton was particularly impressed with the effect of color on the town's appearance. The small town still presented a monochrome appearance, but residents had replaced the Spanish brown of the original townscape with the crisp whiteness of the renovated townscape.

Though he was pleased to find that Shelbyville was a comfortable place to live, what had attracted Hamilton to town in the first place was commercial opportunity. Hamilton was not disappointed. "It is a great place for business," he declared including a litany of busy establishments in the industrializing town. There were "flouring mills, large storehouses, steam furniture and planing mill, cotton factory, weaving mill, two pork packing establishments, steam bucket factory which turns out a bucket cedar, in three minutes." In short, business was booming in Shelbyville—"There [are] a great many people in town every day trading which gives the town quite a business aspect."[27] By the 1850s, people came to town to do business not just on court days, but everyday. But their business increasingly took them to different parts of town.

During the 1850s, territorial expansion and population growth dramatically increased the size of these small towns, fueling the building boom. But adding people and land and buildings was only a small part of the process of architectural renovation. Indeed, a newspaper editor in Columbia insisted that "the tendency of the improvement has been more to refine and beautify the town, than to enlarge its limits."[28] Towns did not simply get bigger; renovation transformed town space.

Redefining the Townscape: Specialization of Space

The building boom of the 1850s compared only to the feverish activity that replaced canebrakes with town grids at the beginning of the century. Fifty years later, the results were similarly consequential. Searching for a way to measure the progress of Columbia, a local newspaper editor in 1860 described its recent architectural transformation: "Within the past five years," he observed, "there has been almost a complete renovation of the town. Numerous buildings—business houses and residences—have been erected, which would be an ornament to any place. Upon the crumbling foundations of old frame houses, new and beautiful houses have risen," along with "new and commodious business houses."[29] Architectural change encompassed all types of buildings in the county seat. Town residents did much more than simply build bigger, more durable buildings than ever before. By the end of the decade, they had completely redefined the townscape itself.

Residents profoundly reconstructed existing town space during the 1850s, creating a distinctive architectural pattern—a townscape that was fundamentally different from its predecessor. The townscape of "houses," with its mixed residential and commercial spaces, was effectively replaced by a new architectural arrangement that segmented town space for increasingly specialized uses.[30] The public square became a more refined retail district. New warehouses and mills created a quasi-industrial zone around the railroad depots. And domestic space was reorganized to serve the increasingly privatized and stratified social life of the town.

Given the economic motivations that underlay their spirit of improvement, town residents targeted the public square as a renovation priority. In 1853, the *Bedford Yeoman* declared, "In the first place, we stand greatly in need of new business houses. . . . There are many old frames standing on the square that if they were taken down, and new, large bricks put up in their stead, would not only add to the looks of the place, but would give additional room to business."[31] Town residents consistently linked appearances and commerce as partners in progress.

As if responding to this pervasive spirit of improvement, a series of fires swept a path for renovation. "Since the burning of the City Hotel" in 1855, observed John Spence, "all the houses round the public square have been burned out and rebuilt with handsome brick buildings, giving the public square round, a fine appearance." Throughout the decade, businessmen steadily replaced the "old frames" on the Square with larger brick stores. Between 1846 and 1861 (when he sold his business), house carpenter Nathan Vaught profited from commissions to build or modify nine stores on or near the public square in Columbia.[32]

With each new brick store, the public square took on a different character. By the end of the 1850s, town centers, which had previously combined residential and commercial structures, became almost exclusively defined as business districts. Merchants did more than substitute brick for frame, however. The stores they built embodied new ways of doing business. Although the dry goods store, which sold everything from hoes to hats, remained an integral component of the public square, it was joined by specialized stores that exclusively sold drugs or books or some particular type of merchandise. For John Spence, this reorganization of small-town trade reflected urban aspirations. "The town was making advances toward city ways," he declared, "doing business in particular branches of trades."[33] Urban models could not have been far from the minds of merchants who continued to travel every year to Philadelphia, and increasingly to New York, to buy products for the small-town market.

The new stores also demonstrated efforts to entice a local clientele that could easily take the train to Nashville to shop. Merchants rearranged store interiors with an eye for "convenience" and "elegance," cardinal principles of small-town gentility.[34] One Columbia newspaper editor took his readers on a tour of "two large business houses" that were "connected with each other by large doors between," located "on the North corner of Main Street and the Square." The interior arrangement made spatial distinctions between storage and display. While the basement was "thickly crowded," the second floor glittered "with every imaginable species of glassware, china, etc.," and the third floor was "closely packed with articles, of which samples are to be seen below." After examining "the entire establishment," he "pronounce[d] it in every way most elegantly arranged."[35] No longer did genteel customers like Virginia Shelton have to climb over saddles and farm implements to view the latest china patterns.[36]

The retail gentility of the public square was reinforced by the removal of wholesale commerce to entirely new industrial zones, clustered around the railroad (Fig. 3.4).[37] Blocks of brick and frame, one- and two-story warehouses and commission stores built near the depot, stored bacon, corn, oats, and other agricultural products awaiting shipment to Nashville and beyond, thereby removing livestock and other agricultural products from town center to periphery. By contrast, the square became a space of increasing refinement, devoted to nonmanual professions or to the retail trade.[38]

If elegance and convenience were the organizing principles of genteel stores on the square, the warehouse and wholesale district was designed for efficiency and profit. In Murfreesboro, William Spence built a mechanized distillery and "hog fattening establishment," which he operated in connection with a flour mill near the depot. In sharp contrast to the elegantly arranged business houses of the square, the four-story brick mill was filled with a "running geer propelled by two twenty-five horse power engines, three twenty feet boilers, shafting throughout the entire building, the necessary bolts for flouring, five pair four feet French bur stones, four for wheat, and one pair for corn grinding." A large cooper shop supplied barrels on site for a production that Spence claimed reached 200 barrels of flour per day. The nearby distillery was "run by a twenty horse power engine, doing its own grinding, shafting, elevators, and steam pipes," with a capacity for "seven barrels [of] whiskey per day, using one hundred bushels of meal for a 'mash.' " The hog-fattening establishment, which used the slops produced in the distillery, was an impressive arrangement in its own right. Penned in "a large floored enclosure, or house, covered sixty feet wide, eighty feet long," the hogs were fed by a series of mechanized troughs. There was even a set of scales at the door "weighing hogs going in and out of the establishment."[39] Spence proudly declared that "a lot of poor, healthy hogs, treated in this manner, will be perfectly fat for market, on an average of four months." He estimated that the establishment could produce "three pens" of fattened hogs in one year. Instead of roaming about town foraging garbage, as they had in previous years, hogs now fattened more systematically in the new warehouse district.

Gentrification and industrialization proceeded hand in hand to reshape space in the renovated townscape. The two principles extended to the domestic environment. Just as commercial areas reflected new spatial distinctions between manual labor and gentility, domestic space—both the rooms inside the house and the town lot surrounding the house—documented a reorganization of work and social life. Labor-intensive household produc-

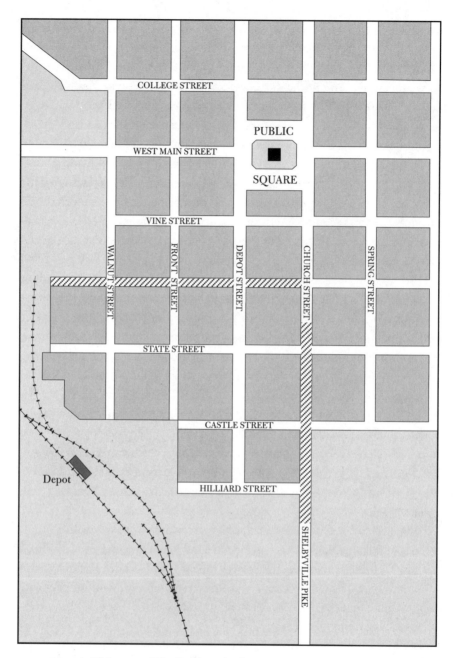

FIGURE 3.4. This map of Murfreesboro in the 1870s shows the development of an industrial wedge and warehouse district south of Sevier Street and west of Church Street. The railroad tracks formed the hypotenuse of the triangle, which encompassed a variety of mills, factories, and commission houses. According to John Spence, this area became known as Depot Hill or Depot Square. It is difficult to reconstruct the exact number and location of antebellum warehouses since most were burned during the Civil War. (Base map source: D. G. Beers & Co., 1878)

tion moved toward the rear of town lots and domestic interiors, while front yards and parlors were devoted to genteel entertainment.[40] The renovation strategy of Virginia and William Shelton suggests how the process worked.

When Virginia and William Shelton moved to Murfreesboro in 1850, they bought a town lot with "a fine garden, stables" and a house with "six rooms & no upstairs."[41] From the beginning, the young couple intended to have the house "*refitted* & *repaired* & *improved* after a while."[42] "All the rooms except two [were] rather small," Virginia complained; nevertheless, the Sheltons reserved several rooms for genteel purposes—dining, sitting, reading—that had little to do with daily operation of the household.[43] Outside the house, their renovations reiterated spatial distinctions between the manual work associated with the service buildings at the back of the lot and the genteel polish of Virginia's garden in front.[44]

Working together, they began with the front rooms, where they entertained guests. Early in the spring of 1851, Virginia wrote, "Mr. Shelton has been painting the front-room & diningroom & I have been helping him to paper the latter. We intend papering the front-room in a few days—& the parlor too."[45] They soon extended their labors beyond the domestic interior. While Virginia developed the garden, William redesigned the service buildings at the back of the lot. Boasting of her husband's industry, Virginia wrote, "Mr. Shelton is having his stable yard enlarged, a crib made & a carriage house & wood house."[46] By November, the proud homeowners could summarize the results of their labor. Inside the house, their improvements included "a neat little Library, just finished the other day," and a "handsomely" painted and papered parlor and dining room. Outside, "the new wood yard & the stables . . . the new crib filled with corn & the *barn loft* with hay & fodder" displayed the fruits of their labor for all to see.[47]

In contrast to the efficient arrangement of service yards like William Shelton's, front yards conveyed new standards of ornamentation. David Dickinson took the opportunity while attending Congress to offer his family in Franklin some advice "upon the subject of planting flowers in the yard," based on his observations in the nation's capitol.

They ought never to be planted unless in cultivated ground. The flowers and rose bushes ought not to be upon the borders, but in beds nicely cultivated in different parts of the yard. The figures of these beds may be stars or any other kind that pleases your fancy. Let the grass grow to the edge of the walks and let only trees be upon the borders and these trees not too thick—cedars, arbor vitae, and the fir tree every now & then one of each, are the most beautiful—and these are all ever greens.[48]

In addition to star-shaped flower beds and evergreen borders, the proper yard ought to have gravel walks flanked by brick gutters, Dickinson continued. The gutters were indispensable because "they will add to the beauty of the garden and will prevent the scars which are made in it by the rains," he explained.[49] The interest in landscape gardening was fueled by Andrew Jackson Downing's immensely popular and influential *Treatise on the Theory and Practice of Landscape Gardening*, published in 1841. Downing argued that tasteful development of the building site was as important as improving the dwelling itself and admonished his readers to place ornamental plants in the yard with as much deliberation as they would use to arrange furniture in the parlor.

Such public displays of gentility and refinement were the hallmark of the renovated townscape. A Columbia newspaper editor noted in 1860: "There has been a growing tendency upon the part of private individuals to adorn and improve their homes. The sums formerly expended upon carriages, dress, and inside show, have been turned and appropriated more to this better and more enduring purpose. Improved yards and well-laid gardens, with their wealth of floral beauty, has been the consequence." Material manifestations of wealth expressed class differences in stark, highly visible contrasts from one town household to another. But architectural change was more than a matter of conspicuous consumption. Significantly, the Columbia editor saw "evidences of a better architectural taste, and the fruits of a more liberal wealth" on "almost every street."[50] Townscape renovation was a pervasive, broadly participatory phenomenon that reached into the households of residents throughout the county seat. The reputation of the entire community was at stake, and prosperity hung in the balance.

Historians have emphasized the conservatism of architectural reform, arguing that elite groups reshaped domestic space to reinforce their own power and social position and to forestall the bewildering pace of change.[51] Although the rebuilding of Middle Tennessee's county seats was every bit as complete and dramatic as the explosive growth of America's cities at midcentury, the change was more comprehensible and therefore less threatening in the small town. Observers of antebellum cities could perceive only one neighborhood at a time, and they saw increasingly stark contrasts in the condition of separate urban regions. Such piecemeal encounters invoked a wide range of impressions—wonder, bewilderment, intimidation, fear.[52] By contrast, small towns could presumably be observed as a whole. The appearance of the entire community thus carried greater weight and required a holistic approach to renovation. Piecemeal improvements could make little impact on the overall reputation of the town.

Above all, small-town elites had a firmer grip on the pace and process of local change. They did not face the riots and civil disturbances among immigrants and native-born Americans, proletarianized urban workers and their bourgeois employers, and controversial reformers (abolitionists and the like) that marked so many antebellum cities.[53] Promoters of architectural change in Middle Tennesseans were not worried reformers who feared social instability.

A diverse cross section of residents eagerly embraced the national spirit of architectural improvement as the measure of communal prosperity and urban aspiration. Architectural change was not limited to elite groups who built fine houses and stores. The 1850s also witnessed the construction of slave-built churches for slave congregations, as well as the creation of new, large colleges for women, which extended female education beyond the older system of academies.[54] This is not to say that all benefited equally from the reorganization of town space. As residents reconstructed their towns with an eye for refinement and gentility, they sought to project a prosperous communal appearance, but their new buildings also clearly and unmistakably hardened social divisions among the residents themselves.

Villas, Cottages, and Commercial Blocks: Social Differentiation and the New Architectural Vocabulary

Segmentation of residential and commercial space generated a new architectural vocabulary that expressed social divisions heretofore hidden. Town residents no longer lived simply in "houses," they owned "villas" or "cottages." Boys and girls no longer went to school together in academies and field schools, young ladies and gentlemen attended their own "institutes" and "colleges." Taverns were transformed into more gentlemanly "saloons." Multipurpose storehouses became specialized commercial blocks. The

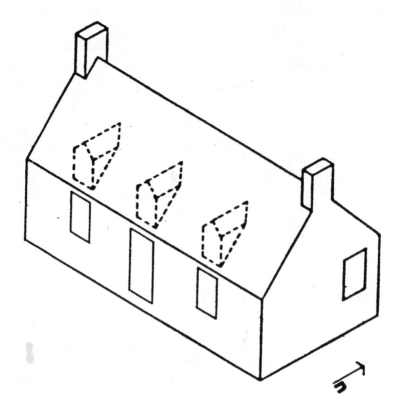

FIGURE 3.5. Original one-and-a-half-story, two-room house of the Maney family.
(Courtesy of Oaklands Historic House Museum, Murfreesboro)

change was more than a matter of semantics. The new architectural vocabulary signaled the construction of entirely new types of buildings in the
renovated townscape.

Town residents did not have to build new villas and cottages from the
ground up. Homeowners like the Maneys in Murfreesboro transformed
existing structures to suit new lifestyles and standards of taste. James and
Sally Maney had moved from Murfreesboro, North Carolina, to Rutherford
County in 1815. They were prominent citizens from the start. Sally had
inherited land there from her father, Col. Hardy Murfree, namesake of
Murfreesboro, Tennessee, and James became a physician and merchant.
They bought a town lot on Main Street, a block from the public square, but
took up residence in a two-room brick house less than a mile from town

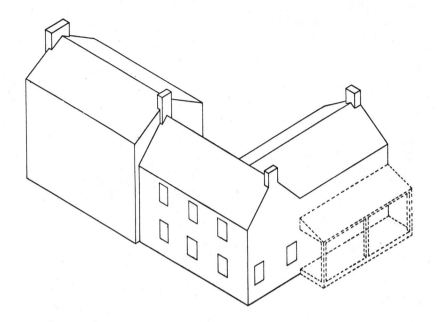

FIGURE 3.6. By the mid-nineteenth century, the Maneys had added a full second story
to the original house (shown here with windows) and made two substantial
additions—a rear ell and a larger Federal-style wing.
(Courtesy of Oaklands Historic House Museum, Murfreesboro)

(Fig. 3.5). Based on this proximity to town, the Maney residence served two
functions. It was both a plantation house surrounded by farmland and a
townhouse integrated into the social world of Murfreesboro. For example,
the Maneys were prominent members of the Presbyterian Church in town
and owned valuable town property.

The Maney family encased their original two-room house within a series
of additions that not only enlarged the living space but also produced
fundamentally new sets of dwellings in keeping with the phases of town
building.[55] During the 1820s and 1830s the Maneys created a two-story,
Federal-style dwelling with a rear ell, appropriate for the townscape of
houses (Fig. 3.6). This was probably the house Virginia and William Shelton saw in December of 1850, when they visited "Dr. Manney's [a] half mile
from town." Neighbors told them simply that "it was a large white house,"
but Virginia was somewhat more impressed. She found the Maney home to
be "an ancient & wealthy looking domicile."[56] Though the house still con-

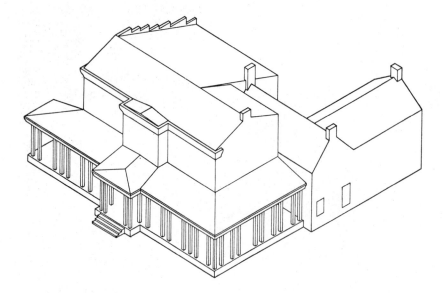

FIGURE 3.7. During the 1850s, the Maney family concealed the older sections of the house behind an impressive new Italianate facade with wraparound porch. (Courtesy of Oaklands Historic House Museum, Murfreesboro)

veyed a sense of the Maney family's prominence in the community, it already embodied an older architectural standard.

A few years after the Shelton's visit, this "ancient and wealthy" house disappeared behind an impressive new facade (Fig. 3.7), probably constructed by a younger generation of Maneys. Sally Maney died in 1857, and her son Lewis moved in with his wife, Rachel Adeline Cannon (daughter of Newton Cannon, who was governor of Tennessee from 1835 to 1839). On the eve of the Civil War, the couple transformed the already sizable house into an Italianate "villa," adding four rooms with wide halls upstairs and down (Figs. 3.8 and 3.9). The new front addition was especially designed for entertaining and genteel pursuits. While the day-to-day operation of the household remained in the older sections at the back of the house, the Maneys added a formal parlor and library, reserved for use only on special social occasions. Outside, architectural embellishments such as bracketed cornice, elaborately ornamented windows, and a colonnaded veranda, conspicuously demonstrated the affluence and refined taste of the inhabitants.

Across town, Virginia and William Shelton were adding a second story to their "little cottage home" in 1855.[57] "The additional story makes the house

FIGURE 3.8. Front view of Maney house, showing Italianate addition.
(Courtesy of Oaklands Historic House Museum, Murfreesboro)

greatly cooler & more pleasant as we have witness[ed] this last warm week,"
Virginia wrote her aunt and uncle, "& . . . we will have room enough, a
pleasant dining-room & and many other conveniences."[58] Though smaller
than the Maneys' "villa," the Sheltons' "cottage" also contained specialized
social spaces, including a library and parlor. Their house no longer stands,
but a dwelling constructed in the same neighborhood during the 1850s
offers clues about the appearance of small-town cottages during the renovation period (Figs. 3.10 and 3.11).[59] Like the Maney house, this one-story
clapboard dwelling was the product of several additions, camouflaged behind a front section that appeared as a single unit. Decorative embellishments were much simpler, though the focal point of the cottage was the same
kind of colonnaded veranda that the Maneys attached to their Italianate villa.
Thus, it was not the application of a particular architectural style that distinguished the cottage from the villa. It was a difference of scale. Both dwellings
displayed a sense of refinement appropriate to their owners' rank in small-
town society.

FIGURE 3.9. This side view of the Maney house shows a corner of the mid-nineteenth-century house (Fig. 3.6) extending a window's length beyond the Italianate addition of the 1850s. A section of the Italianate porch that linked the new addition to the older sections of the house (as shown in Fig. 3.7) has been removed.
(Courtesy of Oaklands Historic House Museum, Murfreesboro)

The cottage was the center of mid-nineteenth-century reformers' efforts to improve the standards of American housing. The term itself was imprecise. Built of wood or brick, embellished with Gothic, Greek, or Italianate ornamentation, the "cottage" encompassed a broad variety of domestic buildings. In fact, the cottage was not so much a particular form or structure as it was a domestic ideal that promoted comfort, taste, neatness, and moral advancement. Typically regarded as modest buildings, cottages were the respectable dwellings of middle-class families. Andrew Jackson Downing's highly influential plans for "cottage residences" ranged from "a suburban cottage for a small family," estimated to cost $1,800, to "an irregular cottage in the Old English Style" complete with a servants' wing, estimated to cost $7,600.[60] In Murfreesboro, by comparison, the Sheltons originally paid about $2,300 for their six-room cottage and town lot.[61] After the couple renovated the house in 1855, Virginia boasted to her uncle that "every person

BUILDING TOWNS

FIGURE 3.10. Front view of cottage on Vine Street, Murfreesboro.
(Photograph by author)

speaks in admiration of the improved appearance of our place. It is the opinion that, it has increased the value of the place so much that it would readily,
sell for a thousand dollars more than it would have done previously—& no
more than half that much will have been expended."[62]

Aside from cost and appearance, cottages and villas tended to be arranged differently within the renovated townscape. Town builders of the
1850s created new, fashionable streets that began to segregate town space
into class-based residential neighborhoods. Prosperous Shelbyville residents moved onto the new Belmont Street, creating a small-town avenue of
wealth, and Columbia's elite moved up to "Quality Hill."[63] Nevertheless,
before the Civil War the wealthiest town residents did not necessarily cluster
together on fashionable streets; instead they tended to live at the periphery
of town, establishing an architectural border between town and countryside.

Horace Rawdon, a Union soldier from Ohio, documented this aspect of
the renovated townscape in his drawing of Murfreesboro about 1863 (Fig.
3.12). The prominent dwelling at the right edge of the drawing appears to
mark the outer limits of town—a perspective exaggerated by the fence,
which seems not only to enclose the farmyard but to form a kind of town

FIGURE 3.11. Side view of Vine Street cottage, showing additions.
(Photograph by author)

boundary. The Maney house (on the opposite side of Murfreesboro from the Rawdon drawing) was part of this band of elite residences encircling the county seat. Indeed, the Sheltons "had some little difficulty in finding the place" on the night of their visit in 1850, "as there are several good-looking residence[s] out in that direction from town," Virginia explained.[64]

Rawdon's drawing emphasized the rural and agricultural qualities of the small southern town. His view of Murfreesboro does not record some of the key elements of the renovated townscape. Rawdon saw extreme contrasts of wealth in the Murfreesboro townscape. Small, one-story houses huddled together to form a humble residential region between the substantial houses at town periphery and the public buildings at the center. The Sheltons' neighborhood, "in a very desirable part" of Murfreesboro, seems nowhere to be found in the drawing. Virginia explained that they lived "very convenient to the square, the churches & the heart of town, yet . . . sufficiently quiet & retired."[65] Rawdon overlooked the cottages neatly arranged to form the heart of the small town. He saw Murfreesboro as a quiet rural village, not as a bustling railroad town.

Though it was impossible for Rawdon to overlook the commercial blocks

BUILDING TOWNS

FIGURE 3.12. Drawing by Horace Rawdon, a Union soldier from Ohio, showing Murfreesboro about 1863. (Courtesy of West Point Museum, U.S. Military Academy, West Point, New York)

that dominated the small-town skyline, their arrangement appears more dispersed than concentrated on the public square. The view of the "cappitol [*sic*]" is unobstructed from his vantage point at the edge of town. Indeed, there is no very strong sense of a street grid at all in Rawdon's view. Notice by contrast to Rawdon's rural image the photograph of the courthouse showing Union soldiers encamped on the public square in Murfreesboro (Fig. 3.13). At this street corner, where Main Street entered the public square, the three-story commercial block at the right edge of the photograph suggests a much more nucleated town center. Rawdon's drawing accurately documents the fact, nevertheless, that commercial blocks had not fully encircled the courthouse before the Civil War.

Commercial blocks have so successfully enclosed the public squares of Middle Tennessee that it is difficult to imagine town space without them. Nevertheless, the tall, boxy buildings began to make their first appearance on the square almost fifty years after surveyors first platted the grid. In 1846—the same year that A. T. Stewart opened the first department store in New York City, a "marble palace" with a ladies parlor on the second floor— Nathan Vaught built the first commercial block in Columbia. Considerably more humble than a "marble palace," Vaught's building was, in his words, "a very deep and extra wide brick storehouse on the north side of West Market Street 2 doors from the corner of the Public Squar[e]." In addition

FIGURE 3.13. West Main Street facade of Murfreesboro courthouse, built in 1859. This photograph, taken during the Civil War, shows Union soldiers encamped on the public square. (Courtesy of Library of Congress, Prints and Photographs Division, Civil War Collection, LC-B8151-10020)

to the building's impressive dimensions, Vaught remembered that "the first open front [plate glass window] in town was put in this building."[66]

The change made an equally dramatic impression on Murfreesboro entrepreneur John Spence, who explained that "merchants, formerly doing business in a twenty feet square room, satisfied with the store and the business, are now making store houses twenty by eighty feet long, still feeling a little crouded [sic]."[67] Old-fashioned "storehouses" were systematically replaced by new "commercial blocks." When the northwest corner of the public square in Murfreesboro burned in 1856, "the ground was immediately covered with a row of brick business houses, running back a hundred feet."[68] Such stores put a new premium on property around the square, maximizing retail space by covering every square inch of a town lot.

In the renovated townscape, the commercial block was particularly suited to retail specialization. In 1859, William J. Dale commissioned Nathan Vaught to build a "brick block of 3 stories high [with] 3 store rooms on the north side of the Square" (Fig. 3.14).[69] The contrast between the Vaught block and the brick storehouse (Fig. 2.3) built on the square in Franklin earlier in the century dramatically demonstrates the new concept in commercial architecture. In a single unit, the three "store rooms" Vaught designed were actually three distinct stores meant to accommodate different retail specialties. The store in the corner building, for example, specialized in selling furniture and the related business of undertaking.[70] Vaught altered the roofline and window styles to define clearly the three separate stores incorporated into the block.

The Vaught building was originally a free-standing structure, but by 1860 it was joined by several equally impressive commercial blocks.[71] Each new block of stores became a segment in a wall of contiguous store facades that surrounded the square. Although the square was not completely encircled until the final quarter of the nineteenth century, the commercial block of the 1850s visually redefined the space, setting it apart from other areas of town (Figs. 3.3 and 3.4). In contrast to cities, where commercial specialization generated brick-walled corridors of trade that visually emphasized the length and trajectory of the street, in the county seat the combination of commercial blocks constructed around a square, produced a striking sense of enclosure.

Architecturally, the commercial block suggested a consolidation of power and authority by wealthy merchants, yet the square itself was a hybrid space charged with diverse meanings. On one hand, the space, lined with com-

FIGURE 3.14. Commercial block built by Nathan Vaught in Columbia around 1859.
(Courtesy of Mrs. Jill K. Garrett)

mercial blocks, turned inward and appeared increasingly separate and contained. On the other hand, the square remained a cultural intersection, the crossroads of Main Streets that became country turnpikes.[72] The space functioned as a kind of public parlor—communal gathering place of farmers and town dwellers, slaves and masters, men and women. Architecture and experience converged on the square, exhibiting new oppositions in the renovated townscape—commerce and domesticity, democracy and hierarchy, urban and rural. These oppositions were drawn in sharper relief as town residents rebuilt their courthouses on the eve of the Civil War.

The Public Square and the Courthouse:
Commerce and Domesticity in the Renovated Townscape

The boxy brick courthouses that had stood at the center of the square since the early days of incorporation seemed out of place in the renovated townscape. Columbia was the first to replace its courthouse, beginning construction in the late 1840s; but just one decade later, residents were complaining about the building. In 1860, even as the Union Guards drilled in the streets, plans to remove the market house and build a city hall on the square brought strong support from one local editor, who urged, "The improvements of fine business houses on the square, by individuals, renders it peculiarly obliging upon the [City] Board to assist in making the Square look better." He could not resist suggesting his dim opinion of the court-house too: "As for the City Hall, it is more needed here than any other building, not even excepting a new Court House."[73] Franklin and Murfrees-boro did not build new courthouses until the end of the 1850s.

Begun in 1859, the Murfreesboro courthouse in particular embodied the new oppositions of the renovated townscape. The brick building stood two stories tall and cost about $50,000 to build. Porticoes rose the entire height of the building, on both the East and the West Main Street facades. Architectural embellishments combined Greek Revival and Italianate elements, such as fluted Corinthian columns, bracketed cornices, and arched windows on the East Main Street facade (Fig. 3.13). In 1860, a bell and clock were installed in the cupola. More than any other feature, the cupola marked the Murfreesboro courthouse as a public building. Without it, in fact, the facade of the building closely resembled several impressive residences built across the Middle Tennessee countryside during the same period of townscape renovation.

In the context of the renovated townscape, the Murfreesboro courthouse embodied a complex set of concerns. Surrounded by new commercial blocks in the heart of the retail business district, the Murfreesboro court-house was built to a domestic standard. Though the cupola signaled its role as a public building, the porches suggested other meanings. Andrew Jackson Downing, the most influential architectural reformer of the period, particularly associated porches with domesticity. He argued in a best-selling book that as "prominent features" of a building, porches conveyed "expression of purpose in dwelling-houses." Indeed, porches were essential; "No dwelling-house can be considered complete without one or more of them," he declared emphatically.[74] The Murfreesboro courthouse was as much a communal habitation as a seat of government. While dwellings were being removed from the square, and the finest houses were being built at the periphery of town, the domesticated courthouse seems an ironic addition to the renovated townscape. Yet the courthouse, with its residential appearance, and the commercial block, embodying new ways of doing business, brought new oppositions into sharp relief on the public square. The renovated square signified the dual elements of communal prosperity—town as desirable home and town as successful marketplace.

County seat residents considered architectural renovation to be an essential component of communal progress at midcentury. The dramatic transformation they wrought was nothing short of a complete reorganization of town space. Nevertheless, renovation was uneven. Stark contrasts between dilapidation and elegance stood out in bold relief, even on the public square— centerpiece of communal identity. In Shelbyville, for example, the courthouse failed to live up to new architectural standards, but the Civil War interrupted efforts to replace it.

One fall day in 1854, Bedford County resident Elvira Moore breathlessly recorded the exciting new sights and sounds she witnessed on an excursion to Shelbyville. "I saw Telegraph wires, heard the [railroad] car whistle," she confided to her diary. In town, she bought several yards of domestic and calico, cotton stockings, a linen handkerchief, and toothbrush. The latter purchase may have been inspired by her visit to the dentist, whose office appeared to her as fashionable as any parlor: "The Dentist's room is well furnished with cushioned chairs[,] a sofa[,] and other furniture, papered walls and carpeted floor. . . . I saw there the first centre table that I have seen[.] It was loaded with books and papers."[75] From the telegraph to the dentist's office, Moore described a townscape that had only recently begun to take shape, and her wonder at what she surveyed came through as she composed her diary entry.

Yet not everything she saw in Shelbyville filled her with awe. Moore was decidedly unimpressed by the courthouse:

> They are fencing in the old court house with iron fence which would
> look nice if it was enclosing a fine edifice but the poor old court house
> is giving away & cracking open so that they have to brace it with straps
> of iron & it never was much good looking I guess, although it is a brick
> building the windows of the upper story are filled with undressed
> plank which looks anything but gay.

Significantly, Moore's description of other buildings in Shelbyville documented the larger patterns of renovation common to other county seats in Middle Tennessee. "There are some elegant buildings on the square," she wrote, "but the most of the handsome buildings are dwellings in the outskirts of town." In particular, the young woman noticed the new female college, though she identified it by an old-fashioned institutional term. "The female academy on the rise in the Northern part of town is a handsome structure, made of brick with a flat roof & was lately built[.] It commands a good view of the town," she wrote with the confidence of an actual observer.[76]

By the end of the 1850s, the building boom had effectively reorganized town space according to specialized uses. New courthouses, commercial blocks, villas, and cottages projected a broad communal image of prosperity and refinement. Residents believed that town progress and architectural improvement were inextricably linked. Nevertheless, the new buildings were clearly designed to reinforce social hierarchies. Architectural change was ultimately an expression of power relations. The public square certainly embodied the dominant authority of merchant and planter. Yet considered in relationship to each other, buildings that composed the space also conveyed other complex meanings—new relationships between domesticity and commerce; town and country.

Though merchants, planters, and other property owners controlled the design and placement of individual buildings, the larger townscape was constructed by a broad spectrum of residents—a product of experience that could never be completely controlled by any one class, gender, or race. Architectural change went hand in hand with changes in lifestyle. Murfreesboro residents had begun the decade with their celebration of Union University, a new kind of school for young men. Female colleges, like the one Elvira Moore visited in Shelbyville, also became important components of the renovated townscape. These new institutions signaled important changes in the roles of young men and women as town residents.

The chronological history of town building described in these first three chapters has shown how town residents worked together to construct not only the material fabric of the town but also their distinctive identity as small-town residents. Their changing uses of town space shaped the border between town and countryside, established hierarchies among town residents, and mingled urban aspirations with small-town spirit. During the 1850s these small towns came of age in a building boom that effectively transformed town space and reshaped social relationships.

The townscapes created during the first half century of town development must be understood as the product of many groups of town residents.

Women and slaves did not design courthouses and commercial blocks, but they were among the architects of the townscape. In the next three chapters we will rewalk town history in their footsteps, visiting the public square and the parlor from the perspective of town residents whose experience shaped the social construction of town space as profoundly as the railroad did.

PART TWO

Walking the Townscape

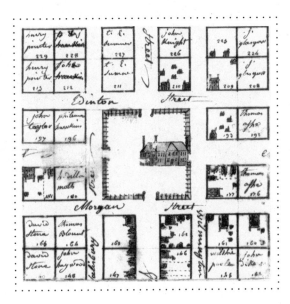

The history of space does not have to choose between "processes" and "structures," change and invariability, events and institutions. Its periodizations, moreover, will differ from generally accepted ones. Naturally, the history of space should not be distanced in any way from the history of time. . . . The departure point for this history of space is not to be found in geographical descriptions of natural space, but rather in the study of natural rhythms, and of the modification of those rhythms and their inscription in space by means of human actions, especially work-related actions. It begins, then, with the spatio-temporal rhythms of nature as transformed by a social practice.

HENRI LEFEBVRE, *The Production of Space*

Part I explored significant stages in the physical construction of town space and the concomitant development of distinctive small-town identities. Yet, the story of small-town life remains incomplete. Carpenters and brick-masons built individual buildings, but townscapes were constructed by more than one gender, class, or race. A highly visual, three-dimensional analysis that connects the built environment to a broad social and cultural context reveals patterns heretofore unseen. The subtle impact of gender and race on spatial development can be understood not as abstractions but as the lived experience of actual individuals. By interpreting architectural meaning as social experience, it is possible to see how groups of residents who had little control over the actual design of individual structures had considerable impact on the social construction of space within the townscape. Conversely, the experiences of these groups also show how space constrained action.

Women, slave and free, constituted half the population of the county seat at midcentury, and at least half of all women were younger than twenty. Ultimately, female rhythms of town life were based on differences in race, class, and life cycle. But gender played a special role in architectural renovation of the 1850s: streets were improved for the refined traffic of "Ladies"; women cultivated gardens for personal fulfillment and in performance of civic duty; and female colleges mediated tensions between contrasting town roles—town as aggressive market and town as peaceful home.

At least half of all men in the county seat at midcentury were younger than twenty. Teenaged sons of merchants and planters worked as clerks, living in stores around the public square. Other young men boarded with town families as students and apprentices. Their free access to the streets—serenading, drinking, fighting, spitting—presented special challenges to the maintenance of public order.

At least 40 percent of town residents in 1850 were slaves and as many as 80 percent of town households were headed by slaveholders. Throughout the antebellum period, slaves lived dispersed, compelled to inhabit the hallways and kitchens of white families all over town. Small towns established patterns of slavery and slaveholding that were distinct from isolated farms or plantations and from urban centers with larger free black populations. The spatial implications of slavery in a small-town context involved critical issues of population control and discipline, privacy and communal intimacy, and opportunities for slave autonomy. Slaves themselves were active participants in small-town life. They helped to shape the distinctive social intimacy that marked small-town society, and they played an influential role in formulating the complex living and working arrangements that distinguished small-town slavery.

Notice that differences in perspective and experience come into focus through narrative parallels built into each of the three chapters in Part II. All the chapters open with a small-town story that follows the daily routines of an individual town resident. In Chapter 4, the teenaged Kate Carney offers a window onto the experience of ladies and other white women. In Chapter 5, the store clerk and eventual lawyer Edmund Cooper reveals the particular rhythms of small-town life for young white men on the make. And in Chapter 6 a laborer named Henry provides a tour of town streets from the unique perspective of a small-town slave.

These individual stories are connected to the larger demographic and social context of small-town life. From day to day the rhythms of town life often took women, young men, and slaves in different directions. Nevertheless, each chapter explores cases in which their paths crossed. For example, the small-town custom of visiting takes on a different set of meanings when viewed from the particular perspective of each group of participants.

Finally, each chapter in Part II ends by exploring a type of building designed particularly for one group of residents—female colleges, male colleges, and African churches. The appearance and uses of these buildings show how town residents applied distinctive spatial strategies for integrating young white women, young white men, and slaves into town life. The complexities and consequences of small-town history come more completely into view when we understand more fully what it meant to be a small-town resident in antebellum Tennessee.

CHAPTER FOUR

Ladies and Other Women

A Small-Town Story: Kate Carney's Walk

Kate Carney was a small-town girl, through and through. In 1859, she had lived all of her seventeen years in Murfreesboro, where her neighbors described the family as "the richest people" in town with "much the finest house."[1] In the northern limits of town, six blocks from the public square, the Carneys had recently built an imposing red brick home (Fig. 4.1). The house, though surrounded by a twelve-acre lawn and twenty acres of orchard and gardens, stood out. Its dominant feature—double, two-story, white-columned porticoes—declared the family's fashionable allegiance to the Greek Revival style. Kate's father, Legrand Carney, owned a dry goods store on the public square and other town property, as well as a plantation in the county. Her mother, Katherine, was a member of the same Lytle family whose patriarch originally owned the land on which Murfreesboro had been built. Kate was the fourth of nine children. Two older brothers were married and living in their own separate households, and her older sister Mary would soon wed a doctor from Nashville and move away to Mississippi. Kate herself was a part-time student at Soule Female College and seems primarily to have studied painting and practiced the guitar. Her best friend was Mary Spence, daughter of Murfreesboro merchant and chronicler, John Spence.

FIGURE 4.1. The Carney family house, Murfreesboro, built during the 1850s.
The Carneys sold the house after the Civil War, and it was torn down in 1910.
(Originally published in Mary B. Hughes, *Hearthstones: The Story of Historic
Rutherford County Homes*, 1942, p. 59)

Kate Carney wrote a chronicle of her own in her seventeenth year.[2] She
kept a diary, remarkable not for its self-reflection or probing analysis of
small-town life but for its straightforward description of what she did almost
every day in 1859. Above all, she walked—not just in her own expansive
yard but all over town, not just on warm, sunny days but on cold winter ones
too. One day in January she "walked up to town four times, . . . three times
this morning, and once this evening."[3] Every night before bed she tried to
record the places she had visited and the people she had seen. Occasionally
she found herself completely overwhelmed by the task. "Mary Spence and I
took quite a long walk, and I got a little tired before getting home. We went
by the store, and, but pshaw! I cannot think of telling everywhere we went,
& ever body [*sic*] we saw for it would take to [*sic*] much time."[4] But most
nights, Kate took the time to record her itinerary.

Katherine Carney did not always approve of her daughter's ramblings.
She was not particularly reluctant to allow her daughter to stroll unattended
through town streets; she was more concerned that Kate's meanderings kept
her from household duties that might otherwise be accomplished. One day,
after Kate took a particularly long and tiring expedition, an exasperated
Katherine Carney told her peripatetic daughter that she "must stop walk-

ing"—as Kate put it, "that I can find enough to do, at home for exercise." Kate admitted, "She must be right, but it is not only for exercise, but for pleasure; for I enjoy those walks very much."[5] Luckily, Katherine Carney did not enforce her rule, and Kate's pleasure in walking never waned. Her diary is a kind of small-town travelogue that suggests some of the ways in which gender operated as a fundamental organizing principle of the mid-nineteenth-century townscape.

On 19 March 1859, Kate "went up town" after dinner with her friend and cousin Nannie Black. The girls walked six blocks, passing Soule Female College and several houses along their way, to the public square (Fig. 4.2). Nannie and Kate zigzagged around the square from store to store. "We first went to Mr. Neilson's & Crichelow's store, then to Pa's, & then back to the same one, & then across to Jordan's & Elliott's." All three of these stores advertised that same year in Murfreesboro newspapers as dry goods establishments.[6] Kate did not record what, if anything, the pair bought.

Having finished their business on the square for the time being, the girls retraced their steps three blocks down the Lebanon Pike "to the College to call" on some friends who were boarding there. "We staid [sic] some time," Kate wrote, "when Nannie saw Ellen & Mary [Spence] going by." So Kate and Nannie "bid the [College] girls good bye, & went out & caught up with them. Nannie & Ellen walked together, & Mary & I until we came to Crockett's store, & we all went in except Nannie, and she went to Mr. Neilson's & Crichelow's."[7] The three girls "did not remain long in at Mr. Crockett's, as Ellen only wished Bob [Crockett] to carry several letters over to the office for her." Kate continued: "We then went in to Mr. Neilson & found Misses Sallie Neilson, Jennie James, & Nannie Black. We all then went to Reed's Bookstore (quite a number six in all) from there we [went to] Mr. Elliott's then walked down Main Street and turned across to College St., stopping only to bid Miss Sallie & Miss Jennie good evening."[8] College Street was one block north of the square, so when Kate realized that she "had forgotten, & left one of Nannie's accountbooks at one of the stores," she and Nannie and the Spence sisters, "walked up & one of the young ladies went in and got it." From the square, the girls took Lebanon Pike toward home, stopped "by Mrs. Spence's & left Mary & Ellen, then came home, as it had grown quite late by that time."[9]

En route from her father's store to Soule Female College to the Carney home, practically every building Kate entered that March day had been built

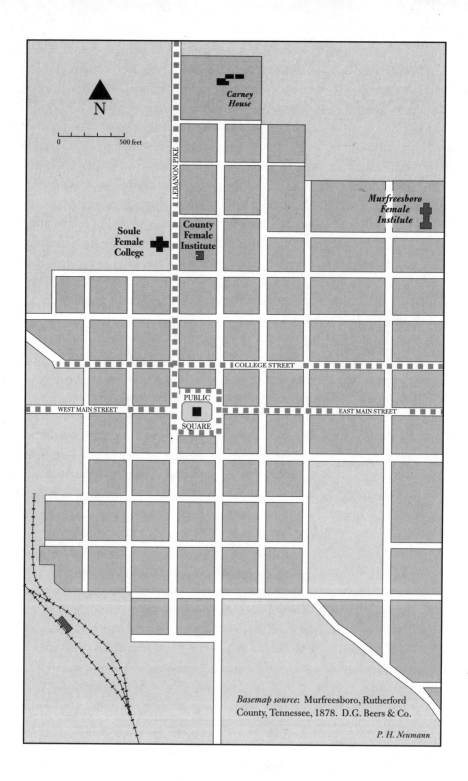

Within the map:

N

0   500 feet

LEBANON PIKE

Carney House

Murfreesboro Female Institute

Soule Female College

County Female Institute

COLLEGE STREET

WEST MAIN STREET

PUBLIC SQUARE

EAST MAIN STREET

Basemap source: Murfreesboro, Rutherford County, Tennessee, 1878. D.G. Beers & Co.

P. H. Neumann

during her adolescence. It was a townscape designed with particular attention to a "refined" female clientele. In the middle decades of the nineteenth century, industrialization redefined the geography of work and home, domesticity was enshrined as the virtuous occupation of the lady, and gender became a volatile national issue.[10] Thus, when Middle Tennesseans reorganized town space at midcentury to create new functional zones—wholesale, retail, and residential districts—their architectural choices also revealed gender as a powerful organizing principle, equally as influential as function, in the design of town space.

At first glance, the public square might seem a uniquely masculine region. Certainly the space was owned by men—Messrs. Neilson & Crichelow and Jordan & Elliot, for example. This impression is reinforced by nineteenth-century photographs that show men lounging on street corners and posing proudly in front of their stores but which rarely include women, even as shoppers (Figs. 4.3 and 4.4). Then enter Kate and Nannie and their four female friends parading around and through the square, and the scene changes dramatically. The band of girls roamed freely, though not indiscriminately, through the space. Significantly, they patronized particular dry goods stores, owned by family and friends in the same social circle. They avoided businesses that were inappropriate for young ladies to enter, such as groceries that sold liquor.

The girls demonstrated how gender worked to organize retail commerce on the Square. Merchants depended on female customers for a profitable season, and they selected their merchandise to capture specific male or female customers. This principal was most evident during the "Fall season," when the latest stock arrived from New York and Philadelphia. As the *Maury Press* reported, "feminine taste and judgment" began to "congregate every day in their stores, to pass sentence upon the styles, to purchase, to prepare themselves" for a winter of parties and fashionable social events. In the fall as at no other time of the year, merchants could see that Main Street was "alive with ladies visiting and shopping. From morning to night their gay and pleasant faces enlivening its walks, . . . bearing down upon the square like gallant ships in full sail."[11]

FIGURE 4.2. (*Facing page*) Map of Murfreesboro, showing the route Kate Carney and her friends took on their afternoon walk. In addition to Soule Female College, the map also shows the location of two other female colleges built during the 1850s.
(Base map source: D. G. Beers & Co., 1878)

FIGURE 4.3. This tailor's shop was located one block from the public square in Columbia, Tennessee. (From *First Autumn Carnival Given Under the Auspices of Columbia Lodge, No. 686 Benevolent and Protective Order of Elks, Columbia, Tennessee, September 16 to 21, 1901* [Nashville, Tenn.: Foster & Webb, n.d.])

But gender pushed beyond the boundaries of the public square to influence the design of entirely new town regions during the 1850s. Kate's walk had taken her to Soule Female College, an educational institution that was architecturally and intellectually distinct from earlier town academies. Housed in large structures containing classrooms, dormitories, lecture halls, and

FIGURE 4.4. The Crichelow & Rice grocery store on the public square in Murfreesboro, Tennessee. (Courtesy of Mrs. Mabel Pittard)

refectories and set on new campuses for women within the town borders, the female college went well beyond the concept of a one-room schoolhouse. Innovative in design, female colleges of the 1850s were nonetheless traditional in purpose—intended to produce ladies, not feminists.[12] Ironically, however, this age that created a privatized, idealized domesticity also redefined female education as a lucrative town industry. Residents enthusiastically promoted their female colleges as instruments of communal prosperity. In fact, small-town residents increasingly pointed to female refinements as an economic as well as aesthetic strategy to enhance the status and reputation of the community.

Kate Carney's narrative provides only a part of a larger women's townscape, which was constructed by a female experience that depended on class, race, and life cycle. As a teenager, Kate had little responsibility for running a household and so was free to spend her afternoons walking with other teenaged girls. As a wealthy young lady, Kate could interpret her walks as "pleasure" rather than work. The young slave, Millie, owned by the Carney family, must have had a very different interpretation of walking while she toted Kate's guitar, paint box, and picture frames back and forth to college for her.[13]

The Demographic Context: Female Rhythms of Town Life

As a member of one of the richest families in town, Kate Carney may have been exceptional, but as a young woman she was far from unusual. In 1850, at least half of all town residents were women, and more than half of this female population was younger than twenty.[14] Such numbers suggest a commonality of experience among young women who had not yet assumed adult responsibilities as wives and mothers. However, more than 40 percent of town women were slaves, among whom, as in the free population, young women were the majority.[15] Kate Carney recorded daily encounters with a wide variety of town women—slave and free, wealthy and poor. Patterns emerge from these interactions that show how female rhythms of town life cleaved along sharp divisions of race and class. Girls like the Carney slaves, Millie and Leathy, began a lifetime of servitude, running errands and tending small children. Their mothers performed the most arduous household tasks, such as cooking and laundering, enabling white mistresses to devote their attention to more refined employment. Female slaves were essential to the creation and maintenance of the idealized, fashionable "lady."

Beyond race, complex social and economic differences separated particular female experiences. Kate and her mother spent much time making and receiving "fashionable calls" with women of their own social standing. But they were also the frequent clients of female entrepreneurs outside the circle of their peers. Among the three white seamstresses whom Kate and her mother regularly employed to make their most fashionable dresses, Mrs. Bumpass received the lion's share of their patronage. Sarah Bumpass, wife of a local cabinetmaker and owner of a fifty-year-old female slave, fit squarely within the middle ranks of respectability.[16] Also included among these ranks of women were the unmarried school teachers Miss Holt and Miss Hines, who taught Kate music at Soule Female College. But Kate's interactions with unnamed women—like the fortuneteller who told her future at the City Hotel, the poor beggar woman who came to the door while the Carneys were eating breakfast, and the itinerant seamstress who arrived at the house one day "with things all ready [*sic*] drawn off ready for working"—reveal a transient female population whose experiences are even more elusive than those of slave women.[17]

In addition to race and class, life cycle was key to female rhythms of town life. Kate Carney and the girls in her social circle enjoyed the freedom of sleeping late in the mornings; performed light housekeeping duties, such as dusting, before the midday meal; and spent their afternoons at school or "exercising." But as she neared adulthood, Kate was painfully aware that her carefree girlhood was nearing an end. She watched her older sister marry and move away to Mississippi, and she worriedly remarked on her seventeenth birthday that her mother "took upon herself to love, honor, and obey" when she was only five months older than Kate. Though at seventeen she was "getting quite old," Kate defiantly declared that she was "not married, and hope I will not be soon."[18] Marriage and motherhood dramatically altered the daily routines of girls like Kate Carney. Sleeping late was impossible when a woman became responsible for the management of an entire household.

Across town, in her "little cottage home," young wife and mother Virginia Shelton eagerly embraced her new role as manager of her first household. Married to William Shelton, a professor at Union University and part-time preacher at any interested church, Virginia took in boarders to "help a little in our expenses" and taught at the Eaton Female College "for a few hours in the afternoon."[19] But Virginia was more than a respectable middle-class lady. She had been raised by her uncle, David Campbell, while he was governor of Virginia, and her brother, William Bowen Campbell, became Whig governor of Tennessee shortly after the Sheltons arrived in Murfreesboro. Such family connections made Virginia something of a local celebrity— courted by the Murfreesboro elite, though counted among the merely comfortable cottage dwellers.

Virginia declared herself "much pleased at the idea of going to housekeeping." To manage her six-room house, she was invariably assisted by three or four slaves, hired yearly. During the first year, the couple hired Bill and Sylva and their son Moses from William's mother in nearby Lebanon, and from Murfreesboro they hired the young girl Jane as nurse to their toddler son David.[20] In addition, Virginia received ample assistance from female relatives living in the vicinity of Murfreesboro, including her mother, mother-in-law, and sisters. "Mother and Martha sew so fast," Virginia declared, "that I have nearly all my work done, curtains, counterpanes, comfits, etc."[21]

William's mother made several extended visits to Murfreesboro from Lebanon, in neighboring Wilson County. Her housekeeping schedule embodied Kate Carney's worst fears. She was "up every morning by 4 o'clock and goes about watching over every thing, now seeing that the cow is well milked again noticing that the pigs are kept out of the garden &c."[22] Clearly, however, managing and doing were two entirely different things.[23] The efficient household operated according to a strict division of labor: Mrs. Shelton "watched over" the work, while an unnamed servant or servants, perhaps Sylva or Jane, actually milked the cow and chased away the pigs.

Yet even Virginia Shelton's industrious mother-in-law devoted much energy to occupations that had little to do with household management. "She is constantly meeting with some old acquaintance's descendant or some kindred of her relations."[24] Virginia's own schedule, as she settled into routine housekeeping, included ample time for recreation as well:

> Mother and Martha and I sew and read and receive visitors and play and caress the dear little fat David [her baby son]. We go visiting and shopping sometimes and mother helps me about every thing. She makes suggestions about the garden and kitchen and smokehouse and house that I would not have thought of and I don't know what I would do if she were to go away.[25]

It is important to note what Virginia was doing and what she was not doing. Instead of cooking or washing she was sewing and reading; instead of milking or feeding chickens she was shopping and visiting. By contrast, her servants in 1853, Vesta and Isaac, found themselves "very busy in cleaning up the house, scouring, washing windows and paint[ing], removing carpets, making preserves, [and] bottling fruit."[26]

Virginia's ability to design a housekeeping routine that left her free to pursue interests beyond the immediate material needs of her household certainly depended on the availability of slave labor. But it was also possible because of profound economic changes revealed most clearly in the renovated townscapes of the 1850s. These changes particularly affected free white women of privilege, who managed town households according to a distinctly different daily rhythm than had the preceding generation of housekeepers. Women of the renovated townscape reconstructed their household routines to eliminate much of the domestic craft production that had previously monopolized the housekeeper's time. In its place they followed new domestic standards that emphasized female responsibility for the comfort and education of the family. Significantly, household managers like Virginia Shelton found their domestic responsibilities to be challenging and time-consuming. When she accepted a part-time job as a music teacher, Virginia expected to relinquish the position before long to a young unmarried woman with "sufficient leisure, which a housekeeper cannot well have."[27] As we shall see, the changing domestic standards and employment opportunities created new distinctions between women who lived in town compared to those who operated farm households.

Space and Society

Virginia Shelton's Piano: Housework Redefined

In 1834, John Shofner, who lived on a farm just outside Shelbyville, attempted to describe for his brother the remarkable transformation that had come over the countryside since his father had first moved to Bedford County about "26 or 27 year ago." The family settled "in a thick forrest of heavy timber and the powerfullest cain brake that was eaver saw."[28] But that landscape had been utterly obliterated in less than three decades. Shofner proudly listed the impressive achievements he had witnessed personally during that brief time. Steamboats had shortened the trip from Nashville to New Orleans from three months to twelve or fifteen days. Market centers replaced nomadic cattle drovers as the chief economic agent for scattered farmers. Large productive farms and water- and steam-powered mills supplanted forests and canebrakes. And prospects for continued progress included a turnpike road from Nashville to Shelbyville and much discussion about building "a line of ralerode from Shelbyvill to Memphies on the grate Massassippi . . . a distence of about two hundred thirty miles."[29]

Embedded in Shofner's list of improvements was an inconspicuous statement with profound implications for women's lives. Before launching into his treatise on the transformation of Bedford County, Shofner remarked that while he was composing his missive, his wife Milley was "a weeving." Her activity must have jogged his memory for, wedged between his tales of steamboats and turnpikes, Shofner mused that during the early years of settlement, "the woman had to spin all thare thread, now thare are spinning factoreys all over the cuntrey and some plases [have] weving factorey[s]." The industrialization and commercialization of the townscape changed the relationship between town and country largely by changing the demands of housework.

At the precise moment that the railroad was shrinking geographic distance, the social distance between town and country was widening. During the early years of town development, town households had functioned much like farm households. Town stores had provided local markets for products manufactured by women in separate households of both the town and the surrounding countryside. In 1833, Thomas Eakin, who owned a dry goods store on the public square in Shelbyville, had assured his customers that he would accept "feathers, tallow, beeswax, hides, and clean rags . . . in exchange for goods."[30] John Spence noted that these "home made articles" were the chief currency in a localized barter economy. Each spring, families came to town to trade "blue jeanes and brown, white linsey, white homespun flax and tow linnen, shoe thread, twine, bees-wax, tallow, feathers, cotton and wool socks, and many other articles." The business of household production was so profitable, he wrote, that "some girls, by spinning and weaving for others, have made money to purchase a bed, and bed stead and side saddle, and similar articles for themselves, beside purchasing their own fine dressing."[31] Town customers like the young Shelbyville lawyer Edmund Cooper completed the economic chain begun by the "frugal housewives and lovely daughters" of unknown country families. "I am myself clothed in a suit of 'Home made Jeans,'" he told his brother, "spun and woven I imagine, by some lovely damsel of the county, for she must be lovely, for no ugly woman could possibly have fabricated such a handsome piece of goods."[32]

During the mid-nineteenth century, however, town factories assumed some of the production processes that had been supervised and performed by women in separate households. In 1854, one weaving factory in Shelbyville housed "one thousand and thirty spindles and thirty looms—worked entirely by white labor," manufacturing "coloured cotton goods" and "pretty checks." It was not the first such establishment in town. One of the project's investors already had about fourteen years of experience "in the manufacture of thread."[33] Such local factories never produced enough to supply the broad range of goods demanded in local markets. Town customers were more likely to buy imported textiles displayed in dry goods stores on the square. Legrand Carney enticed his customers with all kinds of textiles, purchased in the latest styles from Philadelphia and New York: from ginghams and calicoes to Irish linens, laces, and carpets.[34] But whether the cloth or thread was produced in local factories or imported to dry goods stores, the wide availability of commercially produced textiles had a dramatic impact on the role and image of town women.

John Spence measured the progress of industrialization by its impact on female labor rather than by the quality or quantity of factory production. The clearest symbol of change was the substitution of the piano for the loom within the newly refined parlor. While mills turned out "bolts and bales" of "jeanes and linseys" at "lightening speed," he reported that the "old lady" leaned back "in the rocking chair, luxuriating on the happy changes taking place. Looms and spinning wheels never thought of in her times of ease. Daughters, lolling languidly in the parlour, or thumping the piano vigorously . . . shedding smiles, interesting on all around."[35] Spence's characterization of such apparently unproductive women ignores the class structure of town life that shaped women's lives. He omits, for example, the seamstresses who sewed fancy dresses for elite women like Katherine Carney.

Beyond these social differentiations, however, the image of a new generation of leisured daughters defined town women, not their rural neighbors. As late as 1858, six years after the railroad first began transporting people and products between Shelbyville and Nashville, farm women in Bedford County maintained a vigorous schedule of craft production in separate households. One young man, who traveled the Bedford County countryside, got the impression that "nearly every farm house has a loom and weaving and spinning are a part of house or domestic work. The large, old fashioned spinning wheel keeps up its buzzing noise all the fall and winter together with the noise of the flying shuttle. Hence there is quite a quantity of domestic goods manufactured which is so much curtailed from the store bill."[36] Town women continued to sew their own clothes, but weaving was primarily a rural occupation by the 1850s.

Town women, nevertheless, redefined household labor in response to the commercialized and industrialized townscape. They combined new urban standards of housekeeping with traditional forms of production long associated with rural self-sufficiency. The contrast John Spence drew between the productive women of the past and the leisured, even frivolous women of what he called "the new era" was only partly true. While the male-owned economy was highly visible and spatially concentrated along an axis from the railroad depot to the public square, a spatially diffuse female-operated economy continued to provide a local subsistence network linking individual town households.

When Virginia Shelton became mistress of her first home, her mother-in-law from neighboring Lebanon provided the means to make her household a productive unit. "Mother Shelton is going to set us up in the provision line as well as in servants. She is to send not only beds, but flour, lard, butter, bacon, pork, &c., &c. Making us feel quite independent and well-fixed at once."[37] Virginia Shelton received assistance from women outside her family as well. Soon after the young couple moved in, "Mrs. Lieper (my next door neighbor) sent me a waiter of eggs (which cannot be had for money) and apples and pickles."[38] By the spring, Virginia was becoming a productive housekeeper in her own right.

> We have a fine garden and the vegetables most promising. In five days past, I have sold 1.55 cts. worth of things from my garden. Peas, cherries and gooseberries the articles, Jane and Moses my salesman and Mrs. Sublett of one of the Hotels one of my principle customers. My beets and potatoes are very promising and I hope at all events to cover the expence of the milk I have to purchase for Sibby [the family cow] got out the 1st of this month and has not been heard of since. I buy milk at 10 cts. a gallon but half a gallon is enough for Mr. Shelton [her husband], cousin James [a boarder], David [her son] and me and besides I save cream enough during the week to make a very little pint of butter. Mother Shelton sends me butter whenever she has an opportunity and I have been compelled to buy only 35 cts. worth since I've been housekeeping. . . . When we can spare any thing it is proper to sell it, as is the custom here.[39]

At first glance Virginia Shelton might easily be mistaken for a plantation mistress managing the labor of household slaves, Jane and Moses, on a farm complete with vegetable garden and stray cow. But the economic network she outlined unmistakably identifies the Shelton farmstead as a town household in which "housekeeping" was integral to the local market. Thus Jane and Moses were her "salesmen," negotiating the sale of her produce with her best customer at the local hotel. Beyond its ornamental or subsistence value, then, Virginia's garden was an income-producing venture. And she followed what was probably long-standing local custom in selling the household surplus.

Household production was still commercial enterprise in the context of a town. But what distinguished household managers in towns from their rural counterparts was a redefinition of housework that accompanied the commercialization of domestic crafts. John Spence was partly right—middle-class women who lived in or near market towns did exchange their looms for pianos. But he failed to appreciate fully the new domestic standards that kept women as busy as ever. As historian Christine Stansell explains: "Less involved in the productive and caretaking tasks of domestic labor, mistresses in the 1840s and 1850s came to concentrate on housework as the creation and maintenance of comfort and appearance. Cleanliness, tidiness, and care and arrangement of possessions replaced domestic production as house-wives' preoccupations."[40] These preoccupations were the means by which women of the renovated 1850s townscape fulfilled their responsibility for the creation of urbane townscapes. When Virginia Shelton declared herself to be "quite pleased" with the appearances of Murfreesboro, she did not describe the elegance of the courthouse; instead she enumerated the accom-plishments of the town's best women: "Not a dozen ladies have called yet," she declared, "but all I have seen are interesting and agreeable and seem to be perfect ladies."[41]

John Spence notwithstanding, ladies like Virginia Shelton sometimes used their pianos in ways not unlike those in which their mothers had used their looms. Unfortunately, Virginia did not own a piano of her own—a need that became more acute after she had her parlor "handsomely . . . painted and papered and furnished (all except a piano, which I must procure some-time soon)."[42] Virginia proceeded to use her knowledge of music in the same way that her weaving predecessors had bartered their homemade jeans for bedsteads and sidesaddles. She consented to teach piano at Mrs. Eaton's new college to a class of ten or a dozen girls "and thus I shall be enabled in one session to pay for my own piano, the tuition fees being 25 dollars per session."[43] Alas, her predictions proved entirely too optimistic. Enrollment was not as high as expected, and Virginia had to postpone her purchase. In fact, she was never able to earn enough money teaching music to buy a piano. Eventually, her uncle sent the money, partly to boost his niece's spirits after the death of her baby daughter.[44] Virginia had started her piano pur-chasing campaign in November 1851, but it was almost exactly two years later before she and Mr. Shelton boarded the train to Nashville, where they "purchased a beautiful and excellent-toned piano, with the stool and cover, all for $300.00." They returned to Murfreesboro the very next day, "the piano was set up and placed in [the] parlor before sunset," and Virginia entertained her family by playing "several old scotch airs."[45]

The women who produced "scotch airs" instead of "home made jeans" found that the new demands of domesticity could be equally exacting. As men rebuilt the buildings, the standard of the "perfect lady" increasingly became the measure of the cultured townscape. No longer a question of economic survival, town building at midcentury was a quest for prosperity, and the reputation of the entire community depended upon the refined accomplishments of its ladies.

The Cultivated Environment: Gardens and Visitors

As owners of the public square and the railroad depot, as architects and builders, men made the decisions that determined the shape of this architectural townscape. Women provided some inspiration for architectural change. After all, merchants rearranged their stores and selected their merchandise to appeal to a refined female clientele in the 1850s. But town women, especially ladies, refused to limit themselves to such indirect influence. They did more than think about parlor furnishings; they designed highly visual elements of the townscape. In their gardens women cultivated their material and symbolic roles as providers and beautifiers. In their highly ritualized performance as visitors, ladies cultivated a refined, urbane environment within the confines of the small town. The physical and symbolic townscape converged in female responsibilities for gardening and visiting. The stakes were high. The reputation of the entire town hung in the balance of female performance.

After surveying the Shelbyville townscape in 1823, one citizen felt concerned enough to write a letter to the editor of the town newspaper. He worried that Shelbyville's female citizens had failed to perform their civic duty to improve the appearance of the town. "It has been said, and correctly too," he declared, "that the civilization of a country may be ascertained by the attention which is paid to women—and perhaps, the improvement of women, may be correctly ascertained by the appearance of gardens." Unfortunately, the level of civilization in Shelbyville was in serious doubt. Town women, he complained, had neglected their gardens:

> Many of the inhabitants of your village, do not appear, to take much pains to have prime vegetables. This negligence produces astonishment, because most of them have lots of their own, and a good soil. . . . the most important defects which the writer has noticed in gardening, are indifferent enclosures, a want of proper fertility, the use of the plow, instead of the spade, a "beggarly account" of the different species of vegetables which the climate would produce; and too much grass, precisely where not a blade should grow. . . . It is almost impossible, that a woman of an improved taste and understanding can be indifferent to the beauties of art and nature; and, a well planned, and cultivated garden, affords both.[46]

WALKING THE TOWNSCAPE

This citizen interpreted gardening as part of a larger civic role performed by women. To him, the state of their gardens was a visual measure of the level of local civilization.

Significantly, this concerned citizen of Shelbyville applied a masculine standard of evaluation. His underlying rationale was economic, based on the commercial value of the land and a utilitarian definition of beauty. For him the "well planned and cultivated garden" demonstrated the richness of the soil—first by the appropriate and efficient application of agricultural technology and ultimately by the abundance and variety of vegetables produced on one fertile plot. Furthermore, by admitting only vegetables into the garden, he emphasized female responsibility for family subsistence. But gardens were actually more complicated than this concerned citizen imagined. They were the site of a number of responsibilities and ambitions of women— places cultivated not only for household subsistence but for social exchange; places where women expressed their roles as providers and beautifiers.

Gardening was central to female experience, whether in settled landscapes or on the frontier, for, as Annette Kolodny notes, "in the exchange of cuttings, . . . seeds, . . . and information about their garden activities, women shared with one another both their right and their capacity" to shape "landscapes otherwise owned and appropriated by men."[47] Town women derived pleasure as well as profit from their gardens. For them, the successful garden contained not only a variety of prime vegetables, but also many different fruits, flowers, and ornamental shrubs. The female standard of beauty and fertility combined the utilitarian with the ornamental and exotic. Nowhere was this standard expressed more clearly than in Virginia Shelton's garden.

When Virginia moved to her new home in Murfreesboro, she was assured by her neighbors that there was "not a more productive garden-spot in town," and she determined "to raise vegetables in superior abundance and quality."[48] Indeed, Virginia's garden proved to be as fertile as her neighbors promised. She raised a wide variety of vegetables—peas, white onions, radishes, lettuce, mustard, cabbage, beets, and potatoes—enough to sell the surplus to the local hotelkeeper.

But Virginia's garden provided much more than family sustenance; she wanted to make it "quite a pleasant place."[49] Thus, in addition to her vegetables she cultivated a variety of fruits, flowers, and ornamental shrubs, including strawberries, raspberries, grapes, roses, hollies, and boxwood. She turned to other town women to implement her plan. "I want to collect some rare plants & shrubs and there are several ladies who have requested me to send for whatever I may want."[50] Virginia's response was part of a larger pattern of female cooperation. Kate Carney's mother responded to "quite a number of persons [who] sent out for flowers to plant."[51] In the exchange of plants, women affirmed their sense of communal closeness and shared responsibility for the maintenance of their families and the improvement of their communities. Together, these women transformed bare town lots into attractive garden spots.

But town women who owned or hired slaves could choose to weed and plant personally or direct their servants to do it. Virginia Shelton related how she and her husband busied themselves one March evening in 1852, setting out strawberry and raspberry plants, "when Miss Goodrich [a young teacher boarding with the Sheltons] came walking into the garden and seemed greatly delighted with our fine employment."[52] But when Virginia wanted "to collect plants and shrubs" for her garden, she sent her servant, Aunt Chana, "about to several ladies" in town to do the actual gathering.[53]

Gardens, then, were a focus of informal, cooperative social exchanges among women, but they also became part of a ritualized symbolic landscape of polite intercourse between men and women. Kate Carney used the family garden as an alternative to the parlor one spring afternoon when a young gentleman called. "I had not been in the parlor long when he said he wanted to see the yard," she wrote. "I told him to wait a second, and I got a spool of thread, and scissors, and while walking around, gathered a very pretty boquet [sic], and we sat down on the steps fronting the pike and made it."[54] Making a bouquet was much more than a casual afternoon diversion. The careful arrangement of flowers and ornamental plants could create bouquets that conveyed any number of specific meanings—from simple expressions of friendship and concern to highly personal messages of devotion. Whole books were published to interpret this "language of flowers," complete with lists of plants and their individual meanings, recipes for bouquets conveying specific messages, and appropriate poetry to be attached as "emblems" to accompany the bouquet.[55]

Town residents used this etiquette of flowers freely and publicly. When Virginia Shelton's husband William "made an address before the Appollonian Society" at Union University, he spoke to "a large audience of gentlemen and ladies." Afterward, the ladies expressed their approval by presenting him with bouquets.[56] Similarly, when Kate Carney attended graduation ceremonies at Union University in 1859, she went fully equipped with "a beautiful boquet [*sic*] which," she recalled, "I threw at Jessie Sikes, with my compliments on it. He was the first to speak, and received more boquets [*sic*]" than any other boy who graduated.[57] Kate herself was the recipient of bouquets from young men in town upon her departure for school in Philadelphia. John Butler, Tom Tucker, and Nat Butler sent her "some beautiful flowers with a long string of compliments and messages." In return, Kate "sent each a piece of arborvitae with a message," but she worried that she "should have been more politic and sent each a separate flower, with emblems attached." According to Sarah Josepha Hale's contemporary manual on the language of flowers, *arbor vitae*, or "false white cedar," symbolized "unchanging friendship."[58] Perhaps Kate chose the arborvitae with the intention of conveying that message to the friends she would soon leave behind.

Like gardening, the ritual of fashionable visiting mingled female roles in the creation of physical and symbolic elements of the townscape. Wearing their most stylish dresses, walking or riding in carriages through town streets, ladies conducted their ritualized visits as conspicuous acts, making hierarchies among town residents highly visible and competitive. Although the performance depended on the appearance of leisure, women took careful account of their visits and visitors. Virginia Shelton concluded that she "must be quite popular with the citizens here for they come to see me several times to my one visit and seem very anxious to be social."[59] But Virginia was keenly aware of her social responsibilities and so devoted a week to fulfilling her obligations. "This last week I have accomplished quite a talk," she reported. "I have been around and throughout the town and paid up all my visits." In the social economy of visiting, ladies "paid" their obligations, sometimes in marathon days, performing one social call after another. This was, in fact, the distinctive occupation of the lady. Virginia found it noteworthy when her husband once accompanied her. "I think it is so excellent and pleasant a custom for gentlemen also to visit, I would feign have him visit with me constantly," she decided.[60]

Rituals of visiting ranged from the highly formal to the casual, with corresponding demands for social performance. Virginia Shelton noted that her visitors "sometimes . . . bring some work [probably sewing] and sit several hours with me in my room."[61] But when she called on several members of the local elite, she admitted "the visits were all very pleasant indeed. Yet, I generally left just so soon as I could find a sufficient opening in the conversation to allow of my departure."[62] Visits could also be accomplished in large groups, as when "Aunt Mary Lytle, Mrs. Blackman and her baby, Cousin Tabitha Morgan, and . . . Aunt Beck, beside three servants, Little Lizzie and two other grown ones, came out in the Omnibuss [*sic*], to spend the day" at the Carneys.[63] They stayed for dinner.

The sight of all these ladies in their fashionable dresses, walking or riding in freshly cleaned carriages, was bound to call attention to the condition of town streets and sidewalks. Towns launched major campaigns at midcentury for improving streets, which could no longer merely be passable but must be appropriate paths for ladies. As the *Shelbyville Expositor* opined, "Nothing adds more to the *comfort* of a town or city, than good streets always kept in order, and firm, well built pavements upon which *ladies* may walk, even in unpleasant weather, without any danger of impairing their health by getting their feet wet from wading through mud and water."[64]

Beyond its physical impact, visiting was a vital part of the female responsibility for cultivating a refined, even cosmopolitan, atmosphere in a small-town setting. Virginia Shelton fairly beamed when she was visited one evening by Mr. Eaton, president of Union University, and two learned gentlemen from out of town—one the "editor of the Tennessee Baptist in Nashville, and a man of considerable ability," the other "principal of a female Institute in Winchester and quite learned." Virginia could not think of a time when she had "enjoyed a finer literary treat." In fact, she proudly compared her own parlor to a European salon: "I was reminded of some description of literary clubs in England where Johnson & Goldsmith &c. held forth."[65] Her role as architect of this magical literary evening remained implicit in her description.

But not every woman was able to duplicate Virginia's high level of performance. When women failed, the consequences could be catastrophic, or so thought Edmund Cooper. As an eligible young lawyer, he deplored the dullness of Shelbyville, which he disparagingly labeled a "priest-ridden village."[66] But he saved his most damning criticism for the town's female residents. The young women there simply could not compare to the vivacious and accomplished girls he had known when he was a store clerk in Columbia. To his dismay, he found in Shelbyville that

> we have not intellect, or intelligence sufficient among our young Ladies to make them even passable—*Tableaux* [the nineteenth-century fashion for enacting works of art] are to them a sealed book. They have no idea of the mode and manner in which they are gotten up. Hence, all things considered you may deem our town, dull, very dull. . . . If a

stranger comes to town, and he wishes to see our young Ladies, I plead headache or some other excuse, by means of which to escape being *bored to death*.[67]

The success of Virginia Shelton's "salon" and the failure of young Shelbyville ladies were both ultimately determined by a similar standard, based on male pleasure or male judgment. The urban aspirations of small-town businessmen depended on more than successful commercial development; the accomplishments of town women were the final gauge of urbanity. At midcentury, businessmen turned their attention to a new town industry, designed especially to assure that their daughters could fulfill their essential role in the refined townscape.

The Building: Colleges for Women

In the mid-1830s, the citizens of Columbia believed that their town was "about to be the Athens of the West." Town residents had already raised "upwards of ten thousand dollars" to enable the Presbyterian leaders of Jackson College to relocate their school for boys in Columbia. And now the town was launching a bold initiative in the region. As Matthew Cooper reported in 1835, "The people of Columbia are about building a female Academy, which will be conducted on a large scale," managed by none other than the Episcopal Bishop of Tennessee, James H. Otey.[68] Certainly, there were not enough Episcopalians in all of Maury County to support such an institution by themselves. After all, the Rev. Otey himself was forced to preach in Masonic halls, shuttling back and forth between Franklin and Columbia to minister to his small Episcopalian flock. Supporters of the female school in Columbia cast their appeal in broad terms, linking the fate of their experiment with the reputation and prosperity of the entire community.

Their campaign was a huge success. In January 1836, Duncan Brown Frierson described the scene in Columbia for his nephew William F. Cooper, then a student at Yale:

> Literature appears now to be all the Vogue, each person appears to overreach the other in Contributions for the creation of large edifices for the dissemination of learning among male and female. Proposals are now offered for the building [of] a Female Academy of immense size, and they are trying to procure a site on which they intend building a

much larger College for the males, so that in a year from this time *Columbia* will be the Yale of the south.[69]

For Frierson the boldness of this experiment in education was measured not by the innovation of its curriculum but by the scale of its proposed architecture. In the end, the word "academy" simply could not convey the scope of this grandiose vision, and so the Columbia Female Institute was born.

Designed by the northern architects Drummond and Lutterloh, the school was constructed over a period of three years, from 1836 to 1839. Local house carpenter Nathan Vaught, who did "quite a quantity of work on the Female Institute," remembered that "the main building was put up in 1836 but not completed" for several years.[70] Set on a hill at the edge of town, the Columbia Female Institute was one of the most impressive buildings ever constructed in the town. Its massive 120-foot brick facade—resembling a medieval castle complete with crenellated roofline, punctuated by turrets, and supported by Gothic arches—lent the town an aura of antiquity (Fig. 4.5).

But the Columbia Female Institute was actually the product of a completely modern, national revolution in female education at midcentury. Four seminaries established by northern women—Emma Willard at Troy, New York, in 1821; Catherine Beecher at Hartford, Connecticut, in 1828; Zilpah Grant at Ipswich, Massachusetts, in 1828; and Mary Lyon at South Hadley, Massachusetts, in 1837—set the standard for making a higher level of education available to antebellum women.[71] These institutions established a structured curriculum that emphasized the professional preparation of female students for teaching and motherhood and gained an influence far beyond their region. Although male trustees and principals led southern colleges, they employed young, unmarried women from the North as teachers. About 100 women who were trained at Troy alone taught in southern schools.[72] The female teachers at the Columbia Institute were all "employed at the North."[73] And Kate Carney's father, a trustee of Soule Female College in Murfreesboro, interviewed teachers for that school in New Jersey, New York, and Boston.[74]

Increasingly in the 1840s, female schools in the South were being chartered as "colleges."[75] The shift from female academies of the early republic to antebellum female colleges and institutes was more than a matter of semantics. During the early years of the century, Middle Tennessee town builders had opened small academies, where girls learned "all the useful and ornamental branches of an English Education"—from reading, writing, and

FIGURE 4.5. The Columbia Female Institute, built in the late 1830s, was destroyed by fire in 1959. (Courtesy of Mrs. Jill K. Garrett)

arithmetic to French and Italian languages, needlework, and painting.[76] But strangers to town would have been hard pressed to locate these institutions within a townscape of houses. Indeed, private citizens often operated academies in their own homes. The first session of the Shelbyville Female Academy, for example, commenced "in a large commodious room in a retired part of town" in the early 1830s. The school advised the parents of potential students that "young ladies from the county can be accomodated [*sic*] with boarding in respectable families on reasonable terms."[77] Nowhere was the contrast between academy and college clearer than in the stark architectural contrast between this humble schoolroom and the crenellated castle of the Columbia Female Institute.

What had begun in Columbia in the mid-1830s reached fullest expression during the architectural renovation of the 1850s.[78] The Methodists and the Presbyterians built two new female colleges. Like the Episcopalians, these denominations sought broad financial support through subscriptions, which were sold to residents regardless of religious affiliation. The Methodists proposed a school that would be contained in a single, large structure, with "two handsome fronts extending one hundred and four feet, by forty-two, three stories high."[79] But by far the most impressive architectural plan took shape when Franklin Gillette Smith, who served as principal of the Columbia Female Institute from 1838 to 1852, resigned to open his own school, the Columbia Athenaeum, right next door.

Even more ambitious than the massive, single building arrangement of the Female Institute or the Methodist college, the Athenaeum was designed as a multibuilding campus. The Smith family lived in the Rectory (Fig. 4.6), adorned with an exotic, Moorish portico. This building set the tone for a campus that would become an eclectic catalog of mid-nineteenth-century architectural revivalism. In early 1860, Nathan Vaught "built a very large addition" to the main building, called the auditorium or Athenaeum Hall. He later described the most prominent feature of the auditorium as "a very heavy portico at the north and south ends" rising the full two stories of this "very large building."[80] The Doric columns supporting this structure signaled Greek Revival influence. The auditorium was flanked by two octagonal brick rotundas, each connected by a series of two-story, rectangular brick buildings—the whole embellished with Italianate bracketing and colonnaded walks and crowned by fleurs de lis (Fig. 4.7). On the hill above Columbia the enlightened residents of this new "Athens of the West" displayed their knowledge of the great architectural traditions in history.

FIGURE 4.6. Originally built in the mid-1830s as the residence of Samuel Polk Walker, nephew of James K. Polk, this house became the rectory of the Athenaeum when Franklin Gillette Smith opened the school in 1852. (Photograph by Carroll Van West)

Though perhaps less architecturally exuberant than Columbia's Institute and Athenaeum, female colleges stood out in townscapes across Middle Tennessee. In Murfreesboro, a group of prominent businessmen, including Kate Carney's father, organized Soule Female College in 1853 (Fig. 4.8). A few blocks from the public square, on a campus of about four acres, they built a substantial three-story brick building with two recessed wings. The trustees assured their patrons that this structure had been "constructed expressly for a female boarding school." In particular, it was designed with attention "to the convenience and . . . health" of the students. Inside, the rooms were "large, airy, and well ventilated" and the halls were "spacious and well adapted to indoor exercise in bad weather." The campus too was designed especially to accommodate the young ladies, with grounds and a grove of trees that provided "ample room for pleasant and healthful recreation."[81]

Then the trustees of Soule Female College revealed the major distinction between their school and the old fashioned academy: "To protect our reputation and ensure the objects of our school, the trustees have found it necessary to pass an ordinance making it an absolute requirement, that all boarding pupils shall board in the College."[82] No longer were girls from the

FIGURE 4.7. The campus of the Athenaeum in Columbia, showing the auditorium and rotunda. The Athenaeum stood until 1915, when the buildings were razed to make way for a public high school. (Courtesy of Mrs. Jill K. Garrett)

country expected to board with respectable town families. This was one of the reasons that town residents built such large school buildings; they were essentially dormitories. But this decision was significant in the context of the larger townscape for two reasons: first, it indicated a new ambition to extend cultural influence far beyond small-town borders; and second, it produced highly specialized town regions of gender segregation.

In contrast to their smaller academic predecessors, which served a local clientele, female colleges targeted an audience far beyond the town and contiguous countryside; 32 percent of students at the Columbia Institute in 1850 came from states other than Tennessee. Unlike the teachers, who were primarily of northern origin, the students arrived from southern states, especially Alabama and Kentucky, but also Mississippi, Louisiana, and Virginia.[83] Small-town residents conceived of their female colleges as important vehicles for promoting the prosperity and good taste of their communities. The process began when the good reputation of school and town attracted students from far and wide. In turn, those students advertised the advantages of their college communities when they returned to their homes with the small-town lessons they had learned. One female college booster in Columbia was explicit about the potential for extending small-town influence: after all, so many students had gone on to become teachers "and dealt

FIGURE 4.8. Soule Female College, named for Methodist Bishop Joshua Soule of Nashville. After the Civil War, Kate Carney took charge of the academic department for a short time. The school closed in 1917, and the building was torn down and replaced by a public high school. (Courtesy of Mrs. Mabel Pittard)

out in other regions the treasures of culture which they had gathered in this place."[84]

Closer to home, female colleges had a direct impact on the organization of town space. By boarding out-of-state students together in dormitories, female colleges became highly specialized town regions defined by gender more explicitly than any other town space. But this was class-based segregation as well, for these colleges were designed for young "ladies" in particular. Gathered together in their boarding schools, students composed a separate female community, protected but not isolated from small-town society. Total seclusion of the students would have worked against the expansive goals of college benefactors, who linked the accomplishments of students with those of the town itself.

Indeed, spatial segregation made college campuses the appropriate sites for public female performance. In public exams and concerts held at the end of each school session, young ladies demonstrated the skills they had acquired at college for an appreciative local audience. In addition to formal examinations advertised in the local press, periodic social events hosted by the colleges also opened the schools to the local community. For example, the Athenaeum regularly gave "soirees," which were "devoted to Vocal and Instrumental Music, conversation, etc." On such evenings the study hall was "open for promenades," and "friends and patrons of the school" were encouraged to come and "meet the teacher and pupils."[85] These events demonstrated more than the skills of individual students; they reflected the level of refinement of the entire town. Soule College trustees even argued that Murfreesboro itself was one of their school's chief assets. Their list of local resources included "the healthfulness of the locality, the refinement of the surrounding citizenship, [and] the neatness and accessibility of the town, being immediately on the Nashville & Chattanooga R. R." These "external commendations and facilities," they declared, were "equal to those enjoyed by any school in the South."[86]

The trustees of Soule and other female colleges spent considerable sums on these schools at precisely the same moment they were investing large sums in railroads, commercial blocks, courthouses, and elaborate additions to their homes. Soule Female College, for example, cost Murfreesboro subscribers a total of about $25,000, while in Columbia, Methodists confidently sought $10,000 in subscriptions from "the people of Maury and the adjoining counties" to build the female seminary they sponsored.[87] This "preoccupation with buildings" demonstrated more than the trustees' intention to create permanent institutions; they fully expected a return on their investment.[88]

Phil P. Neely, spokesman for Columbia's Methodists, described the proposed female seminary as "an enterprize [*sic*]" that would ultimately benefit the "temporal interests" of the entire community. Significantly, Neely based his claims on a broad argument emphasizing the economic benefits of education—especially female education. He cited the fame Columbia had already earned "throughout the South" for being "attentive to the wants of your daughters." Having supported the Columbia Female Institute for many years, town residents were fully aware that "these schools will enhance the value of your town property—your lands—will open up a fine market in your county town and put in circulation, annually thousands of dollars in your midst, which but for them, would be confined to other sections."[89]

Female colleges occupied a prominent, highly visible place in the renovated townscape because their male designers defined them as integral to larger economic and cultural town goals. One Columbia paper went so far as to claim: "Were our schools permanently to suspend operations, Columbia would be a place of no very great importance in any point of view. Indeed, the rapid growth of the town would be greatly retarded, and business, now so lively, would materially fall below its present standard."[90] In Columbia alone, three female colleges were educating 700 scholars by 1860.[91] A local newspaper editor ranked these schools among the town's most important businesses. They had become a new kind of town industry, in which the production of ladies was a key element of generalized communal prosperity.[92]

But the same editor who enumerated Columbia's business advantages in 1860 also argued that the town's "greatest and main attraction" was that it offered "the best location for a home" to be found "anywhere in the broad limits of the South."[93] Female colleges occupied a strategic position at the center of this new division between commerce and domesticity in the renovated townscape of the 1850s. While they contributed substantially to the economic prosperity of the community, these institutions were ultimately designed to train young ladies in their proper domestic roles. Thus, commerce and domesticity converged in the female college, reconciling inherent tensions between town as market center and town as home.

Conclusion

Like so much of American culture in the mid-nineteenth century, the townscape became feminized as cultural forces reshaped domestic life and commerce.[94] The changes were not intended as aspects of a liberalizing process. Men still controlled small-town politics and economy, and the status of certain women was enhanced at the expense of others. The actual experience of town women depended on their race, class, and place in the life cycle.

Genteel women in particular served a symbolic role in constructing the refined townscape. The fact that town residents increasingly measured their progress by the accomplishments of town ladies was an economic as well as an aesthetic strategy. Town businessmen revealed these connections most explicitly when they explained the importance of investing in female colleges as a method for stimulating small-town business. As we have seen, antebellum residents linked the material appearance of the town with economic success and communal prosperity. The goal of businessmen was to attract productive new residents. As homemakers, women were central to this goal, because local boosters believed that towns must be seen not only as a good place to do business but also as a nice place to live.

Beyond their symbolic importance, women also had a direct and personal impact on the social construction of town space. They set new standards of housekeeping that redefined the relationship between town and country households. They maintained a subsistence network, selling surplus produce in the local market and sharing resources among town households. Above all, in their gardens and through the visiting ritual, women made a direct impact on appearance of townscape. Every day they were out and about on town streets—young girls "exercising," slave girls running errands, ladies visiting and shopping. Women were conspicuous components of street traffic. Their influence on small-town space and society was therefore both symbolic and active.

CHAPTER FIVE

Store Clerks and Serenaders

A Small-Town Story: A Store Clerk's Tale

When Edmund Cooper was fourteen years old, he left his father's household and took up residence in his uncle's store near the public square in Columbia. For the next two years, Edmund lived the life of a semi-independent clerk.[1] By day, he reclined in the counting room or pulled dress goods off the highest shelves for his customers. By night, he roamed town streets with other adolescent boys, who organized themselves into debating clubs and military companies patterned after the adult male associations of their fathers. Between 1835 and 1837, Edmund described his employments and amusements in a series of letters to his brother William, a student at Yale. Edmund composed for his brother a vivid tale of the store clerk's life. The details of his experience—patterns of residence, rhythms of employment and amusement, memberships in youthful male organizations—reveal that young men represented a highly visible group of town residents who experienced town space in distinctive ways.

Edmund was not forced by economic necessity to become a store clerk. On the contrary, it was a natural consequence of family prestige and his father's business interests.[2] Edmund was a son of Matthew Delamere Cooper and his first wife, Mary Agnes Frierson Cooper, whose family included some of the most prosperous businessmen in Columbia and Maury County. By 1827, Matthew Delamere Cooper's success in the dry goods business had provided the nucleus of a small fortune, which he invested in an ambitious scheme to expand his mercantile interests. Maintaining his household and business partnerships in Columbia, Cooper opened a commission warehouse in New Orleans. Until his warehouses were burned during the Civil War, he formed a series of partnerships to sustain a profitable commission business in that busy southern port.

Cooper used his business connections in Columbia to provide a training ground for his sons, who typically worked as store clerks before entering college. From New Orleans, Matthew instructed his eldest son, William, who was managing the household in Columbia, "if possible get my son Henry in a store untill [sic] I return—if you cannot, he had better go to school somewhere."[3] Except for William, who attended Yale, all of Matthew Cooper's sons attended local colleges and served professional apprenticeships with local lawyers, doctors, and businessmen.

The family was large and complicated. Matthew Delamere Cooper had fourteen children in the course of three marriages—a situation that did not always engender family harmony. When he left Mayes and Frierson's store to attend Pleasant Grove Academy, about ten miles south of Columbia, Edmund explained to William that the move was due to "a split in the family." The architect of family division was their new mother. Edmund believed that "father's present wife wanted us all to be sent away" and bitterly bemoaned her success. "She has at length accomplished her wish. We have all been disbanded and sent off for the malice of one woman."[4] Edmund survived this sometimes turbulent childhood to become a successful lawyer in Shelbyville and private secretary to Andrew Johnson.

Adult prosperity and notoriety seemed far, far away, however, to the impatient, adolescent store clerk of 1835. Edmund chafed at his daily obligations at Mayes and Frierson's store. While his brother William studied languages and philosophies at Yale, Edmund "wailed [his] fate of having to live in a store." After spending nearly two years as a clerk, "without a single month being spent in play," he sarcastically told William that "the longer I stay in it the better I am pleased." Eliminating punctuation to compose a narrative of incomplete sentences, Edmund departed from his characteristic literary style to describe for his brother the store clerk's daily routine, as if one monotonous chore flowed seamlessly into another:

I have become used to Getting up at the sun opening the
windows   Going into the counting room sitting down for a
while   Jump up take a pan of water and a brush and sprinkle
the floor   Take the broom and sweep out   Carry it into the
other room   Fling it up in the corner   Set down cross my legs
and think of nothing till the bell rings   Wake up my Contemporary
(Mr. Green)   Wash my face comb my hair and dress Put on my
hat and go to breakfast   Eat my breakfast come down again   Go
into the store take the brush brush off the counter.   Go into the
Counting room kick up my heels & set down while my chum is
gone to the bluff   Presently I hear something Go in and a ladie [*sic*]
says   *Good morning Mr. Cooper have you any pretty calicos,   Oh
Yes Mam!! some very pretty,*   Pulled down all in the store   *None
suit me sir have you any work collars Yes mam*   *Let me look
at them*   Show them to her   She rumbles them about and
throws them all over the counter   *None of them suit have
you any silks of such a colour*   *No mam not any*   (Got plenty
all the time but she don't want to buy)   *Nothing else you will
look at Mam*   *No sir nothin* [sic] *else.   Good morning
sir   Good morning Mam*   Then comes the tug of war putting
up the goods she has pulled down   Hardly had we got the goods
up before in pops some more and perhaps after pulling down the
whole store we may sell them a dollars worth and then they will want
you to fling in a spool of Thread   And if it is a dress they will
want you to fling in a belt so that you have to fling in nearly as much
as the profits you make.   So much for storekeeping and all its
attendant qualities.[5]

Rising with the sun, Edmund was expected to achieve a certain appearance to serve the public—a washed face, combed hair, and a well-swept
floor. His customers, chiefly women, were not free to sift through the merchandise at will. Instead, Edmund climbed the store walls to retrieve goods
from the highest shelves. His decisions to reveal or conceal items, and his
routine negotiations with customers who sought the best bargains for their
money, meant that Edmund had considerable responsibility for the financial
well-being of his uncle's business. Clearly, Edmund internalized much of
this responsibility, identifying more with the profit motive of the merchant-

owner than with the consumer's interest in making a favorable bargain. Murfreesboro merchant John Spence noted that at the same time young clerks were "learning to sell goods," they were "also learning the system of book keeping by double entry, and the transaction of business generally."[6]

Mayes and Frierson's store in 1835 was probably much like the early dry goods stores John Spence described. Built before the dramatic emergence of the commercial block in the 1850s, Spence remembered the stores of the 1830s as small, twenty-foot-square rooms piled high with all manner of merchandise, stacked floor to ceiling. "Dry goods one side, queens and hard ware, groceries, medicines and school books, tin ware and saddlery hung up over head."[7] The store was often so full there was "scarcely room to move round to wait on customers." In the cellar, merchants kept salt and bars of iron that could be broken according to the particular needs of the customer. "This was easy [sic] broken by throwing a heavy weight on it. . . . This work done, clerk wash his hands, enters in the dry goods, shewing muslins, laces and similar articles." In addition to the store room and cellar, dry goods establishments typically had counting rooms, equipped with a locked desk where money and store records were deposited. Nevertheless, male customers were regularly invited into the counting room to warm themselves by the stove or fireplace and to revive themselves from the inevitable bottle of whiskey while their wives examined the merchandise in the store room. Indeed, the difference between store and tavern was frequently inconsequential when it came to the availability of liquor. As John Spence recalled, "Often when men were going home about dark, they were allowed to go in the counting room, take a dram before leaving, and nothing thought of it." Stores stayed open until nightfall, after which young store clerks were at liberty to spend their evenings as they saw fit, eventually retiring to beds in counting rooms or in rooms over the stores where they worked.[8]

Young clerks like Edmund Cooper learned more than bookkeeping, salesmanship, or drinking habits in small-town stores. The sons of wealthy town businessmen and planters also practiced their fathers' disdain for "storekeeping and all its attendant qualities." Although his mercantile career earned him a handsome living and considerable prestige in Columbia, Matthew Delamere Cooper complained, "I would rather live on bread and water than in the way I am doing." Cooper was appalled that his clients looked upon him as a "salesman."[9] As part owner of Mayes & Frierson's dry goods store, Edmund's uncle, Duncan Brown Frierson, explained his objections to the salesman's life in more descriptive terms. His complaints had as much to do with the nature of his clientele as with the business of storekeeping. Frierson begged his educated nephew William to overlook his grammatical inadequacies, for the life of the merchant left no time for study. Indeed, he wrote, he spent "every day of his life measuring calicoes and Lasses weighing nails and coperas, and talking to old women as old as Methusilah [*sic*], and as ugly as a Jackass, or quarelling with some fellow about his account, who couldn't take two from five and tell how many remained, or trying to fit some Gall from the nobs in a pair of shoes, the sight of whose foot would make a Bull bellow, or some other menial office of which a picture is a shadow to the reality."[10] By 1836, Frierson had abandoned storekeeping, at least temporarily, to pursue the more heroic life of the soldier in the Creek War in Florida, leaving Edmund to operate the store.[11]

Confined to the storeroom, Edmund's movements seem highly constrained when compared to Kate Carney's exuberant afternoon explorations of the public square. While Kate and her girlfriends dashed from one store to another, Edmund sat bored and mournful in the counting room or impatiently but politely waited on customers who had no intention of spending their money. However, even though he was obligated to tend the store during the day, Edmund spent much of his time there without adult supervision.[12] Furthermore, despite his protests to the contrary, Edmund's letters reveal that the life of the store clerk left ample time for play—particularly during the evenings.

Edmund spent much of his free time establishing masculine associations that mirrored the social and professional world of his father, an active Mason and devoted Whig. With nine other Columbia youths, Edmund formed the "Columbia Junto," a debating club that met every Wednesday night at Jackson College.[13] The boys gathered, unsupervised by adult guidance, to debate such weighty questions as, "Which has done the most harm, Ambition or Drunkenness?" After careful consideration, they concluded that ambition was the greater evil.[14]

In addition to his debating skills, Edmund honed his drilling techniques as a member of the White Oak Sprouts, a political-military company "consisting of about thirty-five boys." They were outnumbered by the White Guards with its sixty members, "young men of our town friendly to the cause of Judge White." Hugh Lawson White, an anti-Jackson Democrat, carried Tennessee in the 1836 presidential election by drawing a record number of voters to the polls. Edmund really seemed less excited by politics, however, than by the impressive uniforms that identified members of each military company. The White Guards wore "blue coat, white pantaloons, and white straps, plain fur hats with white feathers." But it was the uniform of the White Oak Sprouts that captured Edmund's boyish imagination—"a red round-about with three rows of Bell Buttons, White Pantaloons, and White straps," which every member wore "except the officers, who all have red coats with silver lace and Bell Buttons lower upon them and instead of haveing [*sic*] feathers, we have cockades which dangle from our [hats?], show off in great stile [*sic*]."[15] Such elaborate uniforms readily distinguished young men of privilege as they marched in public parades with leaders of the community, impressively costumed in the regalia of Masons and Odd Fellows.

Edmund's tale highlights some of the distinctive rhythms and spatial experiences that made young men a conspicuous group in the townscape. Young men often boarded away from home when they became store clerks, apprentices, and students, acquiring a semi-independent lifestyle that was unavailable to their sisters, confined to their parents' households or to the segregated world of the female college. Kate Carney and other young ladies spent their afternoons freely walking and visiting, but retreated to the safety of the parlor at night. By contrast, the pent-up energies of store clerks were unleashed after dark as raucous youths roamed town streets together. Their propensity to act collectively in organized, homosocial groups was an im-portant part of their training to assume adult male roles in a world of party politics and vital economic partnerships; nevertheless, their equal potential for disorder made organized youths problematic town residents. Architec-tural choices in the renovated townscape incorporated spatial strategies to harness the energies and refine the behavior of organized town youths. Ultimately, however, town residents sought to keep rowdy young men at a safe distance from the increasingly private domestic spaces they created.

The Demographic Context: The Rhythms of Semidependence

In 1850, the men and women who inhabited Middle Tennessee's county seats were, like the broad population of nineteenth-century America, re-markably young. Three-fourths of all town residents—slave and free—were younger than thirty.[16] Half of all town residents were men, and about a third of all male residents were between the ages of ten and twenty-one.[17] These ages marked the boundaries of "semidependence," a unique stage in the life cycle common to young white men of different classes.[18] The pattern was established during the early years of town development, when boys usually entered the workforce before puberty. At fourteen, for example, Edmund Cooper began work as a store clerk. At ten, the orphaned Nathan Vaught became a carpenter's apprentice. Younger yet, the child Elias came to work as a water boy for James K. Polk and his new bride Sarah Childress when he was "just large enough to stride a barrel."[19] As a slave, Elias had little choice in the jobs he could learn. The experiences of Vaught and Cooper show, by contrast, that free white boys spent the next ten or so years in seasonal patterns of home leaving and homecoming, work and education, until they mastered a craft or profession and achieved autonomy.

Like Elias, more than one-third of male residents were never allowed to achieve autonomy.[20] As slaves, these men were subject to a kind of perpetual semidependence, never to be recognized as independent heads of their own households. Male slaves tended to be slightly younger than their free counterparts; however, there is no indication that town slaveholders made any systematic attempts to limit male slaves to the very young and the old. One-third of male slaves were between the ages of ten and twenty-one.[21]

Racial distinctions in the small town were absolute and inflexible. Slave men swept out stores and started fires to heat them but never worked as clerks. Edmund Cooper outlined this essential difference between white and black with stark efficiency when he recited the whereabouts of three members of his uncle's "family"—two cousins and a slave. "As for Bill," wrote Edmund, "he stays at Mayes & Frierson. As for Bob he stays at J. G. Keebles & Co. . . . As for Cy he is sold for eleven hundred dollars cash. So much for Uncle Jonathan's family."[22] The few free black men who lived and worked in the county seat were confined to very particular trades—especially barbering and shoemaking—or were unskilled laborers. Slaves, on the other hand, clearly worked as skilled craftsmen. But African American men were denied the opportunities for organization that formed the core of white male authority. Their residential and occupational choices were based upon the particular rhythms of town slavery rather than on the forces that shaped the lives of young white men.[23]

While race was an insurmountable barrier against advancement for young African American town dwellers, among white boys distinctions of wealth and social standing had considerable bearing on the experience of semidependence. "In the town of Columbia," a friend informed William Cooper, "there is [sic] two classes of what is called Beaus. Those who belong to the first class are those that own stores together with a few of the counter hoppers. Those that compose the second class are the remaining store keep-ers and the college students of which there is [*sic*] a good many."[24] The elite "counter hoppers" who belonged in the first class of beaus were probably the sons of store owners, whose prospects for future success were predict-able, if not assured. Cooper's correspondent did not even bother to classify the many young apprentices learning a trade in Columbia. But the early career of carpenter's apprentice Nathan Vaught shows that, unlike race, class was not necessarily a barrier to social and economic advancement.

Nathan Vaught lived almost his entire life in Columbia. In contrast to Edmund Cooper's prestigious family connections, Vaught was orphaned when he was about seven years old and then abandoned with his brother three years later by the man who had adopted them. In 1810, when he was ten years old, the county court in Columbia bound Vaught to James Purcell, "as an apprentice to learn the cabinet trade," until he turned twenty-one.[25] At the time, the town was not much more than a clearing, and Purcell quickly forsook furniture-making in favor of the building business, deciding that houses were in greater demand than furnishings. Accident and neces-sity consequently made Nathan Vaught a carpenter.

In 1812, when Vaught was about thirteen years old, he did his "first carpenter's work . . . on a one story log house on the southwest corner of the Public Square."[26] The job involved stripping the roof, raising the walls a second story, replacing the shingles, and refitting the interior for a dry goods store. Vaught noted that for much of his apprenticeship he worked with what he called a "gang," apparently composed of slave and free hands.[27] The gang moved in and out of town, camping for months at a time on construction projects several miles into the country.

This nomadic lifestyle prevented him from attending school, and Vaught reached the age of twenty-one "without an education." Barely literate, he "could spell in 2 or 3 syllables [but] knew nothing of figures nor the pen." In 1820, Nathan Vaught received his only formal education in a country school twelve miles from Columbia. Even then, he worked to pay his way, building "a two story cedar log house all complete" and "covering in several other houses." After ten or twelve months, Vaught returned to Columbia armed with "some knowledge of figures and the use of the pen to a very limited extent." He declined the partnership Mr. Purcell offered him and "went to work as a journeyman at $1 a day."[28]

When Purcell died less than a year later, Vaught bought his tools at the estate sale and went into business for himself in 1822. During the next few years, as he established a reputation as a carpenter, Vaught also joined the fraternal organizations typical of white male experience. His military company, the Columbia Blues, was on hand to receive General Lafayette when he visited Nashville in 1825. That same year, shortly before his marriage to Lucretia Jackson Journey, Vaught was "raised to the sublime degree of a Master Mason in Columbia Lodge No. 31," whose membership included the most elite and powerful men in the state.

Nathan Vaught's experience demonstrates the same broad characteristics of youthful semidependence as Edmund Cooper's. Both boys were expected to work at an early age. They lived as boarders, outside the structure of the single-family household, and they joined fraternal associations. There were, however, notable differences in their experience based on their relative status. Despite Edmund's complaints, clerking was preferable to manual labor, and while military companies were open to boys of different classes, it is doubtful that the orphaned apprentice ever owned a uniform comparable to the store clerk's. Most significant of all was Edmund's membership in debating clubs. Compared to Vaught's paltry schooling, Cooper's access to oratorical skills defined him as a well-educated heir to power and prestige.

Town residents revealed the close association between oratory and the elite in 1841, when "a considerable number of the Mechanic's of Columbia" formed a benevolent society that met "semi-monthly and at night." At each meeting of the Mechanic's Union Society of Columbia, "some suitable and interesting question is discussed, which adds much to the improvement of the members." In contrast to Edmund Cooper's evenings with the Columbia Junto, where young men divided into teams to debate various sides of an issue, there seems to have been little actual "discussion" during meetings of the Mechanic's Union Society. The arguments presented to the group were more like lectures than debates; ladies were encouraged to attend as well. A. O. P. Nicholson delivered the first speech on the question, "whether Mechanics, as a class, occupy that station in society to which they are entitled." Nicholson presented the only argument of the evening, taking the position that the mechanic's status did not fully reflect his contribution to society. According to Nicholson, a mechanic was anyone "employed in severing, compounding or fashioning the products of nature so as to fit them for the satisfaction of our various wants."[29] House carpenter Nathan Vaught was considered a mechanic in this system. In addition to mechanical industry, Nicholson identified two other types of labor—agricultural and commercial or mercantile industry. He grouped mechanics and moderate farmers together as one socioeconomic class in contrast to upper-class merchants, planters, lawyers, and doctors. Despite Nicholson's insistence that mechanics should occupy a place in society commensurate with their considerable contributions, no mechanic was ever advertised as a speaker before the Mechanic's Union Society. Instead, "men of known erudition and ability," local business and professional leaders, were selected to deliver a series of lectures to the group. Oratory and debate were skills of elite men, and the education and fraternal associations of town youths reflected a similar division.[30]

Regardless of class distinctions, young men of working age often lived outside their parents' households. The experience of rooming and boarding was quite different from living in a single-family household, headed by a patriarch who presided over several male and female dependents. Young male boarders spent considerable time in the company of adult male role models and their youthful counterparts. When Edmund Cooper became a clerk, he lived in the store with another clerk, Mr. Green, whom Cooper described as his "contemporary."[31] By the time he was twenty-one, Cooper had graduated from store clerk to lawyer. When he moved from Columbia to Shelbyville to establish a partnership with his uncle, Edmund settled into the small-town bachelor's life. He told his brother, "I have me a room delightfully furnished, near my office—with a large armed rocking chair to loll in of an evening—and the promise of the old sofa, when Uncle Ervin gets him a new one."[32]

By midcentury, the system of training for semidependent boys was changing in the renovated townscape, as young men who formerly would have been clerks became college students, and the apprenticeship system disintegrated. Boys, nevertheless, continued to live as boarders in households often starkly at odds with the single-family domestic ideal. In 1849, when Phillip Nelson walked all the way from Georgia with nothing but the clothes on his back to attend the newly opened Union University in Murfreesboro, he took up residence "with a clevor [sic] man and ten other vary [sic] fine student[s]."[33] Even when young male boarders did find lodgings in single-family households, their hosts often separated them from private family life.

Virginia and William Shelton offered distinctly different arrangements to accommodate male and female boarders in their six-room "cottage." Virginia used at least three rooms—a dining room, a parlor, and what she called the "front-room"—as semipublic spaces where invited guests could be entertained.[34] The Sheltons added a library in 1851, during their first year of occupancy.[35] In 1852, Virginia found herself with "three unoccupied chambers" and decided to put the rooms to more profitable use. The Sheltons

FIGURE 5.1. Small buildings like this one, Dr. McPhail's office in Franklin, and the Polk law office in Columbia (Fig. 5.2) often housed youthful clerks and students. (Photograph by Carroll Van West)

acquired two female boarders—"a scholar, Miss Sayle from the Western District, a very smart and amiable girl," and "the assistant teacher Miss Goodrich, from New York," who seemed "to be a real Northern lady. . . . highly cultivated and deeply pious." Significantly, the two young women were invited into the Shelton home, where they were "very careful to use scrapers and mats before entering" so as not to soil the carpets. Even then, Virginia noted that the two stayed "mostly (when at home) in their own room, which I greatly prefer, as it intrudes less on the sacredness of my own chamber."[36] A year later, their female boarders had been replaced. "We have four young men boarding with us," Virginia told her aunt and uncle. Even though she insisted the students were "really a pleasure in place of a trouble," Virginia and her husband went to much greater lengths to protect their privacy than they had with their female boarders. The Sheltons took on an added expense rather than try to shelter all four scholars under their roof. "Two of them occupy the little office across the street, which Mr. Shelton rented for the purpose," she explained (Figs. 5.1 and 5.2).[37] The two other

FIGURE 5.2. Polk law office in Columbia. Located on the corner of West Main and Garden Streets, the building was razed in the 1880s. (Courtesy of Mrs. Jill K. Garrett)

young men, who lived under the same roof with the Sheltons, occupied the library rather than a private family bed chamber. Virginia insisted that her boarders were "talented, promising, amiable young men," but she did not reveal their names or assess their individual characters as she had with her female boarders.

Young, independent male boarders remained on the fringes of an increasingly privatized domesticity in the renovated townscape. It may be that this actually made boys more attractive as boarders. People like Virginia Shelton, who coveted the "sacredness of their own chambers," could maintain privacy by putting young men in marginal spaces, whereas young women would have to be accommodated closer to protected spaces within the family circle. These residential practices also produced some unintended consequences. Young men who boarded together in pairs or small groups scattered throughout town developed a masculine subculture that was sometimes difficult to control.

Patterns of work, residence, and fraternal organization made free white youths a distinctive, conspicuous group among town residents. In contrast to the townscape of ladies, however, the townscape of apprentices and store clerks was problematic for the reputation of the community. Semidependent boys, not bound by domestic constraints, tended toward disorder. At the very least, young men were prone to disturb the peace. One busy day in Franklin when there was "quite a crowd" in town, John McEwen described "a mele among the boys" that erupted "on the winding up of the day." The fight pitted "the town boys against the country boys." And McEwen seemed pleased that "the town boys got the advantage of the country boys greatly in the fight." More importantly, the fight did not deter trade. "Business was good enough," he concluded.[38] Herein lay the essential community response to managing their youthful, rowdy male neighbors. Periodic disturbances of the peace were not considered a dangerous threat to the social order. However, the semidependent lifestyle of young men was linked to larger economic rhythms of town life. Although occasional boyish misbehavior might be overlooked in a prosperous community, in times of distress it appeared symptomatic of deeper moral and economic failure. The townscape of young men was particularly troublesome in the speculative, unstable economy of the nineteenth century.

Space and Society

Partnerships and Circuits: The Economy of Mobility

While women managed the steady, predictable rhythms of a domestic economy, young men were subject to the volatile rhythms of business in a boom-and-bust economy. Whether one worked as a carpenter, a merchant, or a lawyer, the pace of small-town business was alternately frenetic and lethargic. In this respect, Middle Tennessee's county seats were not unlike antebellum Philadelphia, where, according to labor historian Bruce Laurie, workers experienced "alternating periods of feverish activity broken by slack spells."[39] Aside from periodic financial panics, which were beyond local control, town residents organized weekly, monthly, and yearly business cycles that increased activity on particular days. On Saturdays, town streets filled with shoppers and visitors during the day and drunken revelers at night. The first Monday of every month brought hundreds of country people to town to conduct business at the county court (Fig. 5.3). And on New Year's Day, town and country folk alike settled their accounts, while

FIGURE 5.3. First Monday on the square in Columbia, shown at the end of the nineteenth century. The three-story courthouse on the left was built during the 1840s but had already become the target of much complaint by the 1850s. It was torn down in 1904. (Courtesy of Mrs. Jill K. Garrett)

renters tried their best to negotiate favorable terms for new lodgings.[40] On a daily basis, these cycles made the small-town economy appear dull and stagnant more often than it seemed bustling and vigorous. There were more hours for Edmund Cooper to prop his feet on the counter than there were to negotiate with willing customers. But the appearance of idleness was not always a reliable indication of the health of a town's economy.

Mobility and cooperation were the keys to success or survival in a small-town business. Spatially centralized and highly visible, the public square was the focal point for the business community. But the businessmen themselves rarely confined their activities to its boundaries. The range of movement among town businessmen was an impressive demonstration of their power and authority. It was also an effect of limited economic opportunities in a small town. Entrepreneurs searched out prosperity, extending business connections from one town to the next. The public square itself was a territory of partnerships—testimony to the sharing of risks. Mayes & Frierson; Neilson & Crichelow, Jordan & Elliot, McFadden & McKnight, Crockett &

Co.—sign after sign around the Square proclaimed the cooperation it took to operate a successful small-town store. And newspaper announcements of partnership dissolutions continually reminded town residents that partnerships were fragile and success elusive.

Nathan Vaught learned the hard way that the irregular employment of the house carpenter could be more dependable than the vicissitudes of storekeeping. His career demonstrates that, like merchants, small-town craftsmen depended on clients who lived several miles into the countryside. In 1813, although the first lots in Columbia had only recently been sold, and house builders should presumably have been in demand, Vaught's employer sent him thirty miles into the woods west of town to help build a log cabin for a client who planned to open a "dry goods store to secure the Indian Trade." About three years later, Vaught recalled, his work gang was sent down the [Duck] river "in a canoe with our tools 7 miles northwest from [Columbia,] to build a frame dwelling house."[41] Although Vaught eventually established his own workshop in Columbia, equipped with a steam-powered saw, throughout his career he split his time between building projects in the country and in town.[42]

During the late 1820s, Vaught became particularly disenchanted with his prospects in Columbia. He recalled that he could get only "some small jobs and repairs," such as a front door and stairs for the Nelson hotel and "a long and heavy pair of stairs . . . on the Masonic Hall." Discouraged about the building business, Vaught launched a new career—a move he would soon regret. In 1830, he wrote, "I turned fool as many young men do just starting out in life and thought selling dry goods would be much easier and lighter work than putting shingles on [a] roof in the hot sun. I continued the goods business a year and a half. This brings us to the middle of the year 1831. I sunk a thousan[d] dollars or more. I then laid by the yard stick and took up the jackplane. I done nothing more in 1831 but wind up the goods business."[43] The building business dried up again during the early 1840s. But this time an older and wiser Vaught "kep[t] hammering away" and "got a little to do now and then."[44]

Matthew Delamere Cooper, on the other hand, knew how to make storekeeping pay. He had already been managing his commission house in New Orleans for six years, moving back and forth from Columbia to New Orleans, when his brother sought advice about how to open a store. In general, Matthew told him, "The whole success of a business depends on a proper commencement—do not be hasty." Beyond patience, he counseled, there were two keys to building a profitable business. First, find a good partner:

> All mercantile establishments have a much better chance for success when managed by two or more partners. . . . An establishment when conducted by one person, runs many chances of being neglected by sickness, necessary absence or death. I am therefore decidedly in favour of having partners; but one ought well to know the moral qualities of those, with whom they are about to associate themselves.[45]

Aside from their practical benefit to the daily operation of a store, partnerships also expanded the available capital for sustaining the business. Nevertheless, it was a rare partnership that could accumulate enough cash to finance a storekeeping enterprise outright. Which brought Cooper to the second key to mercantile success: good credit. "In carrying on business cash is necessary but credit is better," he told his brother. "If you associate yourself with anyone he ought to have some means—and you ought at once to establish a credit in Phild. or New York."[46] Good credit was essential because merchants bought their stock once a year, traveling personally to Philadelphia and New York to select the merchandise. In a cash-poor economy, establishing good credit was the only way to afford such large purchases, and working in partnerships was the only way to accumulate the capital to invest in a store. Even so, the routine involved great risk because merchants themselves extended credit to their own customers, who were supposed to settle accounts at the end of every year.

The yearly mercantile circuit from county seat to Philadelphia had been established during the earliest days of town settlement. Trading success predated industrialization and even road building in Middle Tennessee. The first turnpike to link Murfreesboro and Shelbyville with Nashville was not completed until 1838, when the commissioners of the Nashville, Murfreesboro, and Shelbyville Turnpike Company announced that "the whole road from Nashville to Shelbyville, a distance of 55 miles, is now and has been travelled for some time, without obstruction."[47] Yet trading networks had long extended as far away as Philadelphia and raised the standard of living beyond self-sufficiency during the initial stages of town development.[48] As Caroline Nicholson recalled, "All goods were hauled in wagons from Philadelphia, the time for a trip to and from that market occupying, as a rule, six weeks. When a Mr. McDowell claimed to have made the journey in four weeks, we were incredulous and said we did not believe he had seen Philadelphia."[49] Trading paths were well worn long before turnpikes eased the way. The railroad certainly shortened the trip, but it did not fundamentally alter the mercantile circuit.

Professional men followed a similar pattern of mobility and cooperation. Doctors formed and dissolved partnerships almost as often as merchants, but it was lawyers who institutionalized the circuit as an economic routine. Lawyers customarily traveled from one county seat to another, attending courts and seeking clients. Their routes were established by law when the legislature organized groups of counties into a circuit court system. The state assembly periodically redrew the lines of the circuit as it created new counties during the early nineteenth century. Thus the legal landscape of Middle Tennessee consisted of a network of county-seat towns served by an itinerant force of lawyers.

Despite the expansive possibilities of the circuit, there always seemed to be more lawyers than paying cases. John Spence, for example, described the predicament of a young lawyer in Murfreesboro who was "too poor to keep a horse. It was necessary he should attend the courts. When the time come, he shouldered his saddle bags, a law book or two in them, starting off Sunday evening on foot, either to Lebanon or Shelbyville, to be in time the next day at court."[50] In Columbia, A. O. P. Nicholson fortunately owned a horse, but he too found the income of a young lawyer paltry, not even sufficient to support his new wife and household. Financial necessity often made for strange bedfellows. To establish his legal practice on a sound footing, Nicholson combined occupations, forming a partnership with Judge Samuel Davis Frierson "in both the law and [a] printing office." "This was singular," Caroline Nicholson remembered, "inasmuch as they belonged to opposite political parties." Her husband gave up the printing office as soon as he could make enough money practicing law.[51]

The young, single, aspiring lawyer Edmund Cooper moved to Shelbyville, where he assured his brother he had "settled for *life*. . . . I have formed an eligible partnership with Uncle Ervin, which will save me from ever starving, make enough at least to live on."[52] But Edmund soon found that the picture of the starving lawyer was too close for comfort. August of 1842 saw only 100 cases on the court docket. Moreover, Edmund noted, "they are mostly small appeal cases—the fee not being more than from five to ten dollars." In the grip of financial depression, there was "nothing doing in any line of business—Neither the merchant or the grocery keeper—or the Law-yer—doing anything—we meet together on the Corner of an evening—and the conversation is hard times."[53]

During such "hard times" the periodic idleness of young men was viewed as symptomatic of deeper economic and moral weaknesses, which some observers worried might be intrinsic to town life. When they visited Frank-lin in 1841, the Nashville-based editors of the *Agriculturist* found a town "on the retrograde." In a few years the local economy would be reinvigorated by the railroad, but in 1841 Franklin's derelict appearance—its "vacated and dilapidated houses" and its churches "abandoned as the haunts of owls and ghosts"—was surpassed only by its apparent moral degradation. Idle young men presented visitors with the clearest evidence of town vice. "The indo-lent and speculative congregate in the towns," the *Agriculturist* warned, "and their influence is such as to corrupt the youth." Instead of occupying their children at school or at work, the editors argued, "at Franklin a great part of the population seem to have no particular and fixed employment, and hence you will see them by dozens setting about '*doggeries,*' and en-gaged in all foolish conversation." This ready access to "the means of acquiring vicious habits" made it "almost impossible to train up children in the 'way they should go,' in the towns."

The situation threatened not only the soul of the community but its economic well-being as well. "To come short to the truth," they concluded, "there is such a dislike to eat bread by the 'sweat of the face,' and such a disposition to live by speculation and cheating, that the whole community has drunk of the poison, particularly in towns, and the entire system of education and manners must be thoroughly changed, before better times can be anticipated."[54]

The editors of the *Agriculturist* were witnesses not only to the local effects of a nationwide depression but also to the national disintegration of the apprenticeship system. In Middle Tennessee, purposeful patterns of sea-sonal work were gradually being displaced by disorderly rhythms of unem-ployment among the society's youth, as products of local craftsmen were su-perseded by imported, factory-made goods.[55] As if heeding the warning of the *Agriculturist*, Middle Tennesseans did reform the system of education and manners in the renovated townscape. But their architectural choices reflected enduring tensions over the management of organized male youths, whose potential for order and disorder, peace keeping and peace disturbing, self-restraint and violence made them problematic town residents.

The organized activities of town youths were transformed in the renovated townscape. In many ways the changes were subtle. Young men continued to work, room, and board away from home; to form military companies and debating clubs; and to enjoy virtually free run of nighttime streets. Nevertheless, architectural renovation created a new setting for youthful activity that had perceptible consequences. "Doggeries" and taverns were replaced by gentlemanly "saloons" and "family groceries," which reflected new attitudes about alcohol consumption. Nighttime revelry on the streets was further restrained by the domestication of the townscape, as deep, colonnaded porches, landscaped front yards, and improved sidewalks created new buffer zones between home and thoroughfare.

Two activities of young men reveal the interaction between townscape renovation and experience. Serenading was a long-standing community tradition that changed dramatically during the middle decades of the century. The serenade was a ritual of the nighttime streets identified almost exclusively as an activity of young men. In the renovated townscape, the serenade was transformed from a rowdy disturbance of evening peace by apprentice boys to a polite form of visitation by college boys, who performed in newly landscaped yards and tastefully decorated parlors. In addition to refining the serenade, young men enthusiastically joined a new organization, the Sons of Temperance, which emerged as a town phenomenon during the mid-1840s.[56] As cadet members, they paraded alongside adult Sons of Temperance to demonstrate allegiance to the cold water principle. Serenaders and Sons of Temperance appropriated the streets for fraternal rituals that asserted their expansive access to town space and marked town youth as heirs to public authority. Despite the increasing restraint and refinement of serenaders and Sons of Temperance, however, the townscape of young men continued to be potentially troublesome.

The serenade, which originated in the courting rituals of a distant European past, was a vibrant custom in the antebellum county seat. But the romantic figure of a lone paramour standing beneath the window of his lady love, entreating her affections in song, would likely have created quite a stir among Middle Tennessee's town residents. The serenaders they knew traveled in groups, performing outdoors and under cover of darkness. In practice, the serenade was an expansive activity, often involving an involuntary audience of whole neighborhoods or the entire town—anyone within earshot. Nevertheless, town residents usually assumed that women were the ostensible targets of a serenade. Thus it is not surprising that female theatergoers in Shelbyville took particular offense one night in 1835, when the "Show House" became the target of a group of unruly serenaders. A few days after the event, a letter writer calling herself "Amanda" expressed outrage on behalf of "the Female part of the village" to the editor of the *Western Freeman*. Amanda used "the spacious appellation of '*a serenade*'" to describe the "unaccountable and unearthly" sounds that suddenly assailed the unsuspecting audience from the streets. The evening was ruined. "Anticipated pleasures vanished, and fear and alarm came over us," Amanda declared. "Who or what it was aroused our fears, we know not certainly. But presume that the *rattling* of the *bells* was occasioned by *human agency*, and not by the agency of any part of the '*Brutal creation*,' in other words by boys (not Cows)." Amanda assured readers that she was "always greatly delighted" with "serenades in their true and proper sense." But she objected mightily to "the *unmusical* rattling of certain *Cow property*—the *unmelodious* gingle [*sic*] of certain very useful vessels, such as Tin-pans, Buckets and others of far less note." The cacophony, she wrote, was an "outrage upon female delicacy" that provoked the unusual step she had taken to publish her displeasure for public consumption. She felt it incumbent upon female residents to respond with "an expression of our disapprobation, and an earnest desire to do all in our power to prevent a similar catastrophe." Ultimately, however, Amanda and the other women of Shelbyville had little means at their personal disposal to prevent future offenses. "The *young men* have the power," she admitted, "and upon '*them*' we rely for satisfaction for the injury we have sustained, and security against further invasions."[57] Town residents consistently emphasized self-restraint rather than coercion in their attempts to reform youthful deportment.

During the next two decades, serenaders willingly tamed their behavior. Kate Carney's diary provides some clues to the social rules of serenading at the end of the 1850s, twenty-four years after the apprentice boys of Shelbyville had so alarmed "the female part of the village." Kate experienced encounters with serenaders that were dramatically different from the event "Amanda" had described. "We had a serenade tonight, and think [*sic*] it was the clerks from Pa's store," Kate wrote one January evening in 1859. "We had them invited in, and treated on fruit-cake, and cordial, but we were mistaken about them being young men from the store. They performed on two violins and a Guitar."[58] The serenade itself occurred outdoors, where it was dark enough for Kate to mistake the identity of the serenaders. The young men were ultimately invited inside with their violins and guitar to enjoy the hospitality of the Carney household and perhaps to continue their performance. The ritual involved the serving of liquor, but in contrast to the drunken street revelry of previous decades, these serenaders imbibed spirits within the confines of the Carneys' parlor, where access was controlled by Kate's parents, especially her father. Furthermore, it is unclear whether Kate herself shared in the fruitcake and cordial or merely acted as spectator to the ceremony. The Carneys were serenaded on several other occasions during the winter and spring of 1859. Subsequent encounters Kate recorded suggest that the serenade had become a highly ritualized performance based on class or social standing with particular rules and expectations and new sites of action.

Kate's father, Legrand Carney, played a special role in presiding over the ritual. "Before we had retired the serenaders came," Kate noted one January night, "but Ma did not invite them in, as Pa had not come from the store, and she had gone to bed, and she thought Priscy, had too. I was sorry that they were not invited in."[59] A few weeks later, the response was very different when Legrand Carney was at home to host the serenaders. "We have just had a serenade from the College boys," Kate wrote, "and Pa would have them invited in, to treat them."[60] Legrand Carney appears as the central figure of the serenade, the master of ceremonies, while Kate herself, who might have been expected to be the center of attention as a marriageable daughter of one the town's wealthiest families, seems actually incidental to the ritual. Kate's experience suggests that although serenaders usually targeted households with eligible young women, the serenade itself was performed and understood as a keenly masculine ritual.

The masculine dynamic of the serenade is further highlighted by its contrast with other fashionable visits conducted by young men. As in the serenade, young men tended to make fashionable calls in small groups, rather than alone. But the social dynamic of the call was significantly different from the serenade. "After tea Frank Middleton and Jessie Sikes called on us," Kate wrote in May 1859. Like a serenade, this visit involved treats. Unlike with a serenade, Kate's father was not a participant. "Ma sent oranges, beaucorns, and raisins, in to us, and altogether we had a nice time. We named the seed of the oranges, and mine had twelve seen in it."[61] Kate's mother, Katherine Carney, served as the central chaperone and benefactor during this fashionable, late-afternoon call. This time, Kate herself clearly participated with the young men in eating the delicacies her mother provided. Significantly, the group was not served liquor during the call Kate described, in contrast to the serenades her father hosted. Indeed, the presence of alcohol often marked the boundary between male and female territory in the townscape. This is not to say that women were denied all access to liquor. Kate herself seemed powerfully hungover after a late-night party given by the Carneys to celebrate her sister's wedding.[62] Nevertheless, the places where liquor was available outside the home served an exclusively masculine clientele, and public drunkenness was a male prerogative.[63]

In 1836, the teenaged Edmund Cooper had debated with the members of the Columbia Junto whether ambition or drunkenness was more harmful.[64] The boys concluded then that drunkenness was the lesser evil, but a decade later they might have reached a very different decision. In fact, in 1842, when Edmund moved to Shelbyville to work as a bachelor lawyer, he complained to his brother that there was "no fun and frolic because every one of the young men have joined the church and the temperance society."[65] During the early years of town development, liquor was readily accessible, not only in taverns and "doggeries" but also in storehouse counting rooms and at all manner of public events. Liquor was pervasive in the public life of the community. "No election [was] thought to be well conducted without the presence of good Whiskey," John Spence recalled.[66]

At midcentury, Middle Tennesseans joined the national temperance crusade, and what had once been considered, as historian Paul Johnson puts it, "an absolutely normal accompaniment to whatever men did in groups" became redefined as a social ill. The middle-class obsession with temperance in antebellum cities has been interpreted as a direct result of new patterns of work and residence that changed the relationship between master and wage earner. Middle-class employers built a new ethos of bourgeois family life and demanded new standards of time discipline and productive efficiency from their workers. Drunkenness was increasingly inappropriate in either setting. Meanwhile, independent working-class neighborhoods created an autonomous social life that continued to embrace heavy drinking as an acceptable social custom.[67]

In Middle Tennessee's county seats, however, the temperance crusade took a different shape. In these small towns, the working class was largely enslaved and thereby prevented from creating autonomous neighborhoods to compete against bourgeois domesticity. Residents complained about slave drunkenness, but their complaints rarely translated into a concerted effort to control slave drinking habits. Local officials passed ordinances restricting the sale of whiskey to slaves, and intoxicated bondsmen were held in local jails until their masters bought their release. But considering their stated concerns about the resulting disorder, town residents did surprisingly little to interfere with slave drinking on weekends and holidays. Temperance reformers, with their reliance on persuasion, virtually ignored slave drinking habits.[68]

Instead, young men became the particular focus of the reformers' attention. The temperance crusade, like the serenade, united young men with adult men in fraternal rituals. Whereas the serenade took place at night in the semiprivate world of domestic space, the Sons of Temperance took over the public thoroughfares during broad daylight. In the spring of 1849, the Sons of Temperance put on "quite an imposing celebration" in Columbia. The event was a hybrid creation, fashioned from habitual components of civic ceremony, the procedures town residents had long established to conduct evangelical revivals, Masonic rites, and political campaigns. Fragments of civic ritual came together in the temperance "celebration"; nevertheless, to compose a coherent and specific meaning, Sons of Temperance claimed certain town spaces for themselves and differentiated the young heirs to corporate authority.

The festivities began with a parade. At eleven o'clock in the morning a "procession, composed of the Grand Division of the State, and the subordinate Divisions of [Maury] and adjoining counties, with the Cadets, was formed at the Courthouse." According to the *Maury Intelligencer*, the young cadets marched alongside adult divisions "to the grove near Jackson College, where a very large number of ladies and citizens were assembled."

The parade symbolically linked two male worlds at either end of Main Street, where sobriety was increasingly important for success—the adult business world of the public square and the youthful world of academia (Fig. 5.4). Marching down Main Street, the temperance advocates passed a variety of commercial establishments, professional offices, and residences on their way to Jackson College. It is not clear whether the parade route was lined with onlookers, otherwise excluded from the ceremony, but "ladies and citizens" awaited their arrival at the grove near the male college.

The cadets became a focus of considerable attention as events unfolded at the grove. "The ceremonies . . . were commenced by the presentation of a banner to the Cadets, by Miss Elizabeth C. Johnson," who was about fifteen years old.[69] The presentation included a "tasteful" address, which Miss

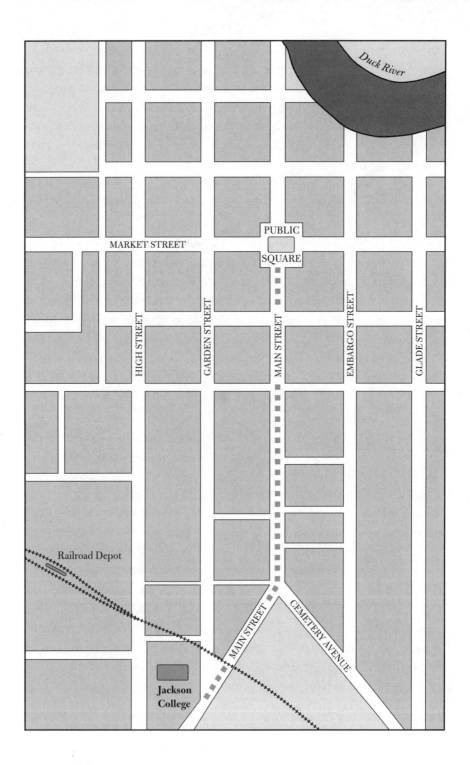

WALKING THE TOWNSCAPE

Johnson "quite prettily delivered." Joseph N. Walker, a sixteen-year-old student, received the banner "on the part of the Cadets" and "acquitted himself handsomely." The presentation was followed by at least two speeches. The first, "of some length," was delivered by the Grand Scribe of the Cadets of Tennessee. Gen. Caruthers of the Lebanon Sons of Temperance spoke next, offering "a spirited and sensible address, which was listened to with more than ordinary attention." After the speeches "the audience was invited to an excellent dinner prepared for the occasion. Dinner over, the procession again formed, marched to the Division-room [at the courthouse] and disbanded."[70]

Temperance became a strategic component of social and spatial differentiation at midcentury. The crusade originated just as residents were beginning to rebuild the townscape. A public square appropriate to the retail traffic of ladies was hardly a suitable location for doggeries, spilling over with inebriated boys who had dangerous tendencies to throw brick bats, fistfight, and use insulting language. The Sons of Temperance in Columbia claimed the territory of Main Street, from the public square to Jackson College, for sober men.

But their celebration was exclusive. Significantly, the particular targets of temperance reform in small-town Middle Tennessee were not working-class laborers and farm boys. Instead, reformers devoted their efforts toward young men of privilege, especially college students.[71] In September 1851, Virginia Shelton attended a temperance meeting at the Murfreesboro Methodist Church, where "quite a large audience assembled." She noted that, at the close of the evening, "an opportunity was given to those between 16 & 21 years of age to join the Circle of Honor & about 25 (mostly students) went forward & joined."[72]

Although temperance meetings and celebrations often drew large audiences and inspired numerous young converts, reformers pursued their course with something less than complete zeal. Virginia thrilled to hear her husband, William, unexpectedly called to speak by audience acclamation. She was, of course, proud of his popularity, but she could not resist smiling to herself. "I don't know when I have felt more amused than when I would

FIGURE 5.4. (*Facing page*) Map of Columbia in the 1850s, showing the parade route taken by the Sons of Temperance.
(Base map courtesy of Tennessee State Library and Archives)

look at him speaking away with the greatest ardor & he no Son of Temperance." Despite enthusiastic participation on the part of some residents in the celebratory aspects of reform, ideological commitment to temperance remained equivocal.

Old habits died hard. During the summer of 1859, Tennesseans were embroiled in a political campaign for governor and congress. "Tomorrow is the election," Kate Carney observed one evening in August. After carefully noting her hope that congressional candidate Col. Ready would be soundly defeated for deserting "his old party, the 'Whigs,' " Kate seemed rather irritated by the antics of some of the young men. "The Serenaders were quite late coming, one was drunk when he came, and laid out on the front porch until four o'clock in the morning though Pa tried to get him in the house to bed." Yet if only one of the serenaders was drunk when he arrived, surely the others made up for lost ground at the Carney house. "Pa treat[ed] them on wine[,] whiskey and cake. They emptied two bottles of wine and commenced drink on the third."[73] So much for the refinement of the serenade.

Architectural change influenced youthful behavior; spatial and social differentiation proceeded hand in hand at midcentury. But there were limits to refinement, especially when town residents consistently depended on youthful powers of self restraint. The architectural choices residents made in the renovated townscape reveal that the role of youth in town life remained problematic at midcentury. Nowhere is this clearer than in the communal response to the male college.

The Building: Colleges for Men

In 1836, the same year that the Columbia Female Institute was built, the trustees of Jackson College moved their school for young men from its rural location on Rutherford Creek into Columbia. Both colleges began in a burst of civic aspiration. Duncan Brown Frierson exclaimed that "each person appears to overreach the other in Contributions for the creation of large edifices for the dissemination of learning among male and female." He proclaimed the female school to be "of immense size" and boasted that the male college would be "much larger . . . so that in a year from this time *Columbia* will be the Yale of the south."[74] A national economic depression postponed local ambitions, and when Columbia residents recovered, they devoted themselves overwhelmingly to female education.

During the 1850s, town residents across Middle Tennessee built substantial and costly women's colleges. Murfreesboro opened three, Franklin had two, and Shelbyville built one college for women during the decade. Thus the renovated townscape was defined in part by a proliferation of colleges for women, but it was also notable for the relative absence of comparable male schools. Despite an extensive building campaign that effectively reorganized town space, residents contributed decidedly little energy and financial support to building colleges for men during the same period. In fact, Shelbyville and Franklin did not build any schools for men to compare with the women's colleges they supported, while in Columbia, residents continued to rely on the old Jackson College. Only Murfreesboro created a substantial new male school, Union University, during the renovation period. At the height of their enrollments, both Union and Jackson served less than 300 students—no contest set against the 700 young women who lived and studied in Columbia's three female colleges by 1860.[75]

One reason that Middle Tennesseans tended not to include male colleges in their midcentury renovation schemes was the availability of established educational alternatives outside the state. Many families that had migrated originally from North Carolina and Virginia sent their sons back to school at the University of North Carolina and the University of Virginia; others went north, chiefly to Yale or Princeton. Nevertheless, the spatial context of the male college in the townscape suggests that the unenthusiastic response to male education was also related to the ambiguous role of young men as town residents.

The position male colleges occupied in the townscape was distinctly different from that of female colleges. Trustees of female colleges located their schools on large lots in residential areas of town. For example, Columbia's Female Institute and Athenaeum stood on adjoining lots at the western border of town in the most fashionable residential district. By contrast, the trustees of Jackson College built their school at the southern end of Main Street, outside corporation limits (Fig. 5.4). Matthew Delamere Cooper described the location as "the margin of the town."[76] Instead of enlarging the building or adding another institution for young men, as they did for women during the 1850s, residents transformed the region around the male school.[77] They built a railroad branch that cut across the school lot, visually separating Jackson College from the town. In a sense, town residents symbolically relocated the college on the "other side of the tracks." They built a railroad depot across the street in a thinly developed section of Columbia that would soon become the wholesale district, complete with stockyards, flour mills, and grain warehouses—hardly a peaceful spot conducive to the study of Greek and natural philosophy.

Meanwhile, in Murfreesboro, town residents celebrated the cornerstone laying at Union University in 1849 (Figs. 3.1 and 3.2). Unlike the ill-fated Jackson College, Union was built on the opposite side of town, far away from the railroad. Nevertheless, it too might be described as part of the "margins" of town, in contrast to Murfreesboro's female colleges, which were deep inside the town borders, in the northern residential section. Significantly, though Union University stood on the principal commercial thoroughfare, it was nevertheless at the easternmost edge of town, just before Main Street became Woodbury Pike (Fig. 5.5). Symbolically, Union anchored one end of Main Street, balanced at the other end by the court-house at the center of the public square. Those entering and leaving town via Main Street could not miss the university and the courthouse—the two prominent institutions of oratory and debate, skills of masculine authority in the antebellum town.

In addition to their distinctive juxtapositions in the townscape, male and female colleges also applied significantly different spatial strategies to ac-commodate their scholars. Most importantly, male schools did not incorpo-rate the chief innovation of the female college—dormitory space. Before the 1850s, local girls from town and neighboring countryside lived at home or boarded with "respectable" families when they attended town academies. In a dramatic departure from this pattern, residential female colleges of the 1850s sought a clientele far beyond Middle Tennessee and housed the students together in buildings designed especially to instruct young ladies in their proper domestic responsibilities. Thus, in addition to classrooms and an auditorium, Soule Female College included a parlor where the boarders entertained visitors, just as they would be expected to do as mistresses of their own households.[78] Union University and Jackson College were both substantial three-story brick buildings, but neither institution housed stu-dents or contained parlors for the reception of visitors. Instead, male stu-dents arranged their own lodging and boarding with local residents, while college space was devoted to classrooms, scientific laboratories, libraries, and chapels or auditoriums for public speaking exercises.[79] At the end of the winter session in 1850, members of the Calliopean Society at Union Univer-sity invited townsfolk to attend their debate. According to Virginia Shelton, "The subject debated was 'ought woman to be as thoroughly educated as man?'" She did not reveal the conclusion the students reached, offering only her own enigmatic evaluation of the evening—"There are some youths of pretty good talents in the University."[80]

Jackson College may not have contained a room large enough to invite townsfolk to public debates. When the Masonic fraternity bought the school in 1848, their hall promptly became an adjunct of the college campus.[81] The affiliation of the two institutions was a natural consequence of long-standing masculine organizational patterns. By the time they reached college age, town youths had already been inured to a group ethos, practicing such youthful traditions as serenading and joining informal debating clubs, like Edmund Cooper's Columbia Junto. Male college students formalized this pattern in elaborately conceived fraternities that established direct connections with adult male organizations. In June of 1849, Jackson College students were finishing exams and preparing for graduation when the Philo Rhetorician Society and the Neatrophian Society, competing student organizations, advertised separate "anniversary" meetings to be held on successive evenings at the Masonic hall. Events at the college and the Masonic hall became inextricably intertwined throughout that graduation weekend. On the final day, the students proclaimed, "there will be a Masonic procession from the Masonic Hall to the College, where it will be joined by the students, and return to the Hall. . . . The Exercises will be public and the public generally are respectfully invited to attend."[82] The Masonic hall stood on Main Street near the public square; thus the student parade incorporated the college at the edge of town into the ceremonial space of the community, thereby linking the school to the larger masculine civic terrain.

The placement and design of male colleges in the townscape embodied the problematic role of young men as town residents. The schools were directly linked to vital commercial and political arteries, yet held at arm's length on the periphery of town. Similarly, organized town youths participated with adult men in the fraternal rituals that constituted official civic ceremony, yet boys had a disturbing potential to violate public order as often as they upheld it. In the spring of 1855, a drunken Union University student was killed in a brawl on the public square. A few months later students organized a strike to resist faculty attempts at more effective enforcement of school regulations. The idle boys loitered on the Square, creating problems for merchants and saloon keepers.[83] In Columbia, female students petitioned the town "for protection while passing on Sabbath night to the Church, from the rudeness of young men, 'who are in the habit of invading

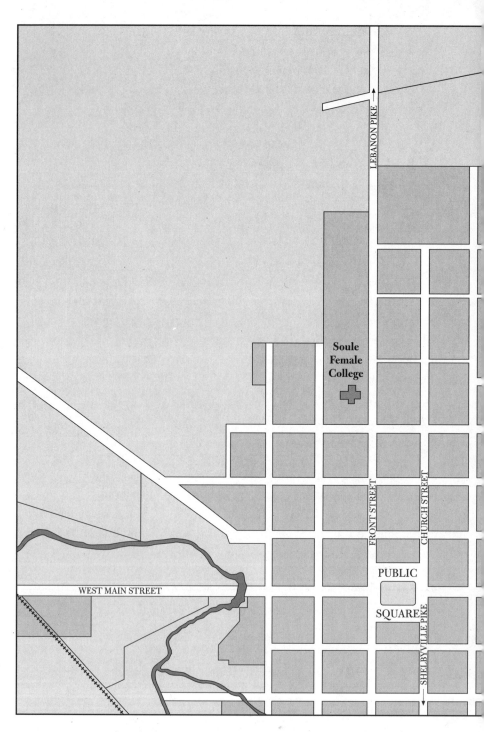

FIGURE 5.5. Map of Murfreesboro, showing location of Union University (at right edge of map) at the opposite end of Main Street from the public square. (Base map source: D. G. Beers & Co., 1878)

L.M. Maney

Union University

EAST MAIN STREET   WOODBURY PIKE

their ranks and insulting them.' "[84] The town responded by hiring additional watchmen, with immediate results. "The order and quiet of our city is now seldom disturbed—and if so only for a moment. Night brawling is incontinently dried up."[85]

The female college successfully negotiated the widening distance between domestic and commercial space. The schools, ostensibly designed to produce ladies who could fulfill ideal domestic roles, became in effect a new town industry that enhanced the prosperity and cultural reputation of the community. Thus, residents enthusiastically supported female colleges in the renovated townscape. By contrast, male colleges in Murfreesboro and Columbia stood outside residential areas on the periphery of town. Male students continued to enjoy expansive access to town spaces, maintaining traditional patterns of youthful organization and boarding out in town households, but their distinctive lifestyle left them on the fringe of an increasingly privatized domesticity. Furthermore, town businessmen, who eagerly invested in female colleges, saw little benefit in recruiting large numbers of young men to attend colleges whose graduates might decide to stay and compete in an already unstable market. The fact that male colleges were not prominent elements in the renovated townscape was not accidental. Such architectural choices reflected the tensions inherent in the lifestyle of young male residents.

Conclusion

While ladies were busy refining townscapes at midcentury, some young men did their best to resist refinement. Rowdy, aggressive, and organized, young men had entirely too much free time, complained many a town dweller, and the townscape of idle boys presented the sharpest of contrasts to the townscape of genteel ladies. While ladies put on their finest dresses to conduct fashionable visits, young men congregated on street corners, smoking and spitting tobacco in its various forms. While young ladies lived together under the sheltered protection of the college, young men found lodgings in smaller groups as boarders scattered throughout town. While young ladies toured the afternoon streets, shopping and "exercising," young men roved the nighttime streets, drunkenly serenading a sometimes reluctant audience.

Yet college youths of the 1850s did refashion traditional patterns of masculine association to suit the renovated townscape. This was particularly clear in the transformation of the serenade from a raucous banging of tin pans and ringing of cowbells through dark town streets into a polite parlor ritual performed with guitars and violins. Town residents also relied on youthful traditions of organization to control drinking, recruiting young cadets into the Sons of Temperance. Architectural choices in the renovated townscape however, suggest the tensions between the integration of young men into the spaces of civic authority and their dangerous potential to challenge or compete for that authority. Thus, businessmen who enthusiastically financed residential female colleges as a profitable town enterprise offered only token support to comparable male institutions. Spatial change embodied the distinctive role of young men as conspicuous, potentially troublesome town residents.

CHAPTER SIX

Small-Town Slaves

A Small-Town Story: Henry's Weekend

Kate Carney habitually took afternoon walks for exercise and enjoyment. Edmund Cooper paraded town streets proudly in his fancy militia uniform. Town streets held an altogether different set of meanings and possibilities for a slave such as Henry. Henry's movements one weekend in the winter of 1850 reveal some of the patterns of work and leisure for slaves in a small town, where streets and shop floors rather than farm fields were the routine sites of action.[1]

Monday, the 25th of February, was no ordinary day in Franklin. It was the day after two white men, John Eelbeck and William Barham, had been stabbed to death by a black man they had suspected of stealing hams. We know something of how Henry spent his weekend not because he kept a diary, but because he was accused of murder. Testimony at Henry's trial offers a rare glimpse of the everyday world of town slavery from the slave's perspective. Many of the trial witnesses were slaves who saw the murders on Sunday night as they walked to their homes from a prayer meeting at Hannah Henderson's house. These witnesses were as guilty of breaking the local curfew as the slave who apparently stole hams from a local smokehouse. They watched nervously as the white men accosted the supposed thief and

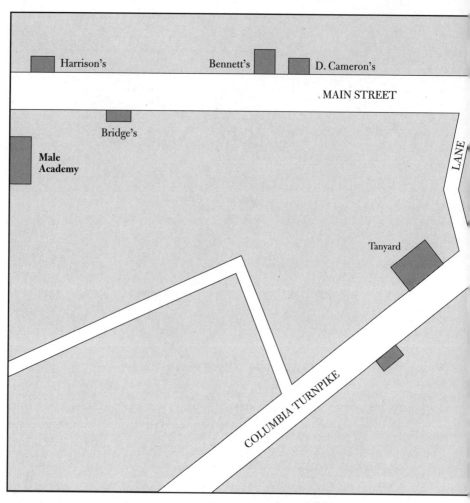

FIGURE 6.1. Map showing much of Henry's route through Franklin in February 1850. Notice in particular the location of the McConnell house at the corner of Margin Street and the Columbia Turnpike, Hannah Henderson's house on Indigo Street, the Bennett house on Main Street, and the tanyard on the Columbia Turnpike. The public

panicked when they saw the two fall to the street, not because they were afraid the murderer would turn on them but because they feared punishment for being out so late. Thus, Henry's story also raises questions about order and control in small towns where slaves made up nearly half the population.

The fact that the murders took place in a small town mattered. The testimony reveals the outlines of a system with its own unique characteristics—a type of slavery that was qualitatively different compared to urban or rural

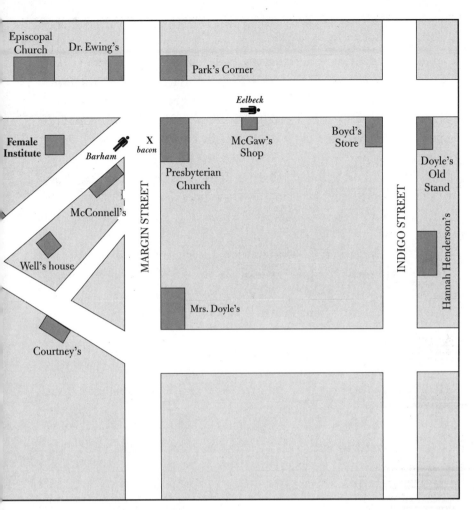

Episcopal Church

Dr. Ewing's

Park's Corner

Eelbeck

Female Institute

Barham

X
bacon

McGaw's Shop

Boyd's Store

Doyle's Old Stand

MARGIN STREET

Presbyterian Church

INDIGO STREET

Hannah Henderson's

McConnell's

Well's house

Mrs. Doyle's

Courtney's

square lies one block east of Indigo Street, just beyond range of the map. The bodies of Barham and Eelbeck were found in the spots indicated on the Columbia Turnpike and Main Street (Base map source: Trial transcript, *Henry v. State of Tennessee*)

forms of the institution. Furthermore, hearing this story from the perspective of slaves enables us to see more fully how slaves were active participants in town life. Questions of law and order in a slave town are addressed more fully later in this chapter.[2] Of particular concern here are the more mundane aspects of Henry's weekend.

Henry worked for Samuel Tenneswood at the local tanyard on the Columbia Turnpike (Fig. 6.1). Before sundown on Sunday evening, the 24th of

February, Henry walked over as usual to Mrs. Doyle's house on the corner of Margin and Church Streets to get his employer's supper, which consisted of "a coffeepot and a plate of battercakes."[3] Catherine Doyle was the widow of a prosperous baker and businessman. Mourning, one of Mrs. Doyle's four slaves, met Henry at the kitchen door. Henry always had to grab a piece of Mrs. Doyle's stove wood to fend off the neighborhood dogs, and Mourning later remembered that she had accidentally kicked over the stick Henry had propped against the wall as she handed him the meal she had prepared. A similar stick would be found at the murder scene a few hours later. Henry balanced the components of Tenneswood's supper precariously, "coffee pot in one hand, and plate and stick in the other," as he set off to make his delivery.

Despite his evening errand for Tenneswood, Henry had had at least part of the day to himself. He spent some of his time off playing cards at Ragsdale's shop.[4] About one o'clock in the afternoon, Henry stopped at Ragsdale's gate to chat with Tom, slave of William P. Campbell, who was on his way to prepare the sacrament for the Sunday service at the Campbellite church.[5] Henry does not seem to have attended church or even the late-night prayer meeting at Hannah Henderson's house.

Henderson, a free black woman, lived on Indigo Street, a block up from Main, where a group of at least eleven or twelve slaves met for Sunday prayer, including Henry's neighbor, Isabella. Isabella worked for the Wells family, who owned a carriage factory next-door to Henry's current residence—the McConnell kitchen. Peter McConnell was a tobacconist from Pennsylvania who owned one slave, a forty-year-old woman named Susan. Henry "was in the habit of staying at night" with Susan in the kitchen, which stood at the back of a V-shaped lot where the Columbia Turnpike met Margin and Main Streets.[6] Susan and Isabella probably broke the monotony of cooking, laundry, and other housework by visiting across the unfenced property line between the McConnell and Wells households. When the prayer meeting at Hannah Henderson's ended around ten-thirty that night, Isabella took a roundabout route back to her employer's house, first visiting the household of her owner and then stopping by the McConnell kitchen to tell Susan the evening's news. Isabella noticed that Henry had returned to the kitchen to sleep.

Early Monday morning Henry rose before daylight and put on a clean, white homespun shirt and his gray roundabout coat with its red flannel lining. His first task was to cut the firewood Susan would need for cooking

WALKING THE TOWNSCAPE

and laundry that day. He made the fire in the McConnell kitchen, slung the ax over his shoulder, and proceeded to his next job—sweeping the floor at King's grocery on the square. James King, who also lived in the store, had hired Jake Childress "to make fires for him." Jake had in turn employed Henry. For the past two or three weeks Henry had walked up Main Street early every morning to clean King's room, sweep out the store, and chop the firewood.

Along the way to King's, Henry was used to seeing Jeff, slave of Hugh Duff, who started his work early at Short's stone yard near the grocery. Town slaves began their work day before sunrise, so Henry and Jeff were among the first town residents to appear on the public square Monday morning. Henry finished sweeping out the grocery just after daybreak, and once again slung the ax over his shoulder and walked back up Main Street to his job at the tanyard on Columbia Turnpike.

These circumstantial details of Henry's life seem insignificant by themselves, but taken as a whole these ordinary activities and encounters begin to outline the contours of small-town slavery. From hard and bloody labor in the tanyard to odd jobs and errands to casual conversations and card games, Henry more often came into contact with other slaves than with white residents. Besides Susan, there was the neighbor Isabella; Jake, who exchanged chores with Henry; Jeff, who worked across the square from one of Henry's early morning jobs; Mourning, who cooked supper for his employer; Tom, a church sexton; cardplayers at Ragsdale's shop; and many others. Whether Henry took his walks in the pursuit of a particular work duty or as part of his own leisure time, town streets offered numerous opportunities for casual conversations with those he met along the way.

What these interactions show is that Henry exerted a certain amount of flexibility and control over his work routine. Small-town streets were full of slaves running errands for their masters or employers, who took the same opportunities that Henry did to choose their own routes and stop to talk to friends and acquaintances along the way.

Besides the flexibility of errand running, Henry was not under the close supervision of an overseer at the tanyard. His employer, Samuel Tenneswood, described Henry as "always attentive" and "perfectly honest." On occasion, Tenneswood left Henry to work alone because, as Tenneswood explained, "he knew what his work was."

Though most slaves were household servants like Susan and Isabella—cooks, washerwomen, stablehands, dining-room servants—Henry was one of the numerous slaves whose work took them beyond individual house-holds. His story suggests some of the ways that slaves used small-town hiring practices to shape their own lives. Samuel Tenneswood was Henry's employer, not his owner. A farmer named John Bennett, whose house stood on Main Street, actually owned Henry and eleven other slaves. But Henry's actions on that February weekend in 1850 show that he neither lived in the Bennett household nor worked as a field hand for Bennett. Before Ten-neswood, George Neely had hired Henry for one year as a butcher.

In addition to his full-time employment at the tanyard, Henry had also taken the initiative to arrange odd jobs to earn extra money. Small towns offered a variety of ways for slaves to earn some extra cash, and those opportunities were expanding in the prosperous 1850s. Indeed, in the last few years, Henry had performed a variety of jobs, including butcher, wood hauler, and meat vendor, selling game he hunted in the vicinity of town. This pattern of localized hiring was more typical than the long-range hiring practices of some antebellum cities, where business was brisk enough to support hiring agents who connected slaves or their masters with potential employers. Hired slaves in the small town tended to have masters who lived in the town or county where they worked. As we shall see, slaves themselves often took an active part in hiring negotiations in a small-town context.

Perhaps it is no coincidence, then, that the antebellum southerner who drew the clearest distinctions among urban, rural, and small-town life was a slave. We can only speculate about Henry's thoughts and attitudes, but the remarkable autobiography of one small-town slave opens a window onto the distinctiveness of small-town slavery. Harriet Jacobs, who grew up in Eden-ton, North Carolina, defined herself explicitly as a small-town slave. "How often did I rejoice that I lived in a town where all the inhabitants knew each other!" she declared. "If I had been on a remote plantation, or lost among the multitude of a crowded city, I should not be a living woman at this day."[7]

The essential distinction of town life, Jacobs felt, was intimacy—a strong contrast to isolation or anonymity. Jacobs exploited the social dynamic of the small town to her advantage when she rejected the unwanted advances of her master, Dr. James Norcum. She reasoned that she was protected by her abusive owner's concern for his own good name as a wealthy doctor and plantation owner in Edenton. "It was lucky for me that I did not live on a distant plantation," she carefully explained, "but in a town not so large that the inhabitants were ignorant of each other's affairs. Bad as are the laws and customs in a slaveholding community, the doctor, as a professional man, deemed it prudent to keep up some outward show of decency."[8]

But Norcum's public image was not the only reputation that mattered. Harriet's grandmother, Molly Horniblow, cultivated a powerful one of her own. Horniblow had secured personal freedom in 1828 and operated a bakery in the heart of town. "Her presence in the neighborhood was some protection to me," Harriet argued. The doctor "dreaded her scorching rebukes," but more importantly, "she was known and patronized by many people; and he did not wish to have his villainy made public."[9] The interactions of James Norcum, Molly Horniblow, and Horniblow's influential white clientele, illuminate the complex racial dynamic that distinguished southern towns.

Of course it was not the complexity of race relations that differentiated small towns from farms and cities. Interactions between white and black were rarely simple anywhere in the antebellum South. It was the spatial and social proximity of mixed-race households that made small-town servitude distinctive.

Henry, who was ultimately executed for murder, might have come to a different conclusion about the protective possibilities of living in a small town where everybody knew each other. His daily movements were widely known. His occupation as a butcher and tanner of hides made him a handy murder suspect. (Doctors who examined the bodies of the murder victims agreed that they must have been inflicted by someone who "had knowledge where the vital organs lay," and "great skill with the use of the knife.") He lived with Susan in the McConnell kitchen along the murderer's getaway route.

And Harriet Jacobs, much as she appreciated the advantages of small-town living, was in fact herself victimized by small-town intimacy. When she became a fugitive, her escape was threatened by myriad possibilities of discovery. For a while, she was unable even to send her grandmother a message because "every one who went in or out of her house was closely watched."[10] For better or worse, lives of white and black were intimately intertwined in a small town where "all the inhabitants knew each other." Slaves managed to turn this situation to their own advantage whenever possible—negotiating employment and housing arrangements, for example—but communal intimacy brought its own dangers and limitations for small-town slaves.

Recent historians have emphasized the possibilities for community building on plantations, where African American slaves were often the majority of residents.[11] Similarly, historians of urban slavery have found that free blacks and slaves who lived in antebellum cities were able to accumulate property, to maintain separate households, to form social organizations, to build independent churches—in short, to create autonomous African American communities.[12] In small towns, by contrast, slaves did not have the opportunity to create physically segregated black communities. Nevertheless, antebellum town space was racially configured, its communities separated by powerful social customs.

Architectural evidence and spatial experience in Middle Tennessee show that the small-town South must be understood on its own terms concerning slavery. Above all, town slavery had the potential to produce extremely complex living and working arrangements that slaves themselves played an influential role in formulating. As much as that of elite female college students or bored young store clerks, the experience of slaves defined the distinctiveness of small-town life.

The Demographic Context: The Distinctive Racial Configuration of Town Space

Slaves were among the earliest migrants to the Central Basin. Robert, slave of James Robertson, worked with the first party of settlers to establish the frontier post of Nashborough in 1779.[13] Twenty years later, one-fourth of the population in Middle Tennessee were slaves.[14] By 1860, four of ten Middle Tennesseans lived in bondage.[15] Most tilled cornfields and tended livestock on rural farmsteads, but a significant proportion of the slave population cleared town streets and managed town kitchens.

There were no direct physical marks of slavery on the antebellum maps of Middle Tennessee's county seats. Southern surveyors and developers drew the same type of town plans—grid-patterned with central courthouse squares—that appeared in northern and western communities, where slavery had become a metaphor rather than a labor system. There were neither slave pens to facilitate the marketing of human property nor specialized urban slave quarters like those found in southern cities such as Alexandria, Virginia, or Memphis, Tennessee.[16] Nothing in the overall designs of small towns betrayed the fact that a significant proportion of town residents lived in bondage. The impact of slavery on physical space in the small town was subtle. For example, town kitchens combined residential and work space by serving as slave dwellings (Figs. 2.5 and 2.6).

Patriarchy and white supremacy, twin principles of town authority, inscribed town space. The most prominent feature of the renovated townscape became the male-centered business axis from the courthouse to the railroad depot, often directly connected along Main Street. But single-family dwellings had always signaled white male authority. Antebellum town residents named their streets but saw no reason to number their houses. They routinely identified dwellings by the names of the men who built them or headed families who lived in them. Nathan Vaught took readers of his memoir on a tour of early Embargo Street that became a litany of Columbia patriarchs:

> Dr. L. H. Estes put up a large 2 story rough log house 2 rooms and a hall below and the same above. This building was on the 2nd lot from the corner east side on Imbargo [*sic*] Street. . . .
>
> The next place improved was on a lot south of Dr. Estes. The house was a one story frame with 2 rooms. I was of the opinion that James Walker had it put up in 1811 or 1812. . . .
>
> William Voorhies put up a one story house (frame) dwelling south on a lot next [to] the one just described. . . .
>
> The next improvement was on a lot south of Mr. Voorhies and was a one story frame house built by Mr. Bird L. Hurt for a storehouse. . . .
>
> The next improvement was a 2 story log house south of Mr. Hurt[']s storehouse on the corner east side of Imbargo [*sic*] Street and on the north side of East Market Street. It is not recollected who built this house. It was occupied at a very early time by Mr. John Bidleman and family for a number of years, and was known for a long time afterwards as the Bidleman house.[17]

Nathan Vaught's tour of Embargo Street suggests that invisibility was one of the potential consequences of spatial integration for slaves. Living scattered in white households meant that there were very few spaces slaves could call their own in a town.

If slavery was not recorded in the town plan, it was readily apparent in the townscape. Slaves worked the spaces that have disappeared from the twentieth-century townscape—the kitchens at the back of town lots, the public wells and cisterns, the woodpiles. During the nineteenth century, they created towns—literally, by clearing streets, making bricks, cutting stones, and building buildings, and figuratively, by serving as message deliverers and errand runners, who connected individual town households and businesses. Spatial mechanisms of control in the townscape of slavery were subtle, complex, insidious. Nevertheless, slaves composed a substantial proportion of town residents—nearly half the population of some county seats—and they actively participated in town life. As much as any town institution, slavery was a defining characteristic of Middle Tennessee's county seats.

In 1830, 556 slaves lived in Franklin—42 percent of the town's population.[18] The proportion remained the same twenty years later. Meanwhile, 46 percent of Murfreesboro residents were slaves, and, although they constituted a smaller proportion of the population in Shelbyville and Columbia, more than one-third of the residents in those towns were slaves in 1850.[19] A town slave was generally young and almost as likely to be male as female. Because they worked primarily as domestic servants, it is not surprising that women in bondage outnumbered men in the small town; nevertheless, the sexual imbalance among slaves was not dramatic.[20] In 1850, 55 percent of slaves in Franklin were women. In Murfreesboro, where 52 percent of slaves were women, the ratio of women to men was virtually equal. Whether male or female, town slaves tended to be children or young adults rather than old people. More than half of the slaves who lived in Franklin in 1850 were twenty or younger; over one third were children under the age of ten.[21]

Slaveowners were far from overburdened with the care of enslaved children. On the contrary, domestic service began at an early age. In her diary, Kate Carney made casual references to at least nine slaves, whose work routines depended on their age and gender. Priscy usually took care of Kate's baby sisters. Peter and Monday drove the Carney family carriage. Mildred seems to have been the family cook, and Josy was simply "a servant." Idella, "cook's youngest," may have been too young to work when Kate wrote her diary and probably occupied the kitchen with her mother. Andrew, a "servant boy," did odd jobs, such as taking dinner to Kate's father at his store on the square and delivering messages to Kate's friends.[22] Millie and Leathy seem to have been young girls who ran various errands for Kate, like the day she "went up to the College, and had Millie" carry her "guitar, [paint] box, and some frames" for her pictures. When Kate discovered she had forgotten the keys to her paint box, she sent Millie home to get them. Leathy returned with the keys, and Kate gave her a finished painting to take home.[23] Though few families were served by so many slaves, work routines followed a similar pattern in households all over town. Slave women were cooks and laundresses. Men were stable hands and drivers. Boys were dining-room servants and messengers. Girls took care of younger children and ran errands.

The geography of antebellum slavery was quite diverse. Small towns differed in terms of the racial configuration of space from urban and rural areas. The daily experience of rural slavery varied widely depending on the size of the farm. Larger plantations supported larger slave communities, while slaves worked more closely with their owners on small farms. Also the type of crops slaves cultivated (rice, cotton, wheat, or corn) demanded different work rhythms and produced diverse landscapes in the southern countryside. Likewise, forms of urban slavery ranged from industrial labor to skilled artisanry to domestic work.

Town residents borrowed from among the spatial arrangements of rural and urban slavery to produce their own distinctive racial configuration of space. The most important factors that contributed to the distinctiveness of small-town slavery include the proportion of black to white residents, the total numbers of free and slave residents, slave residential patterns, and patterns of slave ownership.

By 1850, more African Americans lived in Nashville than in any other city in Tennessee; nevertheless, blacks constituted a higher proportion of residents in county seats than in the city. In 1850, African Americans comprised at least one-third of the small-town population. By contrast, they represented only one-fourth of Nashville's population. The actual work performed by slaves who lived in small towns was similar to the types of work rendered by urban slaves. Some slaves were skilled artisans who worked hand in hand with white workers as carpenters and brickmasons. Most slaves were unskilled domestics or day laborers who worked as haulers, swept out stores, built and maintained roads.[24]

Urban residents were dependent on slave labor for the services that not only made their homes comfortable but which on a basic level made towns and cities function. Given the characteristic intimacy of small-town life, however, slaves had a greater direct impact in small-town society than they did in cities as an urban minority.

Black residents of Middle Tennessee's small county seats were almost always slaves. Altogether, only twenty-three free black men and women lived in Franklin in 1850, about one percent of the town's population.[25] In this respect, small towns presented a dramatic contrast to antebellum southern cities. On the eve of the Civil War, one of the largest concentrations of free blacks in Tennessee resided in Nashville, while the number of free black residents remained insignificant in county seats throughout the first half of the nineteenth century.[26] Despite increasing political and judicial discrimination, urban free blacks educated themselves, accumulated property, and maintained families, creating an independent African American community. One of the consequences of larger free black populations in southern cities was a trend toward racially segregated neighborhoods.[27] Nashville was characteristic of other antebellum cities where intraward clustering of African American residences was producing segregated neighborhoods in the 1850s. In Nashville, 72 percent of the free blacks lived together near the waterfront and the public square, in the second and fourth wards of the city.[28] Urban slaves and free blacks worked together to build churches, schools, benevolent organizations, and businesses that achieved a degree of autonomy from white control.[29] Underlying this cooperation was a multilayered black community where differences in skill level, religion, color, and status mattered. In general, for example, free blacks lived farther away from whites than slaves did in antebellum southern cities.[30]

Small towns produced a less diverse African American society. Yet, despite their small numbers, the evidence suggests that free black residents comprised an influential minority in the county seat. Freemen tended to be skilled or semiskilled; among their number in Franklin were a shoemaker, a chair maker, a wool carder, and a carpenter. Their skills enabled them not only to purchase their own freedom and that of family members, but also to accumulate property, thereby becoming the nucleus for an antebellum black community. Dyer Johnson earned enough money as a carpenter to buy freedom for himself and his wife, build his own house, and donate money to organize the first black church in Columbia. Hannah Henderson, a free black woman in Franklin, hosted Sunday evening prayer meetings attended by slaves.

The community built by men and women like Johnson and Henderson was decentralized. Like town slaves, free blacks seem to have lived scattered throughout town. In Franklin, Martin Scott, a twenty-nine-year-old shoe- and bootmaker, lived in the household of white shoemaker Joseph L. Littleton. Littleton also owned two slaves, a twenty-seven-year-old woman and a four-year-old girl, possibly the wife and daughter of Scott. In another part of town, Susan Philips—a forty-year-old, free mulatto woman with $500 worth of property—headed an independent household that included her daughter Kitty and barber son Frank, both free. In contrast to Nashville's second and fourth wards, there were no separate racial neighborhoods in Franklin. While urban neighborhoods and social organizations were increasingly marked by racial segregation, spatial integration was a distinguishing characteristic of Middle Tennessee's county seats throughout the antebellum period.

White and black residents lived intermingled in the integrated townscape, but there were certain boundaries that could not be crossed. Though slaves lived in white households all over town, racial integration did not extend to cohabitation across the color line. Soon after he moved to Shelbyville, Edmund Cooper learned to appreciate the rules that separated slave and free, black and white, in the integrated townscape. "My first Law suit in Bedford was the defense of a man who permitted his negro to live as a freeman, contrary to an act passed in 1840," Cooper explained. "I made a long and lengthy speech in proving that the boy did not come within the cases provided in the act, exerted myself in giving the boy a *good* name and character, and abusing the corporation for endeavouring to move him without their limits." His client's subsequent behavior brought Cooper to a new understanding of the law and a more circumspect attitude:

> Judge of my feelings a few days ago, when it was proven, that the *rascal* had forcibly compelled a *white girl* to cohabit with him. Before I had been bragging of my success in his defence [*sic*], now I say not a word when he is abused. I did not before see the necessity of the act passed by the legislature, but it is perfectly plain that slaves must be kept within strict bounds for if you give them an *inch*, they take a *yard*. The scoundrel has fled.[31]

Edmund Cooper's client went beyond the pale when he extended the privileges of living as a freeman beyond those of autonomous work and residential arrangements to include a sexual liaison across the color line. As much as any insurrectionary plot, interracial cohabitation between a black man and a white woman struck at the very foundations of patriarchal town authority. Cooper emerged from the experience convinced that the leniency of white residents only encouraged slaves to take greater liberties. He was by no means alone in this opinion. But Cooper's case was an isolated example that served as a warning to civil authorities that race-based slavery must be managed with a firm hand. Slaves rarely provided white residents with such direct challenges to the system. More often, whites resorted to a vague mistrust of their labor force.

In fact, white residents in small towns were more successful than their urban counterparts at restricting the free black population. The relative absence of free blacks in these small towns was not accidental. It was the result of systematic discrimination. During the first two decades of the nineteenth century, there were few restrictions on masters who wished to emancipate their slaves. Then in 1831, in the wake of the Nat Turner rebellion, the Tennessee state legislature outlawed emancipation except for slaves who agreed to leave the state. The state constitution of 1834 made it illegal for the general assembly to pass laws emancipating slaves without the consent of their masters and denied freemen the right to vote (a right they had enjoyed under the old constitution).[32] John Spence reported that, in 1838, twelve free blacks lived in Murfreesboro. "They were required to give a bond and security for good behavor [sic], and keep themselves entirely from the society of slaves, or remove from town." The twelve freemen complied with the order, but Spence admitted it was "a heavy pressure on free persons."[33]

In addition to the relative absence of free blacks to build African American neighborhoods in the small town, spatial integration was largely the product of slaveowning patterns and hiring practices that distributed slaves throughout town. Slave ownership in the city, by contrast, was becoming the privilege of an elite few. During the 1840s, 59 percent of Nashville households had owned slaves, but by 1860, only 37 percent did. In the most affluent neighborhood, the fifth ward, 78 percent of households owned slaves. The middling wards recorded 45 percent ownership, and the poorest only 14 percent.[34]

During the 1850s, wealth was more evenly distributed across the county seats, and as a result, slave ownership was more common in small towns than in the middling wards of Nashville. In fact, the distribution of slave ownership in these county seats approximated patterns of slaveholding in Nashville's wealthiest ward. In 1850, 77 percent of households in Murfreesboro owned slaves, compared with 68 percent of households in Franklin and 52 percent in Columbia. Even in Shelbyville, the poorest of the four towns, 51 percent of households held slaves.[35]

Slaveowners occupied a broad range of social and economic positions in the small-town hierarchy. Franklin's slaveholders certainly included the wealthiest town residents—merchants, physicians, lawyers. But slaveholding was far more than the privilege of an elite few. There was also John Burch, a shoemaker who owned a twelve-year-old boy; and John Short, a stone cutter who owned a twenty-year-old woman; and Elijah Porter, a mulatto laborer who owned a thirty-year-old woman, a four-year-old girl, and a two-year-old girl, possibly his wife and daughters.[36] Indeed, these small slaveholders were typical in Franklin, where 42 percent of slaveowners held only one or two slaves.[37]

But actual slave ownership was only part of the story of town slavery. Many householders not counted among slaveowners customarily hired cooks, laundresses, and stable hands on yearly contracts or for specific jobs. Thus, widespread slave ownership and hiring practices distributed the slave population evenly across the townscape. African Americans lived and worked throughout the county seat, from the public square to the railroad depot, from Italianate townhouses to middle-class cottages and even a few laborers' cabins.

The spatial integration that was the hallmark of small-town slavery also differed significantly from rural patterns of the institution. Southern plantations were often described as townlike by observers searching for a metaphor to encompass the many buildings that composed the plantation landscape—from the master's dwelling to the barns and service buildings to the slave quarters.[38] Samuel Perkins, for example, accumulated more than 1,000 acres on his plantation in Williamson County. His slaves worked the fields and maintained a blacksmith shop, cotton gin, tobacco shed, gristmill, slaughterhouse, wagon scales, waterworks, and icehouse.[39] Though the clustered buildings suggested a townlike appearance, the racial configuration of the plantation, where the dwelling of one white family was outnumbered by the dwellings of multiple slave families, was quite different from the physical integration of the races found in the county seat. Like the urban free black neighborhood, the plantation slave quarter offered the possibility of a separate African American community.[40]

Likewise, small-town slavery was also distinct from that in rural neighborhoods, where slaves lived widely scattered on smaller farms. Just as slave experience shows that small towns were more than urban microcosms, so it also demonstrates that the small town should not be subsumed seamlessly into the rural landscape.

The agricultural landscape of Middle Tennessee was substantially different from the cotton plantation region of the Deep South, so often associated with slave experience. Most rural Middle Tennessee slaves lived in small groups of four or five laborers on farms that averaged 100 acres. Some slaves cultivated cotton, but corn and livestock were the principal products

FIGURE 6.2. Rear service entrance of the Carter house near Franklin.
(Photograph by author)

of Middle Tennessee agriculture.[41] Large plantations, housing twenty or
more slaves, were rare, and over half of rural families were not slaveholders.[42] Indeed, slaveholders represented a higher proportion of town residents than of rural folk. In 1850, for example, about 44 percent of farm
families in Maury County owned slaves, in contrast to its county seat,
Columbia, where more than half of all town households owned slaves.[43]

In some cases, proximity to a town could blur the distinction between
town and plantation slavery. A few expansive farmsteads encircled the county
seat, near enough for census takers to include their owners as town residents.
Peter A. Perkins, a physician and farmer who owned eighty-one slaves, was
listed as a resident of Franklin; likewise William L. Murfree, a farmer who
owned 101 slaves was listed among Murfreesboro residents in 1850. Large
slaveowners like Perkins and Murfree built plantations at the edges of county
seats, where their slaves lived in quarters and followed rural work routines.
But located in close proximity to a town, these quarters were hardly isolated
rural communities (Figs. 6.2 and 6.3).

During the turnpike era, six miles was the radius of town accessibility for
regular social calls among white residents.[44] Slaves who lived on nearby
farms took the opportunity to visit town as well, with or without their

FIGURE 6.3. Row of service buildings at the Carter house, a working farm within walking distance of Franklin. (Photograph by Carroll Van West)

master's knowledge. Harriet Jacobs suggests that such visits to town by rural slaves were not uncommon. When her owner moved Jacobs to his plantation, six miles from Edenton, she refused to be banished from town. Visiting family members who lived in town was a particularly powerful motivation. "I had been three weeks on the plantation," she remembered, "when I planned a visit home." She made the first trip on foot under cover of darkness with a young man who "often stole to town to see his mother."[45] Without her master's knowledge, Harriet made these nocturnal walks to town "again and again" to visit her children.[46]

Besides slaves who lived within walking distance of town, rural slaves also came to town at their owners' behest. Members of slaveowning families shared slaves with each other, creating a transient labor force that traveled between plantation and county seat. Caroline Nicholson and her husband borrowed her father's plantation carpenter to renovate their Columbia town house.[47] Judy Lytle sent her cook Maria into town to help Kate Carney's mother prepare for the wedding of Kate's older sister.[48] It is reasonable to assume that slaves who came to town on their masters' business caught up with the local news and pursued some of their own interests as well.

The antebellum county seat was less segregated by race than either plantations or cities. Town slaves occupied kitchens, hallways, and occasionally independent households scattered all over town near the white families they served.[49] In a town where black residents were almost exclusively enslaved, racial roles were much clearer than in a cities where significant populations of free blacks created a multileveled African American community. In a small town, racial difference—white dominance and black subordination—was measured in social distance rather than physical separation.[50] The demographics of the small town tell only part of the story. To fully understand the distinctive experience of small-town slavery, it is necessary to examine interactions among town residents—to reconstruct slaves' participation in the social townscape.

Black and white residents shared close living quarters, yet, of course, there were clear racial boundaries in the integrated townscape, where social custom built walls as palpable as any physical separation of neighborhoods or households.

Space and Society

From Public Wells to Parlors:
Communal Intimacy in the Integrated Townscape

One night in 1859, Kate Carney recorded the physical closeness between slave and free who shared sleeping quarters in the Carney home. "Rosa [her little sister], Cousin Jane, & myself, besides the servant Mildred, are sleeping over the nursy tonight," Kate wrote.[51] Black servants and white masters may have slept in the same rooms, but such physical proximity did not preclude other mechanisms for establishing racial hierarchy within the Carney household. For example, Kate Carney identified the privilege of getting a good night's sleep explicitly as a privilege of her race. "All the whites, are [a]sleep except Jennie [her baby sister]," she confided to her diary one night in 1859, "& Priscy has taken her, to get her to sleep, so I must follow my own color's suit."[52] The reference was not accidental. One month later, Kate reiterated, "It is after eleven o'clock, all whites asleep."[53] The implication was that blacks were still awake and at work.

The same combination of physical closeness between black and white residents and temporal boundaries that established racial divisions in the Carney household also extended into town streets. The boundaries that divided black and white town residents were temporal rather than territorial. Thus, as Henry's experience as a laborer in Franklin demonstrates, slaves were often the first residents to appear on the public square in the early morning—sweeping out stores, chopping firewood, walking to work.

Spatial integration created conditions for strong communal intimacy that bound white and black residents together in the townscape of slavery. The physical closeness of black and white residents enabled slaves to acquire intimate knowledge of their masters' lives. As John Spence put it, people in towns lived "as one family, what one knew, the whole community knowing and understanding the same thing."[54] Slaves played a central role in this process. Though the racialized rhythms of town life were intended to sustain white supremacy, they also opened up considerable periods of time during which slaves were not directly supervised by their masters. These periods of autonomy, combined with the personal knowledge slaves had of the white families they worked for, made them significant architects of communal intimacy. Nowhere was the process more evident than at the public well.

For the first half of the nineteenth century, individual town households used public sources of water rather than sinking private wells on their own lots. Hauling water was one of the routine jobs assigned to slaves that gave them some degree of unsupervised mobility. Each morning, long before white residents crowded into the streets to attend their business, slaves headed for the public well to collect the daily household supply of water. While there, they often took time to draw more than water, transforming the uses of the town well in the process. If the courthouse was the official center of town business, the public well was its unofficial information center—John Spence called it the "News Depot"—and slaves controlled the content and distribution of news:

> At this place negros commenced gathering about day light with water vessels to get supplies. The usual number meeting for an hour and a half, coming and going, averaging from twenty to forty men, women and children, all after water. Necessarily delayed at this place, all news collected transpiring during the night over town. A general exchange made of what was on hand with the water carriers, then distributed again throughout town. By breakfast time every family was familiar, having heard the morning news, all then ready for work. It was a cheap mode [of] publishing morning news. No telegraph lines up, still there were many sensation[al] reports afloat in the community.[55]

Being scattered as domestic workers in households throughout county seat, slaves were familiar with the private lives of white town residents, powerful and lowly alike. Because they were often the last residents to sleep and the first to wake, slaves were in a perfect position to know what had happened overnight in town. As they interacted at the well, slaves collapsed the boundaries that protected the privacy of white families and enhanced the sense of communal intimacy.

John Spence leaves the distinct impression that whites readily supported the slave "news depot" as a way of keeping up with their neighbors. Gossip was a more powerful force in a small town than on plantations, which contained only one white family, or in cities, where family gossip was diluted by population size. Harriet Jacobs insisted that the unique intimacy of the small town had been powerful enough to protect her from an abusive master.

But if whites were eager to hear the local gossip, they were not in full control of the system. Slaves had the potential to be very influential because of their position in the process. They could include or omit details to shape the overall meaning of the information they circulated. Surely slaves must have preserved important limits in their communication with whites. John Spence and his neighbors likely did not hear all the news that slaves discussed at the well.

Though slaves were burdened by the weight of full water buckets on their trek home, the public well no doubt held attractions as a meeting place for those whose duties took them there. The house girl, Betty Haddox, revealed her strong desire to know "what went on among the other negroes" in Franklin and her keen sense of isolation and confinement when she was prevented from going out.[56] The slaves who gathered each morning at the well were likely as interested in finding out what was happening among themselves as they were in spreading rumors about the white households where they worked.

There were other kinds of messages being delivered at the town well. Slaveholders used the site to reinforce the social hierarchy among white residents. Caroline Nicholson of Columbia remembered that when Sarah Childress married James K. Polk in 1822, her new father-in-law sent her "a little negro boy, just large enough to stride a barrel." He worked partly as a dining-room servant, but his responsibility for hauling water was the job that made the most important public statement of the Polk family's position. "In those days," Nicholson recalled, Columbia residents hauled their water from White's Spring, and "Major Polk had sent mule, cart, water barrel, and little driver, a complete outfit."[57] Such an "outfit" stood out in contrast to the other slaves who, according to John Spence, ordinarily balanced water vessels on their own heads.[58]

White families may have been moving away from this communal water system in the 1850s renovated townscape, where architectural choices revealed increasing concern for ensuring privacy. The Carneys used their own well to supply water for the new house they completed during that busy rebuilding decade. The Sheltons did not have their own well, but Virginia bragged frequently to her aunt and uncle about her "fine cistern of water just at the kitchen door."[59] The renovated townscape enhanced the connections between social status and slaveholding, producing new sites of action for new standards of refinement. White masters took their slaves into the world of the parlor and the ritualized visit, a decidedly more controlled environment for gossiping than the public well.

Through their presence at the public well, slaves were the primary agents of town news, choosing what to tell their white owners and what to keep to themselves. In the parlor, whites considered their slaves to be part of the stage dressing for the visiting ritual, intended to be seen but not heard. The formal visiting ritual thus documents the social mechanisms by which racial boundaries were reinforced in the integrated townscape.

Slaves' roles in the ritual emphasized their subordination to whites at the same time that they underscored the pivotal position slaves occupied in small-town society. Virginia Shelton was accompanied on a three-day visiting marathon by her driver Peter, who dressed especially for the occasion. "If I were of a vain temperament," she bragged, despite herself, "I might have indulged some of the weakness when the neat & elegant little carriage drawn by two beautiful, round fat & gay horses, came 'round to convey me out. Peter too, was looking very neat indeed in his clean clothes & Mr. Shelton's old coat & hat."[60] Peter did not follow his mistress into the parlors she visited, but his role was essential to her success nonetheless. The visiting ritual in the small town began with the stylish parade through the streets in freshly cleaned carriages with respectably attired drivers holding the reins.

While drivers stood outside with the horses, waiting maids accompanied their mistresses into the parlor. Mothers frequently made social calls with infants or young children and the nurses (often little more than children themselves) who attended them. Kate Carney reported that three servants, "Little Lizzie and two other grown ones, came out in the Omnibus to spend the day" with their mistresses, one of whom brought her baby.[61] Kate did not record any information about the opportunities Little Lizzie and the others may have had to interact with the Carney family slaves. In any case, such visits could not offer the kind of unrestricted exchange of information that took place at the well.

Slaves, nevertheless, were more than passive onlookers; they could become key participants in the visiting ritual. As domestic servants, carriage drivers, and waiting maids, slaves were in a position to directly influence the success or failure of a particular social call. Virginia Shelton could not resist a chuckle at the embarrassment of a male visitor who intended to pay a call on her unmarried sister-in-law. "Margaret (our servant Albert's sister)," she explained, "had made a mistake in thinking he asked for Mr. instead of Miss Shelton, & the poor fellow thought he had to wade through the whole family to get to see Miss Martha."[62] Mistakes such as Margaret's might have an effect on the ultimate success or failure of a potential courtship! Whether they were backstage in the parlor or central stage at the public well, slaves were integral to the construction of communal intimacy in the small town.[63]

Slaves for Hire: Work and Family in the Integrated Townscape

Small-town residents in Middle Tennessee followed national housing trends during the mid-nineteenth century as they built increasingly segmented domestic spaces. White residents replaced one- or two-room houses, in which rooms had multiple functions, with multiroom houses, in which domestic spaces had specific functions—bedchambers, parlors, libraries. The change embodied evolving conceptions of family life and privacy.

In the context of the integrated townscape, the segmentation of white households was also an expression of racial dominance.[64] In contrast to the individuation of white space, with its emphasis on the control of domestic privacy, slaveowners provided no separate spaces for their servants. Instead, slaves occupied hallways and slept in the rooms of white family members. They passed through white-owned spaces rather than inhabiting their own. Not only were they denied separate quarters within white households, town slaves were generally prohibited from building independent households.

Detached kitchens were the closest thing to separate slave housing in the small town (Figs. 2.5 and 2.6). Slaves and free blacks in southern cities had a greater variety of housing options than their small-town counterparts.[65] Living at the back of a town lot in a kitchen, however, did offer a better chance for privacy than living in the same house with an owner or employer.

But white residents never recognized the kitchen as a separate slave household. For example, while a second story was being added to their house in the 1850s, Virginia Shelton and her family moved into the kitchen already occupied by their cook, Vesta. Virginia approached the temporary inconvenience as an adventure and took the opportunity to improve her cooking skills. "Tell Aunt she would be amused could she see me in the kitchen early these mornings," Virginia wrote her uncle. "We have breakfast an hour earlier than usual & I can (without bragging) make better biscuit & cofee [*sic*] than most persons." We have no way of knowing how Vesta felt about giving these cooking lessons or to what degree this arrangement displaced her personal living quarters. She must have kept any objections to herself because Virginia did not complain of any disagreements. On the contrary, residence in the kitchen made Virginia more aware of her cook's skills. She noted with admiration that "Vesta makes uncommonly good light bread & I will try if I can equal her in that also."[66] The kitchen obviously offered only limited privacy for slaves in the integrated townscape.

Not only were slaves unable to gather together in separate quarters or neighborhoods, their primary occupation as domestic servants suggests that isolation in separate households must have severely limited opportunities for interaction with other town slaves.[67] Betty Haddox, a "house girl" in Franklin during the 1850s, shows that this was certainly a problem for some town slaves. "I did the house work, sweeping, building fires, and playing with the children," she remembered in an interview conducted long after the Civil War. Like many of the other slaves in Franklin, Betty "slept in the house with the white folks." She complained bitterly about her sense of isolation from other black town residents. "I don't remember much of what went on among the other negroes," she said, "because they [the white family she worked for] never allowed me to go out."[68] In fact, the severely constrained circumstances of Betty Haddox were the exception rather than the rule.

The apparent isolation of Betty Haddox provides a sharp contrast to her Franklin neighbor, the enterprising and peripatetic slave Henry. Recall his errand to retrieve Tenneswood's supper, his cardplaying at Ragsdale's shop, his sweeping out the grocery on the public square, and his various jobs in and around town. Furthermore, though her housework kept his companion Susan confined to the McConnell kitchen and yard much of the day, she developed a close friendship with the next-door housekeeper, Isabella. And though the details of Henry and Susan's courtship are lost to history, they must have had multiple opportunities for casual encounters about town in order to develop a personal relationship.

Denied their own households and neighborhoods, slaves nevertheless managed to construct their own small-town community. As Henry's story suggests, their primary building blocks were the seemingly casual and inconsequential encounters that took place daily in town streets. Most white residents found it convenient to own or hire slaves not only to perform dirty and tiresome household tasks—cutting firewood, cooking, laundry—but also to deliver messages and run errands all over town. Slaves in the Carney household spent as much time traveling town streets as they did working at the Carney house. "Ma sent Uncle Peter [the family's carriage driver] up to Dr. Avent's, to see how Sister Amanda was," Kate wrote one cold day in February 1859. Peter "came back with the news, that Ma had another Grandson, born last night at ten oclock."[69] Amanda was the young wife of Kate's brother John, and their child once again became the subject of an unnamed servant's message a few months later. Kate and her family "were ready to go to church" one Sunday in June, "when a servant came from Uncle Tom Turners [to] say Brother John's child was quite ill, so we gave out going to church, & Pa, & Ma went out there."[70]

One of the most striking aspects of town slavery was the apparent freedom of movement and broad access to town space that was an everyday part of the work town slaves performed. Slaves filled town streets to report births and illnesses, to make deliveries, and to conduct all sorts of business for the convenience of their masters or employers. Town streets even served as the full-time job site for a few slaves. The town of Franklin purchased "three negro men, with mules, carts, and other tools and implements," in order to "keep them all the time at work in cleaning and improving the streets and alleys of the place."[71] But such broad access to town streets also worked to the advantage of slaves, who crossed each other's paths along the way and exchanged messages of their own. Thus errand running served as a mechanism for slave residents to interact with each other.

Because the primary building blocks of the small-town slave community were transitory—conversations and shared work routines, family ties and friendships—little material evidence of its vitality in town life remains. Census takers in 1850 had no column in which to record the outlines of this community. They listed the number of slave residents by age, gender, and color under the names of their masters. The resulting survey presents a simple, ordered townscape, suggesting that slaves lived and worked exclusively in their owners' households. In practice, as Henry's story suggests, labor relationships in the townscape of slavery were intricate, even labyrinthine. Masters frequently hired out their slaves to other town residents, who may or may not have owned their own servants. Meanwhile, slaves themselves refused to be confined to isolated household labor and negotiated their own bewildering network of associations with black and white town residents. The actual townscape of slavery was a tangled maze of associations that mediated the relationship between master and slave. The census obscures the active role African American residents played as negotiators in the small-town hiring process working to preserve their families and construct a loosely defined black community in the spatially integrated townscape.

Evidence from the Shelton household in Murfreesboro reveals the complications of small-town hiring practices and the participation of slaves in the hiring process. Virginia and William Shelton moved to Murfreesboro in 1850 and took up residence with their son David in a six-room "cottage." They had two more children during their stay in Murfreesboro. The Shelton cottage must have been filled to capacity with the frequent boarders and visiting relatives who shared the dwelling for extended periods of time, so it is not surprising that they added a second floor to their house. But they needed the extra space for more than their children and boarders. Throughout their sojourn in Murfreesboro, the Sheltons depended on the services of slaves they did not own.

The couple had no objections to slave ownership. In fact, they tried repeatedly to buy a girl named Amanda, who, Virginia noted, was "willing to leave her mother & father" to become David's nurse. Unfortunately, Virginia complained, her owner "asks so much for Amanda or I would wish to buy her at once." The price of slave ownership was rising in the boom economy of the 1850s, so the Sheltons settled for hiring Amanda for a few weeks, and even that seemed costly. "We pay five dollars a month for her. Is not this extravagant?" Virginia exclaimed.[72] It seems that the Sheltons considered it less extravagant to hire several slaves than to buy one.

As long as they lived in Murfreesboro, the Sheltons consistently hired three or four slaves at a time. In 1851, it was Billy, Sylva, Moze, and Jane. In 1852, Peter and Chana replaced Billy, Sylva, and Moze; Jane seems to have worked for the family throughout their time in Murfreesboro. Vesta and Tom became the principal adult servants from 1853 until the Sheltons moved away in 1856. By 1856, Sarah and Binkey were routinely helping the sickly Vesta. The Sheltons also employed additional temporary help for special jobs. Jane's brother Alex helped serve at a dinner during a religious convention, and Clarissa helped wash while Vesta was recovering from a persistent illness.

Whether owned or hired, domestic help did not come cheap. In 1851, William was "on the eve of closing a bargain for a man at a hundred & a woman at 75 dollars" to work for one year, when he made a much better deal to hire two slaves for a total of only ninety dollars for the year.[73]

The slaves hired by the Sheltons were more than interchangeable domestic servants; they were family groups in their own right. The first three servants who came to work for the Sheltons were members of a family borrowed from William's mother, who lived in neighboring Lebanon. The young Moze "waited" and acted as "diningroom servant." His mother Sylva "cooks, washes, &c.," and his father Billy handled the horses and wagon.[74] When Billy, Sylva, and Moze returned to Lebanon, the Sheltons quickly learned that slaves themselves could be aggressive participants in the negotiation process.[75] They were inundated "for several weeks" with applications from interested servants. Virginia was mildly entertained and even flattered by all the attention. "It is really amusing what a number of servants have been here to get us to hire them. We seem to be quite popular," she told her aunt and uncle.

Virginia's description of the servants who "presented themselves" for employment suggests that slaves shaped hiring practices to preserve their families. "Today there was a man & woman (husband & wife) came to us & we like their character & appearance better than any we have seen yet."[76] Peter and Chana, this husband and wife, could not have approached the hiring process with the same lightheartedness Virginia displayed. For slave families, finding work in the same household could mean the difference between staying together and being dispersed among separate masters, perhaps in distant places. In fact, Virginia noted casually that Peter and Chana belonged to "Col. Bellows who has sold out & is expecting to remove to Texas next year."[77] Nevertheless, slave experiences documented in Virginia Shelton's letters suggest that patterns of domestic service in a small town offered significant opportunities for slave families to live and work together. Indeed, the Shelton household was generally composed of two separate families at any given time—one white, the other black.[78]

Of course, not all slave families were able to work together in the same town households. The teenaged slave Amanda was "willing to leave her mother & father" to become a nurse for the Shelton's children.[79] Members of the same family often worked across town from each other. But when they could not work together, slave families found other opportunities to spend time together. Jinney and her daughter attended a prayer meeting together at the home of the free black woman Hannah Henderson in Franklin. According to Oney, who also participated in the prayer meeting, Henderson's house was "full of negroes."[80] They gathered from households all over town. When the meeting ended, Isabella took the time to visit other slaves (presumably members of her family) who worked for her owner, a shoemaker, before returning to the household of her employer, a carriagemaker.

The Shelton's slaves—Peter, Jane, and Moses—joined a busy traffic of slaves sent out into the streets to conduct their masters' business. Like other town residents, the Sheltons depended on the slaves they hired to connect their household with the local market and to convert the household surplus to cash. The Sheltons apparently left much of the actual bargaining up to their slave agents. Negotiating on Virginia's behalf, Jane and Moses sold peas, cherries, and gooseberries from the garden to one of the local hotels. William Shelton bought a two-horse wagon at the same time he hired Peter. "When employed all day he brings in his two dollars. In the summer he can make three [dollars] & in this manner he can more than pay for his own hire, the price of the wagon & keeping the horses," Virginia proudly declared.[81] Thus households operated as small businesses of a sort, and white residents depended on the slaves they owned or hired to negotiate the best deals on their behalf. Beyond domestic work, small-town slaves performed essential service in local town trade.

Their work as carters and peddlers of the household surplus offered slaves certain economic and political advantages. Slaves must have used this loosely supervised arrangement to earn some cash of their own whenever they could negotiate deals beyond the expectations of their masters. In addition to the possibility of earning extra cash or favors from local merchants, their negotiations presented opportunities for forming useful alliances. Each time they interacted with merchants, hotel owners, and other customers, slaves expanded connections to other white residents who might hire them in the future.

In the social politics of small-town slavery, these business interactions might also have offered a limited measure of protection from abusive masters. Harriet Jacobs emphasized the protective potential of establishing liaisons with influential white residents in a small-town context. Their work as errand runners, carters, and household traders gave slaves a more extensive and detailed knowledge of small-town streets and neighborhoods than most white residents possessed.[82] This information proved useful for creating a kind of privacy for slaves in the integrated townscape. They knew how to alter their routes to escape unwanted observation.

Despite their forced dispersal as domestic servants in privatized white households, slaves managed to form interpersonal relationships that constituted a separate, decentralized black community. Slaves themselves played an active and influential role in formulating the complex living and working arrangements characteristic of small-town slavery. Above all, they shaped the small-town hiring process to preserve their families. Furthermore, their work took them outside individual households and made them active agents in the local economy. Their broad access to town streets offered numerous opportunities throughout the day for interactions with other slaves. Such interactions formed the building blocks for a discernible black community.

Black and white town residents composed an integrated community of unequals. They were not physically separated in the integrated townscape; nevertheless, slave and free composed distinct communities in small-town society.[83]

Murder, Theft, Arson, and Suspicion: Law and Order in the Integrated Townscape

White residents overlooked the activities of the slave community as long as they did not seem to threaten the social order. For instance, town residents like the Sheltons supported slave families in their hiring decisions, and Franklin slaveowners tolerated the prayer meeting at Hannah Henderson's house. An estimated 100 slaves in Franklin even had a party in the market house one rainy afternoon during the Christmas holiday in 1852.[84] But tensions lurked beneath the calm surface of the integrated townscape. Small-town hiring practices and work rhythms had the potential to obscure the lines of authority between master and slave. Furthermore, it was often difficult to distinguish work time from leisure time in a small town. Unlike rural farm labor, town business depended less on long agricultural cycles and more on a weekly routine that left many slaves with spare time, especially after business on Saturday night until work began again on Monday morning. In their free time, slaves exercised the broad access to town streets that was customary of their work routines. Certainly, this situation did not go unnoticed by white residents.

In 1828, an irate "private citizen" of Murfreesboro wrote a bitter letter to the local newspaper, denouncing "masters of the most indulgent and respectable characters" who had refused "to restrain their servants within lawful bounds in their conduct—especially in allowing them to stroll about town and country without passes." He expected town authorities to step in where permissive slaveholders failed and enforce restrictions on slave residents. "Last year we had no town police," he grumbled, "and the effect was, that the negroes and vagrants, and grooms, had unrestrained liberty."

The freedom of movement that was necessary for the work of slave draymen and messengers became a nuisance for white residents when slaves continued to exercise their access to town streets for their own purposes. Imminent insurrection was not the issue; the town's reputation was. Unrestricted slaves "gave to certain parts of our peaceful village, in the estimation of strangers, a very under-the-hill like kind of character." Furthermore, "the most retired citizens were constantly subject to the most unpleasant arrogances from the disorder of which prevailed always on the Sabbath day among negroes and their more disreputable associates. The negroes . . . were in the habit of prowling about the streets, stealing everything they could lay their hands upon, from Saturday night till Monday morning."[85] Disturbing the peace and petty theft were the two most common complaints about slave residents, particularly the men. Given his disdain for the "unrestrained liberty" of town slaves, this unnamed citizen of Murfreesboro would not have been surprised to learn about the events that transpired when a slave was caught stealing slabs of bacon one fateful winter weekend in Franklin.

The moon shone very bright on Main Street Sunday night, the 24th of February 1850. Most of Franklin's 1,500 or so residents were at home asleep, but sometime between ten and eleven o'clock the quiet street filled with people. A prayer meeting had just ended at Hannah Henderson's house on Indigo Street. The slaves who had worshipped there walked leisurely toward their various places of residence, chatting in small groups spread out along Main Street. The tranquil scene changed abruptly when the moonlight revealed three men—two white and one black—wrestling in the street up ahead, near the Presbyterian Church corner. Someone cried, "Look there, they are about to take that negro." But the "scuffle" took a deadly turn. Before they could cry out for help, both white men lay dead in the street as the black man disappeared up the Columbia Turnpike, pursued only by the barking of dogs.

The victims, William P. Barham and John G. Eelbeck, described as "respectable citizens" of Franklin, had both been stabbed in the heart.[86]

Beside the bodies lay four slabs of bacon which the murderer had dropped during the fight. It appeared that Barham and Eelbeck had attempted a citizen's arrest of a black man they accused of stealing the meat. Barham's heart had been "laid open, a piece cut off," along with one of his ribs. Drs. Ewing, Cliffe, and Morton all examined the bodies and determined that they must have been murdered by a powerful and skillful man, one who "had knowledge where the vital organs lay." Investigation of the crime scene and the search for the murderer continued through the night and into Monday morning. Sometime after breakfast on Monday, authorities arrested Henry, whose job at the local tannery made him skilled with the knife and thus a likely suspect. Henry was ultimately convicted and hanged for the murders of John Eelbeck, son of a prosperous carriagemaker in Franklin, and William P. Barham, whose family owned a grocery store near the public square.[87]

Franklin residents were predictably alarmed by the murders. "The deepest solemnity of feeling as well as intense excitement, prevailed throughout our whole community," the local paper reported. The funeral was "attended by an unusually large and deeply affected gathering of friends and mourners," and stores closed to mark the solemn occasion. "A deep and settled gloom pervaded every heart and every home."[88] The news quickly spread beyond Franklin to Nashville and surrounding small towns.[89] But their "deep and settled gloom" did not lead to hysterical retaliation against the small-town slave community as a whole. Unlike the riotous aftermath of the Nat Turner rebellion in many southern communities, the murders of Barham and Eelbeck were not linked to an insurrection plot.[90] They were viewed, instead, as the act of a thief, working alone, caught in the act. The fact that the crime was initially reported by slave witnesses, probably averted any widespread suspicion of the slave community. Thus, when Henry was arrested, residents let the law take its course, confident of the outcome. Twenty years later, when the power of white residents was less assured, Henry might have been lynched. But in 1850, white residents emphasized the systematic deliberation and ultimate justice of the process, and so, "after a patient hearing of all the evidence and the able argument of counsel, the jury . . . returned a verdict of guilty."[91]

Despite the local editor's supreme confidence that justice had prevailed, Henry was convicted primarily on circumstantial evidence. Only one eyewitness, a slave named Oney, identified him by name as the result of repeated questioning. The other eyewitnesses admitted only vaguely that one of the three men looked like a negro. Jinney "could not say from his face whether he was white or black, only thought he was a negro because he had a load and had the dress and form of a negro." Similarly, Malinda believed that one of the men was a slave, not because she could distinguish the color of his skin, but "from his dress and walk and form—that he had on a sack coat and black cap. . . . She thought the other two men were white from their dress." Even Oney insisted that she "could not say positively" that Henry was the man she saw run up the Columbia Turnpike on the night of the murders. Henry, who did not testify during the trial, declared his innocence on the gallows to a crowd estimated at about 4,000 spectators, "a great portion being negroes."[92]

Yet, beyond the putative guilt of Henry, evidence presented at the murder trial raises larger questions about law and order in a slave town. Testimony revealed that the accused murderer was not the only potential criminal in attendance. The slave witnesses themselves were guilty of breaking several laws of the town. For example, it was illegal for Hannah Henderson, a free black woman, to "entertain any slave in . . . her house or residence on Sunday, or between sunset and sunrise of any day."[93] Nevertheless, slaves testified that "there was a house full of negroes at prayer meeting that night."[94] Furthermore, it was illegal for these slaves to "be found from home after 10 o'clock at night" without written permission from an "owner or manager."[95] As a consequence, the same streets that thronged with slave messengers and draymen during the day were forbidden territory after dark, when slaves presumably would be engaged in something other than their masters' business. They risked arrest, not only by the watchmen but by any "citizen" of the town. This explains the reaction of Oney, who saw the "scuffle" between the three men on her way home from the prayer meeting. Believing that "white men were whipping [a] negro for being out so late . . . she pushed on home."[96]

Despite such flagrant violations of town laws as the illegal prayer meeting at Hannah Henderson's house, testimony at Henry's trial suggests an almost casual disregard on the part of Franklin slaveowners for enforcing the letter of the law. They expressed no surprise or dismay about the prayer meeting at Hannah Henderson's, which seems to have been a routine gathering for the slaves in attendance. Dr. Ewing and Peter McConnell slept peacefully in their houses a few steps from the scene of the murders until their nervous slaves woke them to explain what had happened. Although laws regarding slaves convey an impression that social control in the county seat was rigid and absolute, town officials were never willing or able to enforce strict compliance from either white or black residents. Custom was frequently at odds with the law in the antebellum town, a situation that becomes more understandable when viewed in the larger context of small-town slavery.

The ten o'clock nighttime curfew was part of a new set of town by-laws that had been written during the 1830s, a turning point in the regulation of slavery. In 1831, William Lloyd Garrison began publishing *The Liberator*, and Nat Turner led his bloody insurrection in Southampton, Virginia. Middle Tennesseans interpreted these events as matters of immediate local concern. In Tennessee, as elsewhere in the South, legal restrictions on slaves and freemen became increasingly repressive. In 1835, abolition hit close to home when an angry mob in Nashville publicly whipped Amos Dresser after they discovered abolitionist pamphlets in the Lane Seminary student's possession. Town residents rewrote their by-laws in this context, establishing stricter rules for governing slaves. Shelbyville published a new set in 1833, and Franklin was not far behind in 1838.[97] For the next twenty-five years, white paranoia fluctuated, gaining intensity as the South moved toward secession.[98] Compared to other regions, Middle Tennesseans considered themselves to be moderates. In 1850, as the national debate between proslavery and abolitionist forces intensified, the Franklin *Western Weekly Review* treated its readers to an article titled "Ravings of the Southern Fanatics and the Northern Abolitionists."[99]

By the 1830s, repressive legislation set clear racial boundaries that circumscribed the movements of slave residents. But lax enforcement and casual disregard for the letter of the law demonstrate that white residents rarely felt any concerted threat from the slave community. As we have seen, the demographics of the antebellum county seat reassured white residents that any black person within town limits was almost certainly a slave. Widespread slave ownership and hiring practices among white residents fostered an enlarged sense of ownership that extended to African American town residents in general. Whites were confident that racial dominance was secured by more effective means than legislation and found it more convenient in practice to disregard the law. Efforts to regulate time and space in the townscape of slavery were, ultimately, contradictory.

Town slaves recognized the inconsistencies between law and custom and kept steady, though subtle, pressure on the system to enlarge their modicum of independence. They could exploit relationships with numerous whites to limit the authority of their individual masters. But control of this process was tenuous at best. Small-town whites compensated for the weakened authority of individual masters by giving white residents extensive powers over town slaves. For example, even though they were not officially deputized, Barham and Eelbeck had the authority to stop and take into custody the slave they had suspected of stealing hams. In effect, small-town slaves had multiple masters.

Despite their confident authority in the integrated townscape, white residents did not entirely trust the slaves who inhabited their kitchens and hallways. As white paranoia increased over the "incendiary" language of abolitionists and what whites perceived to be the "unrestrained liberty" of town slaves, fire became the pervasive emblem of danger and disorder. In towns built primarily of wood, where open fires served as the chief household energy source, residents had always prepared themselves for the possibility that buildings, and even whole sections of town, could burn to the ground. Town ordinances required householders to provide a leather fire bucket for each story of their dwellings and businesses, and designated all "free male inhabitants within the limits of the Corporation, under the age of fifty-five years" as a town fire company.[100] During the 1850s, a series of fires swept through the public square in Murfreesboro. On one hand, John Spence concluded that the fires had a beneficial effect, removing dilapidated structures that store owners quickly replaced with more modern brick commercial blocks. But Spence could not resist troubling implications, "the frequent fires occurring [sic], having much the appearance of a fire epidemic in town."[101] White residents increasingly interpreted these conflagrations as the result of slave arson.

To some extent, the association between slaves and fire was a natural consequence of the slave work routine. Cutting firewood was the job that made the most memorable impression on James Thomas, who spent his childhood as a slave in Nashville. "Wood was brought to . . . Eight feet in length. When cut once, the four foot log just fit the fireplace. An Ax was made for me (of light weight) & I cut the wood," he later remembered.[102] Fire was integral to jobs slaves, regardless of gender or age, performed— chopping wood, building fires for heat, cooking, laundry. It seemed logical to white residents that arson would be a practical option for a discontented labor force.

In 1854, "a goodly number of the citizens hastened" to Mrs. John Eakins's burning dwelling in Shelbyville, "and before it had done any material damage extinguished the raging element." The local newspaper reported that "the fire took place in the second story of the building, in a closet, and was

Small-Town Slaves   219

without doubt, put there by some one of the negroes."[103] The charge was increasingly automatic. In 1859, when Kate Carney heard that "there had been another fire on the side [of the Square] where Pa keeps his store," she immediately concluded that slaves must have been involved in the destruction. "Mr. Joe Nelson's drugstore was the place," she wrote,

> burned all the floor, & injured it a good deal by tearing the things up to put it out. They don't know how it happened, one negro was put in jail for stealing a pair of shoes, where is the place he should be, as I would not be surprised if the object for setting that house, was to steal from others that would be alarmed for the safety of their goods, & remove them, & thereby offer an opportunity to theives [*sic*] to steal.[104]

There were clear limits to communal intimacy in the integrated townscape. Mutual suspicion divided slave and free. Kate Carney trusted Millie and Leathy with the keys to her paint box, but other town slaves were potential thieves and arsonists. From the slaves' perspective, white residents could not be trusted to let them walk the streets in peace. Vulnerable to the arbitrary decisions of white residents, slaves might be punished for breaking curfew—or not. Families might be hired to work together, or they might be split apart. Though suspicion percolated ever nearer the surface in the 1850s, small towns were models of peaceful coexistence compared to riotous antebellum cities, torn by class, ethnic, and religious strife. Whereas white fears had led to repressive legislation during the 1830s, in the 1850s mutual aversion led increasingly toward racial separation—a potentially radical change in the integrated townscape.

The Building: African Churches in the Renovated Townscape

The defining characteristic of slave experience in the county seat was living dispersed among white households. Scattered throughout town, slaves became architects of communal intimacy as they hauled water, delivered messages, and ran errands for white employers. But forced dispersal constrained the slaves' ability to create their own communal institutions. This was their predicament—they lived everywhere and nowhere. Unlike the plantation slave quarter or the urban free black tenement, black space in the small town was subsumed by and almost inextricably intertwined with white space. Still, in casual exchanges on the street, card games in the back rooms of storehouses, the neighborly sharing of household duties across unfenced back lots, slaves managed to create a kind of community in the midst of white space. Families arranged to live together as much as possible, but in general slaves were prevented from creating the kind of social organizations that defined white experience. In the slave community there was nothing to compare to the segregation of young white ladies in residential colleges or to the organizational ethos of young white men who drank together, debated together, and marched together in groups that mimicked adult male associations. The black community was invisible, denied its own landmarks, with one crucial exception: black churches.

Slave churches have been called "invisible institutions" because they flourished without the tangible structures that buttressed mainstream religious life—houses of worship, educated ministers, membership records. Nevertheless, some of the earliest separate black churches in the United States were built in the South, long before the end of slavery.[105] In the late eighteenth century, black churches emerged on South Carolina plantations and in Virginia towns. During the nineteenth century, the pace of racial separation fluctuated with white fears that religious meetings could be used to plot insurrection. One of the leaders of Gabriel's Rebellion of 1800 in Richmond, Virginia, was a preacher. Most of the accused insurrectionists in Denmark Vesey's 1822 conspiracy were members of the African Methodist Church in Charleston, South Carolina. And the infamous Nat Turner had a reputation as a preacher, seer, and prophet among slaves in Southampton, Virginia. Harriet Jacobs noted that slaves had built their own church in Edenton, North Carolina, before Turner's rebellion. When news of the bloodshed reached the town, white residents attacked the church. According to Jacobs, "the slaves begged the privilege of again meeting at their little church in the woods, with their burying ground around it. It was built by colored people, and they had no higher happiness than to meet there and sing hymns together, and pour out their hearts in spontaneous prayer. Their request was denied, and the church was demolished."[106] Gradually the hysteria subsided, and southern congregations continued to separate along racial lines.

During the 1840s and 1850s slave residents of Middle Tennessee began to establish their own separate churches. Slaves had periodically gathered in groves of trees on the outskirts of town to conduct their own religious celebrations. For example, before they built their new church, the White's Spring congregation in Maury County met together for some time on the rock ledges that formed a natural auditorium at the spring.[107] But separate African American churches appeared for the first time in the renovated townscape. In 1847, black and white Baptists began to meet separately in Nashville, although full independence remained elusive because white ministers and church leaders insisted on monitoring slave worshipers.[108] By 1860, the city directory listed four African churches.[109]

Black Baptists in Columbia had already been meeting on their own for four years by the time their urban neighbors in Nashville gained autonomy. The Burns' Spring church, organized in 1843, became the first African American church in Columbia, and one of the first independent black churches in the state. Other slave congregations followed suit. In 1860, a Columbia newspaper sarcastically noticed "that a new church has been erected for and by the negroes, (of what creed, it is hard to tell)." Slaves had built "a good looking and quite large frame house, capable of seating about two hundred persons." According to the newspaper's count, "this makes three African Churches here, in which every Sunday the negroes regularly hold meetings. One we have mentioned, near the White Spring, another near Greenwood Cemetery, and the third, near Burns' Spring."[110] Doubtless there were many other less visible groups in Columbia comparable to the prayer meeting that convened at Hannah Henderson's house on that moonlit night in Franklin. Given their diversity, white residents monitored these religious gatherings with varying degrees of attention.

Free blacks played a crucial role in building African churches in antebellum southern cities. Labor shortages and increased wages during the 1850s produced unprecedented prosperity in the free black community.[111] Similarly, the communal prosperity that financed the town building boom during the 1850s also gave slaves (including domestic servants who bargained in the local market on behalf of their employers) greater access to cash.[112] Dyer Johnson, a carpenter who managed to buy his freedom sometime before 1850 and the freedom of his wife Elizabeth in 1852, was one of seven founders and chairman of the first deacon board. Johnson donated more than half of the money to purchase the church lot and built his own house next door (Fig. 6.4).[113] Known to its members as the Mt. Lebanon Baptist Church, the slaves and free blacks who attended became leaders in the post-emancipation African American community.

Free blacks played a vital role in organizing African American religious groups. Hannah Henderson, a free woman of color in Franklin, led prayer meetings in her home, and George Cherry, a seventy-year-old free black

FIGURE 6.4. Dyer Johnson house in Columbia. (Photograph by author)

resident of Columbia, listed his occupation as "preacher" in the 1850 census.[114] But given the extremely small numbers of free black residents, slaves must have played a larger role in small-town churches than they did in urban ones, where free blacks tended to dominate leadership positions.[115]

Conclusion

Slave experience in the antebellum small town embodied a unique blend of advantages and disadvantages. The social dynamic of town life was marked by a degree of racial intimacy that was altogether different from both plantation and urban conditions. Harriet Jacobs argued that communal intimacy constrained white slaveowners, thereby offering some protection to vulnerable slaves. At the same time, it forestalled attempts to create an autonomous black community, until slave churches emerged in the renovated townscape.

It is impossible to know what solutions slave and free town residents would have worked out, because the Civil War and emancipation dramatically altered the material townscape and the social rules of engagement in this biracial society. After emancipation, freedmen established their own schools, churches, and households almost overnight, profoundly reshaping town space. Hastily constructed shantytowns at the corporation limits became the first visible, separate African American communities in the county seat. But these institutions did not appear in a vacuum. They were deeply rooted in the invisible antebellum community—the slave families who worked together in white households all over town, the small but influential free black population, the churches and religious gatherings that carved out a particle of black space in the townscape of slavery. Though the fact of spatial integration often obscured its outlines, the slave community was a vital force in small-town life.

Remnants of the Antebellum Townscape

In 1927, the home of William Lytle was torn down to make way for the new Carnation milk plant—an inglorious end for the birthplace of the town of Murfreesboro. In the years after his lavish barbecue had persuaded the citizens of Rutherford County to choose his land for the new county seat, William Lytle built his home into a showplace at the edge of town. The two-story, brick dwelling had five bays with double chimneys at each gable end. The central bay was defined on the first floor by the front door with its fanlight, side lights, and colonnaded porch and on the second floor by three arched windows. Brick dependencies flanked the dwelling on both sides, connected to the main house by colonnaded passageways. The site was a marriage of two worlds—a grand plantation house only a short walk from the small-town public square.[1] In the end, town consumed plantation. One of the dependencies—the former plantation office—was the only building that survived demolition in 1927. Pieces of the Lytle house were salvaged—doorways, columns, mantels, fanlights—and found their way into new homes in Murfreesboro.[2] Thus the antebellum past was destroyed and fragmented as residents constructed new townscapes for a changing society.

Of course the fate of the Lytle plantation was nothing new. From the beginning, small towns were invented and mutable or even disposable places, remade by successive generations of residents. Because they had carved town grids out of canebrakes, residents did not have a past to preserve. Instead, they created the suggestion of antiquity—each town employing the Greek Revival to become an "Athens of the West." Furthermore, residents showed little sentimentality for their own architectural heritage, encasing log buildings behind painted clapboards or transforming old-fashioned Federal-style dwellings into fashionable Italianate villas. Local boosters eagerly embraced new types of buildings and new ways of doing business, from commercial blocks to female colleges. Just as antebellum town dwellers replaced one townscape with another, their descendants have reshaped town space and rebuilt the material fabric of the town many times since the Civil War.

The fate of the Lytle house speaks volumes about the relationship between history and progress in the small towns of Middle Tennessee. Towns have long since burst their original grids and spilled out into expansive suburbs and strip malls, swallowing farmland by the square mile. Ironically, even as they disappeared from the landscape, subdivided into small-town neighborhoods, plantations became enshrined in local memory. Stories of antebellum town life were overshadowed by more compelling narratives of the Civil War. Today, for example, historic house sites such as Oaklands, antebellum home of the Maney family in Murfreesboro, and Carter's Grove and Carnton in neighboring Franklin commemorate a plantation rather than a small-town past.

These sites also have connections to dramatic Civil War events. Oaklands played host to Jefferson Davis as well as the wounded from the Battle of Stones River (Fig. 3.8). At Carter's Grove, visitors hear the unbearably sad story of the Carter family, who emerged from their root cellar after the Battle of Franklin to discover the body of their brother and son. Tod Carter enlisted in the Twentieth Tennessee Regiment in 1861 and survived almost four years of war only to die at his father's doorstep in the Battle of Franklin. The most prestigious Civil War pedigree, however, belongs to Carnton (Fig. 7.1), where

> For over a hundred years Franklin people have cherished the fact that the bodies of five generals—those of Pat Cleburne, John Adams, State Rights Gist, Hiram Granbury, and Otho Strahl—rested on this porch in pathetic dignity. . . . Carnton, as all houses where battles were fought, brooded over the strange scenes it witnessed and was honored yet sorrowful over the dead and wounded heroes it embraced.[3]

FIGURE 7.1. The back porch of Carnton, where the bodies of five Confederate
generals were laid in the aftermath of the Battle of Franklin.
(Photograph by Carroll Van West)

The emphasis on a heroic Civil War past coupled with aggressive destruction and rebuilding has obscured much of the antebellum small-town past.
Nevertheless, by the end of the Civil War small towns had established a
meaningful role in the southern landscape. In 1864, one defiant Rutherford
County slave was explicit about the freedmen's view of small-town opportunity when he refused to leave Murfreesboro with his mistress. "You have
no business to take me out of town," he insisted adamantly, "I intend to stay
and go to school & be free."[4] Clearly the small town occupied a compelling
place in the imagination of nineteenth-century Middle Tennesseans.

The antebellum townscape lies buried now under new layers of town
building. A drive up Main Street toward the courthouse reveals the town's
finest architectural heritage, the substantial residences that line the avenue.
Closer to the square these residences give way to public houses of worship,
financial institutions, and commercial establishments. The courthouse itself
stands at the center of the square, surrounded on four sides by a variety of
stores and offices. This pattern, so commonplace today as to be considered

the defining characteristic of a county seat, was new to the towns of late-nineteenth-century Middle Tennessee.

As we have seen, by the time of the Civil War, new commercial blocks were only just beginning to enclose the public square within a box of brick storefronts. Most of the finest houses encircled the town, hugging its borders, rather than congregating along prominent streets. What remains of these antebellum towns are shards and remnants—produced from the combined efforts of decay and neglect, deliberate destruction, and purposeful reconstruction.

Among the victims of subsequent building cycles have been the finest homes as well as the humblest. The home of Hannah Henderson, the free black woman who played host to slave prayer meetings in Franklin, no longer stands (Fig. 6.1). But neither does Kate Carney's house, once known by local residents as the finest house in Murfreesboro (Fig. 4.1). Yet even if every building from the antebellum town had survived into the twentieth century, it would still be impossible to walk the same streets as Kate Carney or Edmund Cooper or Henry and Susan. Their streets belonged to a historically specific time and place.

The first half of the nineteenth century marks a discrete episode in the story of small-town development. From their modest creation as centers of government to their dramatic growth into railroad towns during the 1850s, the history of architectural change in county seats of Middle Tennessee shows that small towns played a dynamic and influential role in shaping the culture of the region. Despite their diminutive size, small towns invested in urban ways of doing business. Commercial blocks on the public square linked Middle Tennesseans to an expanding market economy in the nineteenth century that extended all the way to Philadelphia and beyond. Turnpikes connected one Main Street to another, creating small-town networks traveled by circuit-riding lawyers. Small-town lawyers like Andrew Jackson and James K. Polk became the architects of a national party system; while the mass rallies and illuminations of Whigs and Democrats inadvertently revealed the competing claims of town and country identities. By the 1850s, small-town residents were feeling so confident of their influence that they invested large sums in women's colleges in an effort to export their reputation and cultural influence far beyond local county boundaries.

This history of change and development shows that small towns were much more than a passive backdrop for the rituals of rural planters and yeomen. Furthermore, studying the material context of social interactions within small-town space makes possible a more nuanced understanding of the distinctive experience of small-town life compared to urban and rural patterns. Viewing town space from the varying perspectives of different groups of residents reveals the subtle but profound impact of gender and race—the layered meanings of town space. The antebellum small town was a place where all the inhabitants knew each other and slavery imposed a distinctive spatial pattern of racial integration.

This world took new directions in the aftermath of the Civil War. More powerful than any of the economic or technological changes that had come before, the social and political force of emancipation profoundly reshaped small-town life. The spatial integration of antebellum townscapes obscured the presence of black residents, but in the aftermath of slavery, race inscribed town space. Insurance maps carefully noted the location of "colored" cabins and tenements in the heart of town, while small-town slums in flood-prone areas (usually called "the bottoms") housed mostly black residents.

Race played a decisive role in the reorganization of commercial space as well in the aftermath of war. Competing merchants carved up the public square as they sought to attract or exclude freedmen as a new clientele. In Murfreesboro, W. N. Doughty & Company advertised their dry goods establishment as a "freedmen's store." Announcing that their merchandise was "selected with special reference to the colored trade," the merchants insisted that freedmen would find the cheapest prices but "No trashy goods."[5] Meanwhile, across the square, another merchant declared that "his store is now a 'white man's store.' "[6]

Emancipation created new social relationships and new material contexts that redefined small-town life. Nevertheless, given the distinctive patterns of antebellum race relations, it seems reasonable to suspect that small towns continued to work out different social arrangements compared to biracial urban and rural communities. We need to know more about the potentially unique patterns of segregation that developed in the context of the post-emancipation small town. Preliminary evidence shows that by the early twentieth century white residents lived among black inhabitants of the "bottoms," and both black and white entrepreneurs operated businesses side by side on streets leading from the public square.[7]

Though small-town society developed in new directions after the Civil War, these profound changes had strong links to the antebellum past. For example, the African American churches that multiplied in the post-emancipation townscape were actually based on antebellum slave congregations.

FIGURE 7.2. Today this postmodern skyscraper, viewed from the public square in Murfreesboro, is the most visible landmark of town space. (Photograph by author)

"During their slavery," African American Baptists in Columbia "preached out in the open air." In 1869, "they commenced [building] their chapel, and, after spending all they had, succeeded in getting it covered and weatherboarded."[8] By 1870, there were five separate African American churches in Columbia—two Methodist, two Baptist, and one Presbyterian—and about 250 black students attended a freedmen's school on West Main Street.[9] In Murfreesboro, black residents attended two Methodist and two Baptist churches.[10] The churches they built, against all odds, became both the symbols and the guarantors of autonomy in the beleaguered black community. John Spence admitted that "it was common mixing politics with religious matters in churches of the colored people. At these places they could speak their sentiments without fear of molestation."[11]

The bitter truth of small-town history in the aftermath of emancipation was unprecedented racial violence. In Murfreesboro, where John Spence insisted that black residents found refuge in their own churches, a group of armed white men attacked "a lot of noncambatant blacks who are quartered in the basement of the M. E. Church, and routed them" during a series of street battles between negro guards and white soldiers.[12] In fact, racial

Epilogue

violence was so pervasive as to be one of the distinguishing features of the post-emancipation townscape. Heroic narratives of the Civil War have effectively erased local memories of the armed combat in town streets during Reconstruction. Too painful to be commemorated in official memory was another battle of Franklin—an ambush of the parading Union League by white merchants who took up strategic positions in second-story, commercial block windows and fired on the black soldiers as they marched into the public square.[13] The Ku Klux Klan created such anarchy in Maury County that martial law had to be imposed to restore some semblance of order.

The racial warfare of the post-emancipation townscape is best understood when linked to the antebellum experience that prepared the ground for it. Given the pervasive pattern of racial integration that marked antebellum town space, segregation represented a loss of territory for white residents and a territorial gain for black residents. Though small towns often played a more prominent role in the history of Reconstruction and the New South than they had in pre–Civil War histories, these events occurred in the context of places with a deeper past. The political and social battles of the late nineteenth century were strongly influenced by the antebellum experience of small-town residents.

Any map of the antebellum South is incomplete without the small towns that shaped southern society. A simple quantitative measurement of town size is an inadequate measure of the distinctive cultural influence of small towns in the region. Town residents—black and white, male and female, rich and poor—constructed ever-changing, multilayered townscapes redefining town space to shape the demands of fluid societies.

Today, a postmodern skyscraper towers over the courthouse residents built in 1859 on the public square in Murfreesboro (Fig. 7.2). The streetscapes of the late twentieth century were unimagined by the small-town surveyors of the early nineteenth century, but the central courthouse squares they created remain the signifiers of contemporary small-town identities. The plantations are long gone, but though they are no longer intimate communities where all the inhabitants know each other, towns continue to shape society in the region.

NOTES

Introduction

1. Virginia Shelton to her uncle, 4 May 1854, Campbell Family Papers, Duke University.

2. Virginia Shelton to her uncle, 4 May 1854, Campbell Family Papers.

3. *Maury Press*, 7 March 1860.

4. See, for example, Cash, *Mind of the South*; W. R. Taylor, *Cavalier and Yankee*; Genovese, *Roll, Jordan, Roll*; Oakes, *The Ruling Race*; and Fox-Genovese, *Within the Plantation Household*. While these scholars construct very different arguments about the nature of southern society, they all assume the centrality of the plantation. For two exceptions to this rule, see Robert C. Kenzer, *Kinship and Neighborhood in a Southern Community* (Knoxville: University of Tennessee Press, 1987), which develops the concept of distinctive plantation neighborhoods in Orange County, North Carolina; and Orville Vernon Burton, *In My Father's House Are Many Mansions: Family and Community in Edgefield, South Carolina* (Chapel Hill: University of North Carolina Press, 1985), which examines town and country in one district of South Carolina.

5. See, for example, Goldfield, *Cotton Fields and Skyscrapers*; Brownell and Goldfield, *The City in Southern History*; Goldin, *Urban Slavery in the American South*; Ernst and Merrens, "'Camden's Turrets Pierce the Skies!'"; Curry, "Urbanization and Urbanism in the Old South"; Dorsett and Shaffer. "Was the Antebellum South Antiurban?"; Brownell, "Urbanization in the South."

6. Fox-Genovese, *Within the Plantation Household*, 5, 74.

7. Ibid., 5–6.

8. Oakes, *Ruling Race*, 92.

9. Stephen Ash estimates that about twenty-five towns contained "what may be called the urban population of Middle Tennessee." During the mid-nineteenth century this population doubled. In 1850, 10 percent of whites lived in towns. Ten years later that proportion had reached 21 percent, and included about 1 of every 5 families in the region. "Slaves were far less likely than whites to live in towns: only about 7 out of 100 did so. Free blacks were far more likely, but their numbers were comparatively few." These numbers changed after the Civil War, but so does Ash's definition of "urban." He set his "cutoff point" in 1860 at 1,500 to designate "rural" and "urban" districts; his 1870 cutoff was 2,000. Ash interprets 1870 census data as evidence of a "pronounced agrarianization of white society" while black society was becoming increasingly urbanized. See Ash, *Middle Tennessee Society Transformed*, 23, 258, 237.

233

10. Jacobs, *Incidents in the Life of a Slave Girl*, 35.

11. Quantitative analysis of Middle Tennessee is based on Ash, *Middle Tennessee Society Transformed*, 1–12.

12. Ash (*Middle Tennessee Society Transformed*, 257) notes that the distinction between rural and urban "was recognized by contemporaries but did not preoccupy them as it does modern students of society. . . . [Census takers] did not specify towns . . . few town populations can be specifically calculated and in any given district the town and country families cannot be distinguished. There is, moreover, no general agreement on just what constituted a 'town' in the nineteenth-century South."

13. Rutman, "The Village South," 233.

14. As Darrett Rutman puts it, nineteenth-century census marshals were "eclectic in their labeling of the aggregations they reported." The emphasis on "townships" in the north has led to overestimation of town population there, while town residents in the South are "for the most part subsumed in counties" (Rutman, "The Village South," 237–39).

15. Ash, *Middle Tennessee Society Transformed*, 9.

16. Meinig, *Continental America*, 275.

17. This places Tennessee within the general eighteenth-century trend toward town building in the South. See Earle and Hoffman, "Staple Crops and Urban Development in the Eighteenth-Century South." According to Earle and Hoffman, "at least in the Carolinas, the lonely frontiersman living apart from all urban contacts never existed in any significant number" (64). They suggest that the quickening pace of town building in the South during the second half of the eighteenth century "constituted the predictive foundations of future Southern economic development" (11). This assertion holds true for Tennessee, largely settled by North Carolinians, where the frontier closed quickly and towns were built early.

18. Edward T. Price followed the development of county seat plans as a product of cultural diffusion in the settlement process from Pennsylvania to the Midwest. He found that the simplified block square was first articulated in Shelbyville and quickly followed by Fayetteville, Pulaski, and Winchester, all laid out between 1810 and 1812; thus he calls the block square pattern the "Shelbyville plan." See Price, "Central Courthouse Square in the American County Seat." For an examination of the county seat form in the South, see Pillsbury, "Morphology of the Piedmont Georgia County Seat."

19. Alfred Hamilton Letters, undated (ca. 1858), TSLA.

20. Spence, *Annals of Rutherford County*, 1:193.

21. Ibid., 1:87.

22. Upton, "Imagining the Early Virginia Landscape," 71.

Introduction to Part One

1. Dell Upton has pointed out that landscapes appear as a unity but actually include buildings constructed over time to serve particular cultural needs; see Upton, "The Southern Cultural Landscape as Meeting Ground and Debating Ground."

2. In "Domestic Architecture as an Index to Social History," Clifford Clark measured the success of social reform movements in the mid-nineteenth century by comparing reform literature to the plans of houses produced during the Romantic Revival. Clark

used architecture, much like traditional documentary sources, as a record of change—an "index" that codified cultural innovation after the fact. But buildings are more than reflections of change; they help to generate change as residents learn new ways of using space. Thus it is important to understand not only the information contained in a building as document but also to evaluate it as an experiential phenomenon composing a variety of meanings. On the semiology of space, see Lefebvre, *Production of Space*, 142–43. Lefebvre argues that the semiologies of space and language work in significantly different ways. The messages contained in social space are intrinsically different from those written on a printed page. Above all, he argues, " 'reading' follows [spatial] production in all cases except those in which space is produced especially in order to be read" (143). Thus the act of interpreting space is fundamentally different from the act of reading a text. For example, he argues that Gothic churches were built in a specific context: "this space was *produced* before being *read*; nor was it produced in order to be read and grasped, but rather in order to be *lived* by people with bodies and lives in their own particular urban context" (143). In fact, Lefebvre warns, spaces that have been produced to convey intentional messages are often "the most deceptive and tricked-up imaginable" (143).

Chapter One

1. Spence, *Annals of Rutherford County*, 1:85.

2. Ibid., 1:86.

3. Ibid., 1:101. Maj. John Lytle's house stood on the lot that became the southeast corner of the public square, known thereafter by town residents as the Lytle lot.

4. Nicholson, "Reminiscences of an Octogenarian," 1, SHC. Caroline O'Reilly Nicholson (1811–94) moved to Columbia in 1822 and married A. O. P. Nicholson, United States senator and Tennessee Supreme Court justice, on 17 June 1829.

5. From the reminiscences of Nathan Vaught, transcribed in Tinker, "Nathan Vaught, Master Builder," 95. Photocopies of the original memoir, titled "Youth and Old Age," are also available at the Tennessee State Library and Archives in Nashville, Tenn., and at the Maury County Public Library in Columbia, Tenn.

6. Earle and Hoffman, "Staple Crops and Urban Development in the Eighteenth-Century South," 51–59. Earle and Hoffman emphasize market functions in the creation of backcountry towns, a different process than county seat formation. Nevertheless, many of the towns they consider were also established as county seats.

7. Hofstra and Mitchell, "Town and Country in Backcountry Virginia." Hofstra and Mitchell describe the development of a "town-country settlement system" composed of county seat and smaller subsidiary towns by the beginning of the revolutionary war in the Shenandoah Valley. The evidence for Middle Tennessee supports their observation that "the forces that had earlier integrated the small town and dispersed farm replicated this world on the trans-Appalachian frontier with greater speed and less discontinuity to create one of America's most indelible settlement landscapes and most powerful cultural symbols" (646).

8. Arensberg, "American Communities." Arensberg outlines regional differences in the construction of American communities, arguing that the town was the organizing principle of New England society while the county was the fundamental building block

of southern society. Subsequent historians of the South have used the county as the primary focus for community studies. See, for example, Burton, *In My Father's House Are Many Mansions*; and Kenzer, *Kinship and Neighborhood in a Southern Community*.

9. Petition to form Rutherford County, Legislative Papers, TSLA.

10. See Goodstein, *Nashville, 1780–1860*, 8, for information about Weakley and for a description of the role speculators played in land development during this period in Middle Tennessee.

11. Spence, *Annals of Rutherford County*, 1:31. According to Goodspeed, Robert Weakley was also one of the first purchasers of lots in Jefferson; see *Goodspeed Histories of Maury, Williamson, Rutherford, Wilson, Bedford, and Marshall Counties of Tennessee*, 814.

12. Rutherford County Deed Book H, January Session, 1813. See also Spence, *Annals of Rutherford County*, 1:72.

13. Shepard, " 'This Being Court Day.' "

14. The classic analysis of this phenomenon is Wade, *Urban Frontier*.

15. This pattern was not necessarily unique to small towns of the early national period. In Philadelphia, "slow physical expansion was accompanied by rapid population growth" (Twiss-Garrity, "Double Vision," 4).

16. Paul Groth argues that street grids are much more than interchangeable templates; rather, they contain important historical evidence of city development. By recognizing the nuances in streetplans, he asserts, "we can learn to see street layouts not merely as sterile initial plans . . . but as a collection of artifacts which reveals the processes of urban building." He notes that "In general, *the plot is more permanent than either the building or the street*. The grain of plots, set not by the original plan but by initial occupance and building on urban land, is perhaps the most enduring physical aspect of the city" (Groth, "Streetgrids as Frameworks for Urban Variety," 69, 72).

17. *Goodspeed Histories*, 766.

18. Ibid., 766.

19. See Price, "Central Courthouse Square"; Reps, *Town Planning in Frontier America*; and Pillsbury, "Morphology of the Piedmont Georgia County Seat." Price attributes the popularity of the central courthouse square to Scots-Irish influence. Early-seventeenth-century English towns of Northern Ireland were often planned with central courthouse squares, for example, Londonderry in 1622.

20. Reps, *Town Planning in Frontier America*, 204–23.

21. Philadelphia firms established trade with the Shenandoah Valley during the late 1750s, and the city linked the backcountry to the consumer revolution of the late eighteenth century (Hofstra and Mitchell, "Town and Country in Backcountry Virginia," 641). See also Doerflinger, "Farmers and Dry Goods in the Philadelphia Market Area, 1750–1800." See also Meinig, *Continental America*, 275–76, on the combined cultural influence of Virginia and Pennsylvania on the distinctive development of the Upland South region.

22. Hofstra and Mitchell, "Town and Country in Backcountry Virginia," 619–46. See also Meinig, *Continental America*. According to Meinig,

This characteristic architecture [dog trot and I-house] confirms that this expanding frontier was not in fact a simple projection from classic Tidewater Virginia but was, rather, an extension of what came to be known as the Upland South, a distinct regional complex formed in the Great Valley and Piedmont during the late eighteenth century, drawing strongly upon the Delaware Valley and Greater Pennsylvanian sources as well as those of Greater Virginia. The towns reflected the same antecedents, in various combinations and adaptations" (274).

Harriet Simpson Arnow likewise noted the cultural influence of Philadelphia on frontier Tennessee in *Seedtime on the Cumberland*.

23. Pennsylvania played an especially influential role in setting the standard for American town design. See Pillsbury, "Urban Street Pattern as a Culture Indicator."

24. In his article "The Central Courthouse Square in the American County Seat," Edward Price went so far as to suggest that Middle Tennessee was a secondary culture hearth where new cultural forms were synthesized and spread to other regions, especially the Midwest. Henry Glassie also found Tennessee a "dynamic area" for cultural experimentation at the beginning of the nineteenth century: "it was here that, in what was apparently a brief period, the transverse-crib barn and dogtrot house were developed" (Glassie, *Pattern in the Material Folk Culture*, 88–89).

25. According to Price, the Shelbyville plan is the earliest example of the central block square. Whereas the Philadelphia and Lancaster central squares had clear European antecedents, especially in the towns of Northern Ireland, Price argues that the Shelbyville plan was a particularly American development, produced in the waves of migration across the Appalachians ("Central Courthouse Square," 133–36).

26. Pillsbury, "Morphology of the Piedmont Georgia County Seat," 120. See also Price, "Central Courthouse Square," 136, for a map showing spread of the central square plan throughout the Midwest.

27. Price traces the first example of this type to Harrisonburg, Virginia, platted in 1780 before the first planned example of the block square, which he asserts to be Shelbyville, Tennessee. He explains that geometrically the plan at Harrisonburg "lies halfway between the Lancaster [or Philadelphia] and Shelbyville types" ("Central Courthouse Square," 137). Pillsbury reasons that in Georgia the plan "may be a mutation of the central and secanted Philadelphia squares" ("Morphology of the Piedmont Georgia County Seat," 120).

28. *Democratic Clarion and Tennessee Gazette*, 29 March 1811.

29. Burdette and Cook, "Original Town Lots of Shelbyville."

30. Spence, *Annals of Rutherford County*, 1:149.

31. Ibid., 1:144.

32. Ibid., 1:ix.

33. Quoted in Tinker, "Nathan Vaught, Master Builder," 95.

34. In his memoirs, James Norman Smith noted that in 1825 the Columbia Masonic Lodge "consisted of the First Class of Citizens—of Lawyers, Judges, Merchants, and Farmers" (Smith Memoirs, TSLA).

35. Vaught claims to have constructed seventy-six buildings, only ten of which are still standing. This suggests the scope of the rebuilding processes that have dramatically reshaped Middle Tennessee county seats from the first phases of development.

36. Spence, *Annals of Rutherford County*, 1:93.

37. Ibid., 1:93.

38. Ibid., 1:153.

39. Ibid., 1:150.

40. Ibid., 1:149.

41. Nicholson, "Reminiscences of an Octogenarian," 1.

42. Glassie, *Pattern in the Material Folk Culture*; more recently, Meinig, *Continental America*, 274.

43. Quoted in Tinker, "Nathan Vaught, Master Builder," 113, 131. Similarly, the architectural historian Gregg D. Kimball found that "Richmond's domestic architecture just after the Revolution was not significantly different from the folk housing that dominated the surrounding countryside" ("African-Virginians and the Vernacular Building Tradition," 125).

44. Roberts, "Tools Used in Building Log Houses in Indiana." Roberts identified seventy-six different tools used in building log houses and concluded that it was unlikely for a single individual to own a complete set of them. Whether a housebuilder worked in town or in the country, pooling resources was necessary for constructing log buildings.

45. Spence, *Annals of Rutherford County*, 1:149.

46. Ibid., 1:87, 149–50. See Stilgoe, *Common Landscape of America*, 166–70, for discussion of American preference for white paint in the early Republic.

47. Quoted in Tinker, "Nathan Vaught, Master Builder," 135.

48. Spence, *Annals of Rutherford County*, 1:87.

49. According to Meinig (*Continental America*, 277), churches "were never the symbol and focus of community life as in New England. In Nashville, for example, a Masonic hall faced the courthouse square years before any permanent church building existed in the town, and Methodist Bishop Asbury, on his third visit in 1812, recorded his bitterness about 'a community that put the courthouse in the central location, where the church "ought to be." ' "

50. Spence, *Annals of Rutherford County*, 1:149–50.

51. Ibid., 1:150.

52. Ibid., 1:156.

53. Ibid., 1:157.

54. According to Meinig, the importance of the courthouse in the trans-Appalachian west was a sign of Virginia influence. "A marked tendency toward greater formality and regularity in town planning that laid out a grid with a designated public square owed more to Pennsylvanian than Virginian models, but a large courthouse in the middle of that central square symbolized a polity that was assertively Virginian" (*Continental America*, 275–76). See also Lounsbury, "Structure of Justice."

55. The first brick courthouses were built in Franklin about 1806, in Columbia about 1810, and in Murfreesboro and Shelbyville about 1812.

56. John Spence describes a slightly larger building, but the published specifications are otherwise consistent with the courthouse that apparently was built. "J. M. Ditches bid off the contract for building court house. . . . Contract calling the dimension of court house fifty feet square, two storys, twelve and fourteen feet high, of good brick, a chimney on each corner, stair way leading from the lower room, above, roof terminating to a point at the center, a cupaloe proportionable hight [*sic*], the top finish, iron rod with a spread eagle. All other parts regularly finished. The building completed, made a

handsome appearance for a new country. The expense about four thousand dollars. . . . No offices in this building for clerks," see *Annals of Rutherford County*, 1:88.

57. Charlotte in Dickson County is home to the oldest remaining courthouse in Tennessee. Originally built between 1806 and 1812, the present building was reconstructed on the original foundation after a tornado destroyed the first courthouse in 1830. Wings were added in 1930, but the central block of the building was left essentially intact. This original core matches the pattern described in published specifications for other courthouses in the region. Harper, "Antebellum Courthouses of Tennessee," 3–5.

58. *Nashville Whig*, 25 November 1812. See also Harper, "The Courthouses of Williamson County."

59. For specifications of the Franklin courthouse, see *Impartial Review and Cumberland Repository*, 8 November 1806; for specifications of the Shelbyville courthouse, see *Democratic Clarion and Tennessee Gazette*, 17 August 1810 and 29 March 1811; for specifications of the Murfreesboro courthouse, see *Nashville Whig*, 25 November 1812. These are all Nashville newspapers.

60. *Nashville Whig*, 25 November 1812.

61. Courthouses in eighteenth-century Virginia, though "an integral part of county life," typically stood in relative isolation at country crossroads (Lounsbury, "The Structure of Justice," 214).

62. Harper, "Antebellum Courthouses of Tennessee."

63. For example, Nathan Vaught built "a double cedar log house" on Garden Street in 1844 (quoted in Tinker, "Nathan Vaught, Master Builder," 113).

64. Spence, *Annals of Rutherford County*, 2:5.

65. Franklin was incorporated in 1815; Columbia and Murfreesboro in 1817; see *Acts Passed at the First Session of the Twelfth General Assembly of the State of Tennessee, Begun and Held at Knoxville, on Monday, the Fifteenth day of September, One Thousand Eight Hundred and Seventeen* (Nashville: T. G. Bradford, Printer to the State, 1817). Shelbyville was incorporated in 1819; see *Acts of a Local or Private Nature, Passed at the First Session of the Thirteenth General Assembly of the State of Tennessee, Begun and Held at Murfreesborough, On Monday, the Twentieth Day of September, One Thousand Eight Hundred and Nineteen* (Nashville: Printed for G. A. & A. C. Sublett, Printers to the State, by George Wilson, 1819).

66. Spence, *Annals of Rutherford County*, 1:244.

Chapter Two

1. Folmsbee, *Sectionalism and Internal Improvements in Tennessee*, 101. The editor of the Nashville *Republican and State Gazette*, 27 November 1834, argued that a good turnpike from Columbia to Nashville was the best way to ensure the commercial dominance of Nashville.

2. Dell Upton has called this piecemeal effect the "paradox of landscape." In particular, he writes, "an apparently unified landscape may actually be composed of several fragmentary ones, some sharing common elements of the larger assemblage" ("White and Black Landscapes in Eighteenth-Century Virginia," 59).

3. This argument takes issue with two separate sets of arguments about the southern

landscape. The prevailing interpretation is that small towns reflected the countryside; see, for example, Fox-Genovese, *Within the Plantation Household*. Urban historians have effectively shown the importance of urban development in the region; see, for example, Goldfield, *Urban Growth in the Age of Sectionalism*. Both urban and plantation historians, however, have tended to overlook the distinctiveness of small market towns like Middle Tennessee's county seats at the same time that they have generally agreed about the ubiquity of small towns in the region.

4. According to estimates in Eastin Morris's *Tennessee Gazetteer* of 1834, Columbia and Franklin each had 1,500 residents; Murfreesboro had about 1,000; and Shelbyville, having recently suffered the double calamities of tornado and cholera epidemic, had only about 600 inhabitants.

5. John Shofner (in Bedford County) to his brother Michael (in Orange County, North Carolina), 28 August 1834, Shofner Papers, SHC.

6. John Shofner to his brother Michael, 28 August 1834, Shofner Papers.

7. Morris, *Tennessee Gazetteer*, 252.

8. "An Act to amend the laws heretofore passed, for the better regulation of the towns of Fayetteville and Shelbyville," 9 October 1817, in *Acts Passed at the First Session of the Twelfth General Assembly of the State of Tennessee, Begun and Held at Knoxville, on Monday, the Fifteenth day of September, One Thousand Eight hundred and Seventeen* (Nashville, Tenn.: T. G. Bradford, Printer to the State, 1817).

9. John B. McEwen to David Campbell, 3 February 1822, Pope Family Papers, TSLA.

10. Betsy Blackmar notes that the construction industry in New York City was extremely unstable from 1800 to 1840. There was some regional variation in economic cycles. Building booms occurred in New York during the early 1820s and again in the mid-1830s (Blackmar, "Re-walking the 'Walking City,' " 144).

11. Hugh Robinson laid out the first seventy lots in 1813; two lots were added to the town in 1817. See "An act to enlarge the town of Murfreesboro," in *Public Acts* (Nashville, Tenn.: Printed for G. A. and A. C. Sublett, Printers to the State, G. Wilson, Printer, 1820), 101.

12. Spence, *Annals of Rutherford County*, 1:214.

13. From the reminiscences of Nathan Vaught, transcribed in Tinker, "Nathan Vaught, Master Builder," 104.

14. Quoted in Tinker, "Nathan Vaught, Master Builder," 112.

15. Morris, *Tennessee Gazetteer*, 135, 158, 209–10, 251–52.

16. Ibid., 251.

17. *The Western Freeman*, 29 May 1835.

18. Morris, *Tennessee Gazetteer*, 251.

19. Ibid., 252.

20. Conger Diary, January and May 1813, TSLA.

21. Fannie Blount O'Bryan to Martha Ann Maney Douglass, 3 March 1848, Douglas-Maney Family Papers, TSLA.

22. *Maury Intelligencer*, 15 February 1849.

23. Virginia Shelton to her uncle and aunt, 3 November 1850, Campbell Family Papers, Duke University.

24. Quoted in Tinker, "Nathan Vaught, Master Builder," 127–28.

25. Spence, *Annals of Rutherford County*, 1:239.

26. According to Lounsbury, *An Illustrated Glossary of Early Southern Architecture & Landscape*, 184, the term "house" was used to refer to "a building for certain activities or, in general, any building. In modern usage, the term is synonymous with dwelling, a place of human habitation. However, from the time of settlement through the early 19th century, the term usually had a prefix to describe certain activities, occupants, or relationships associated with the building, such as almshouse, back house, cowhouse, courthouse, meetinghouse, slave house, storehouse, smokehouse, and tobacco house. Thus the term dwelling house was not redundant, as it would be today."

27. *Tennessee Democrat*, 20 November 1844.

28. This house was subsequently moved to its present location on Third Avenue North in Franklin. It has long been known in Franklin as the home of Elizabeth Eaton, mother of U.S. senator John Henry Eaton. John Eaton was a cabinet member in the Jackson administration, but he became more famous as the husband of young widow Peggy O'Neill, who was snubbed by the Washington social set. The furor over their marriage caused a split in the cabinet and precipitated the resignation of Vice President John C. Calhoun. Recent research has shown, however, that the Eaton association probably derives from the purchase of the house in 1841 by a grandson-in-law of Elizabeth Eaton. Apparently, neither the senator nor his mother ever owned the house. See Hasselbring, *National Register Properties*, 33.

29. Patrick, *Architecture in Tennessee*, 91–92; Weaver and Eidson, "James K. Polk Home"; Bowman, *Historic Williamson County*, 123–24.

30. See Gowans, *Images of American Living*, 217–21, for his discussion of the Polk house as an expression of Adamesque style on frontier.

31. Darby and Darby, "Maury-Darby Building."

32. This common house type for the Upland South—two stories tall, one room deep, two rooms wide, with a central hall—has been termed the "I-house" by vernacular architecture historians. See Kniffen, "Folk Housing: Key to Diffusion"; Glassie, *Pattern in the Material Folk Culture*; Meinig, *Continental America*, 274.

33. Virginia Shelton to her uncle, 6 June 1855, Campbell Family Papers.

34. Spence, *Annals of Rutherford County*, 1:150.

35. *Western Weekly Review*, 21 April 1831 and 8 July 1831.

36. *Murfreesborough Telegraph*, 13 November 1845.

37. Mary Louise Polk to Sarah Polk, 8 October 1848, Polk Papers, TSLA.

38. Quoted in Tinker, "Nathan Vaught, Master Builder," 111.

39. Also, wealth was expressed in architecture differently during this period than it would be in the 1850s. Emphasis was on the quality of the construction rather than on extravagant embellishment. Catharine Bishir argues that this is a kind of "architectural politics"—an elite strategy for maintaining their position by emphasizing republican simplicity rather than the appearance of opulence. See Bishir, *Architects and Builders in North Carolina*, 56–60.

40. Spence, *Annals of Rutherford County*, 2:10.

41. Beyond skin color, clothing also distinguished slave from free in the small town. Witnesses of a fight between two white men and one black man on a nighttime street in Franklin identified the race of the combatants by their clothing. According to one

witness, she "could not say from his face whether he was white or black, only thought he was a negro because he had a load and had the dress and form of a negro." Similarly, another witness believed that one of the men was a slave, not because she could distinguish the color of his skin, but "from his dress and walk and form—that he had on a sack coat and black cap. . . . She thought the other two men were white from their dress" (*Henry v. State of Tennessee*). I explore more fully the issue of race and status in small-town society in Chapter 6.

42. Duncan Brown Frierson to William F. Cooper, 31 December 1834, Cooper Family Papers, TSLA.

43. Mary Louise Polk to Sarah Polk, 8 October 1848, Polk Papers.

44. John Shofner to his brother Michael, 28 August 1834. Shofner Papers.

45. Boniol, "Walton Road," 403.

46. Folmsbee, *Sectionalism and Internal Improvements*, 24.

47. *Western Freeman*, 18 December 1832.

48. Spence, *Annals of Rutherford County*, 2:20. For explanation of the development of the Rutherford County road system, see also Annable, "History of the Roads of Rutherford County," 29.

49. *Republican and State Gazette*, 27 November 1834, quoted in Folmsbee, *Sectionalism and Internal Improvements*, 17; see also 101 n. 74.

50. Bracegirdle, *Archaeology of the Industrial Revolution*, 66, 71–72. See also Reader, *Macadam*.

51. G. R. Taylor, *Transportation Revolution*, 16, 26–27. Taylor argues that throughout the United States, "country roads . . . were really much more important . . . than were the turnpikes, which were chiefly designed for travel between the larger towns or to the westward across the mountains." He concludes that turnpikes were "a boon to travelers" but "generally did not cheapen and stimulate land transportation sufficiently to provide satisfactory earnings from tolls." See also Folmsbee, *Sectionalism and Internal Improvements*.

52. Spence, *Annals of Rutherford County*, 1:240. Spence suggests that spring was the typical season for such annual visits. If so, road conditions must not have been the primary consideration for traveling, given the chance for spring rains.

53. Folmsbee, *Sectionalism and Internal Improvements*, 17, 184; *Western Weekly Review*, 18 May 1832. The 1830s and 1840s became a major road-building era in Upland South. For examples of road-building activity, see Shirley, *From Congregation Town to Industrial City*; and Bishir, Brown, Lounsbury, and Wood, *Architects and Builders in North Carolina*, 130–92.

54. John Shofner to his brother Michael, 28 August 1834, Shofner Papers. The *Daily Republican Banner*, 25 April 1838, announced that the turnpike from Nashville to Shelbyville was complete "a distance of 55 miles."

55. Virginia Shelton to her uncle, 24 November 1853, Campbell Family Papers.

56. Fannie Blount O'Brien to her sister, 21 November 1845, Douglas-Maney Family Papers.

57. *The Mayor & Aldermen of The Town of Franklin vs. Job Mayberry*.

58. *Columbia Observer*, 19 July 1838.

59. From the reminiscences of Nathan Vaught, transcribed in Tinker, "Nathan Vaught, Master Builder," 110–11.

60. See Warner, *Private City*, 3–45, for a vivid description of Philadelphia as "eighteenth-century town." See also P. E. Johnson, *Shopkeeper's Millennium*, 48–55, for discussion of a similar pattern in Rochester that changed quickly after 1825. Betsy Blackmar distinguishes between "walking distance" and "social distance," arguing that mixed-use does not entail harmonious social relations. Class differences in New York were expressed between property owners and renters as well as by differences between multiple-family and single-family housing (Blackmar, "Re-walking the 'Walking City,'" 131–48).

61. *Tennessee Herald*, 29 August 1818.

62. *Tennessee Herald*, 20 June 1818.

63. *Tennessee Herald*, 29 August 1818.

64. *Tennessee Herald*, 20 June 1818.

65. On 9 April 1854, Murfreesboro resident, Virginia Shelton, wrote that her husband, William, had "attended the funeral of Strickland the Architect of the Capitol, who *died drunk* a day or two before" (Virginia Shelton to her aunt, 9 April 1854, Campbell Family Papers).

66. Patrick, *Architecture in Tennessee*, 141–42. Gilchrist, *William Strickland*.

67. Bowman, *Historic Williamson County*, 104–5.

68. Joanna Rucker to Sarah Childress Polk, 7 February 1849, Polk Papers.

69. Carnes, *Secret Ritual and Manhood*.

70. *Philadelphia Gazette and Daily Advertiser*, 13 May 1818, quoted in Gilchrist, *William Strickland*, 53.

71. *Port Folio*, September 1821, quoted in Gilchrist, *William Strickland*, 55.

72. Ibid.

73. Patrick, *Architecture in Tennessee*, 125. The Nashville bank was designed by Pennsylvania-born architect David Morrison, who came to Nashville sometime before 1828.

74. Quoted in Tinker, "Nathan Vaught, Master Builder," 102.

75. Dell Upton explores the increasing divergence between nineteenth-century architects and builders in "Pattern Books and Professionalism." Two advertisements in the same issue of Franklin's *Western Weekly Review*, 21 April 1831, demonstrate the changes taking place in building trades during the early nineteenth century. Philip A. Yancey assured potential clients he was prepared to perform "according to the most approved system of modern architecture," but he described himself in traditional terms as a "house carpenter and joiner." In contrast, John Gadsey called himself an "architect & joiner," and built a "substantial kiln, for drying plank," signaling small-town industrialization of the building trades.

76. Quoted in Tinker, "Nathan Vaught, Master Builder," 111.

77. Tinker, "Nathan Vaught, Master Builder," 63; and Patrick, *Architecture in Tennessee*, 125.

78. *Port Folio*, September 1821, quoted in Gilchrist, *William Strickland*, 55.

79. *Columbia Observer*, 27 June 1834 and 24 December 1839; *Maury Intelligencer*, 12 April 1849.

80. Quoted in Tinker, "Nathan Vaught, Master Builder," 111–12.

81. JoAnna Rucker to Sarah Polk, 1 December 1847, Polk Papers.

82. According to Joanna Rucker, for example, slaves filled the streets after a public

celebration in Murfreesboro (Joanna Rucker to Sarah Polk, 5 October 1847, Polk Papers).

83. Elizabeth Bowman to Martha Ann Douglass, ca. 1845, Douglas-Maney Family Papers.

84. Ryan, *Women in Public*; S. G. Davis, *Parades and Power*; Wilentz, *Chants Democratic*.

85. Stephen A. Mrozowski and Mary C. Beaudry, in "Archaeology and the Landscape of Corporate Ideology," studied the nineteenth-century industrial village of Lowell, Massachusetts, to understand how landscape affects the production of a corporate ideology. In contrast to Lowell, where architecture was designed to make a unified corporate statement, Middle Tennessee's county seats were built in a more piecemeal fashion. As a result, ceremonial uses of town space were particularly important for fashioning communal identities.

86. See Chapter 3 for a description of an interesting exception to this rule. Upon completion of a new university building in Murfreesboro, black and white brickmasons paraded and picnicked together.

87. *Tennessee Democrat*, 20 November 1844.

88. Joanna Rucker to Sarah Polk, 5 October 1847, Polk Papers.

89. *Columbia Observer*, 27 June 1834,

90. *Columbia Observer*, 24 December 1839.

91. John Shofner to Michael Shofner, 22 October 1841, Shofner Papers.

92. Joanna Rucker to Sarah Polk, 5 October 1847, Polk Papers.

93. *Western Weekly Review*, 8 July 1831.

94. For descriptions of typical celebrations, see *Tennessee Democrat*, 30 June 1842; *Columbia Beacon*, 8 Jan. 1847; *Tennessee Democrat*, 13 October 1842; *Tennessee Democrat*, 12 October 1844; Joanna Rucker to Sarah Polk, 5 October 1847, Polk Papers.

95. *Tennessee Democrat*, 30 June 1842.

96. John Shofner to Michael Shofner, 29 November 1844, Shofner Papers, SHC.

97. John Spence describes the excitement and rituals of the election campaign in Murfreesboro in *Annals of Rutherford County*, 2:66–69. See the *Tennessee Democrat*, 9 November, 20 November, 19 December 1844 for election news in Columbia.

98. John Shofner to Michael Shofner, 29 November 1844, Shofner Papers.

99. Ryan, *Women in Public*; Davis, *Parades and Power*; Wilentz, *Chants Democratic*.

100. John Shofner to Michael Shofner, 29 November 1844, Shofner Papers.

101. Ibid.

102. Ibid.

103. Ryan, *Women in Public*, 19–57.

104. John Shofner to Michael Shofner, 29 November 1844, Shofner Papers. See Chapter 4 for a more extensive analysis of the role of women in constructing townscapes.

105. Ibid.

106. Ibid.

107. Quoted in *Tennessee Democrat*, 19 December 1844. Illuminations were popular forms of political demonstration in the mid-nineteenth century. Four years after Polk won the White House, he followed his hometown custom and lit up the presidential residence in honor of Zachary Taylor's victory. Back in Murfreesboro, Polk's neice,

Joanna Rucker, heard about her uncle's generous tribute to the success of the opposition. "A few days since it was reported here that the President had the White House brilliantly illuminated in honor of Gen. Taylor's election." She compared the response at the White House to Whig celebrations in Murfreesboro, the place where Polk had launched his political career: "The Whigs have carried on highly here with joy at their success," she informed her uncle. In particular, she mentioned that "they had quite a pretty illumination" (Joanna Rucker to Sarah Polk, 9 December 1848, Polk Papers).

108. Quoted in *Tennessee Democrat*, 9 November 1844.

109. *Tennessee Democrat*, 9 November 1844.

110. West, "Democratic and Whig Political Activists of Middle Tennessee," 7–8. West found that "Whig political activists tended to reside in the county seat more than the Democrats in counties which had not experienced significant economic development." And that Whigs and Democrats were equally represented in more prosperous county seats. His findings reveal some subtle differences in the patterns of political activism in town and in the country.

111. Spence, *Annals of Rutherford County*, 1:244.

Chapter Three

1. The following description is based on an event recorded by John Spence in his *Annals of Rutherford County*, 2:84–88. Union University was originally founded in 1842 in Somerville, a West Tennessee town where John Spence was a merchant from 1832 to 1847. He moved to Memphis for about two years before returning to Murfreesboro in 1849, about the same time that Union University was moved from Somerville to Murfreesboro. Spence suggests inaccurately that the event was the first cornerstone laying in Rutherford County.

2. Ibid., 2:84–88.

3. Probably the Murfreesboro Freemasons applied a procedure similar to one described in Albert G. Mackey's *Encyclopedia of Freemasonry and Kindred Sciences* (Chicago: Masonic History Company, 1929), 243: "The stone, when deposited in its appropriate place, is carefully examined with the necessary implements of Operative Freemasonry—the square, the level, and the plumb, themselves all symbolic in meaning—and is then declared to be 'well formed, true, and trusty.'"

4. 1850 manuscript census, Murfreesboro.

5. Barbara Myerhoff defines rites of passage as "a category of rituals that mark the passages of an individual through the life cycle, from one stage to another over time, from one role or social position to another, integrating the human and cultural experiences with biological destiny: birth, reproduction, and death" (Myerhoff, "Rites of Passage: Process and Paradox," in V. Turner, *Celebration*, 109). I am applying this concept to the larger life cycle of a community at its own moment of transition. Roger D. Abrahams elaborates a useful distinction between seasonal festivals, which "commonly take place on the plateaus of the year when in fact nothing important occurs," and rites of passage, which are organized in response "to the crises of the transitional events of life like birth, death, marriage, initiations, or physically moving on." Rites of passage provide "an organizing set of principles, traditional ways of momentarily binding the

opposing forces within the community and tying together the past with the present" (Abrahams, "The Language of Festivals: Celebrating the Economy," in V. Turner, *Celebration*, 167).

6. Columbia, Franklin, and Shelbyville also established impressive universities for male and female students during this period. This phenomenon is analyzed in greater detail in Chapters 4 and 5.

7. William Shelton to David Campbell, 1 March 1851, Campbell Family Papers, Duke University.

8. Virginia Shelton to her uncle, 4 May 1854, Campbell Family Papers.

9. William Shelton to David Campbell, 1 March 1851, Campbell Family Papers.

10. Spence, *Annals of Rutherford County*, 2:98–99.

11. Ibid.

12. Virginia Shelton to her uncle, 28 September 1851, Campbell Family Papers.

13. Virginia Shelton to her uncle and aunt, 7 December 1851, Campbell Family Papers. The Sheltons did not actually buy their piano in Nashville until two years later (see Virginia's letter to her uncle, 5 December 1853).

14. Edmund Cooper to Matthew Delamere Cooper, 16 January 1855, Cooper Family Papers, TSLA.

15. For the link between railroads and the building boom of the 1850s in Virginia and North Carolina, see Goldfield, *Urban Growth in the Age of Sectionalism*; and Catherine W. Bishir, "A Spirit of Improvement: Changes in Building Practice, 1830–1860," in Bishir, Brown, Lounsbury, and Wood, *Architects and Builders in North Carolina*, 130–92.

16. Anita Goodstein has described the 1850s in Whig-controlled Nashville as "a kind of watershed in city activity as the corporation also became involved in a public school system and, to a greater or lesser extent, in a fire department, a hospital, and a gasworks" (Goodstein, *Nashville*, 181). On a smaller scale, county seats also significantly increased their public investment in these services.

17. *Bedford Yeoman*, 20 April 1853; *Goodspeed Histories*, 753, 791–92.

18. *Shelbyville Expositor*, 10 December 1850.

19. Cleaveland, Backus, and Backus, *Village and Farm Cottages*, 46.

20. C. E. Clark, *American Family Home*, 15. In North Carolina, for example, beginning in the 1830s and cresting in the 1850s was a period of "such effective and widespread rebuilding that from these years, as from none before, buildings have endured by the hundreds to the present day" (Bishir, Brown, Lounsbury, and Wood, *Architects and Builders in North Carolina*, 135).

21. Virginia Shelton to her uncle, 4 May 1854, Campbell Family Papers.

22. Hincheyville did not begin to be fully developed until after the Civil War.

23. *Columbia Beacon*, 7 January, 21 January, 4 February 1848.

24. *Maury Press*, 7 March 1860. The definition of town resident did not always correspond to legal corporation boundaries. Often people who lived just outside town limits thought of themselves as county seat residents whether they paid city taxes or not. This attitude was also held by census takers, who interpreted town boundaries loosely. This is one of the reasons why town population totals are difficult to calculate from manuscript census returns.

25. Alfred Hamilton letters to his father John Hamilton in Lewistown, Pennsylvania, 28 November 1858, Hamilton Letters, TSLA.

26. Ibid.

27. Ibid.

28. *Maury Press*, 7 March 1860.

29. Ibid.

30. In her study of Philadelphia, Elizabeth Gray Kogen Spera found that specialization of retail space began in the late eighteenth century. Before 1800, she argues, urban space was already organized around separate, clearly distinguishable commercial, financial, manufacturing, and residential zones. See Spera, "Building for Business."

31. *Bedford Yeoman*, 12 October 1853.

32. From the reminiscences of Nathan Vaught, transcribed in Tinker, "Nathan Vaught, Master Builder."

33. Spence, *Annals of Rutherford County*, 2:123.

34. *Maury Press*, 4 April 1860.

35. *Maury Press*, 4 April 1861.

36. Tolbert, "Commercial Blocks and Female Colleges."

37. John Spence describes the creation in Murfreesboro of "Depot Hill" just after the arrival of the first train. The buildings were apparently constructed as blocks of warehouses. "The first [ware]house . . . was thirty feet wide, one hundred and fifty feet long, [and] one story" high; three subsequent two-story brick warehouses were built "one hundred and ten feet long" (Spence, *Annals of Rutherford County*, 2:102).

38. Stuart Blumin examines the development of urban retail centers specializing in nonmanual business interests of the middle class. See *Emergence of the Middle Class*, 83–107.

39. Spence, *Annals of Rutherford County*, 2:119–21.

40. Bushman, *Refinement of America*; Grier, *Culture and Comfort*.

41. Virginia Shelton to her aunt and uncle, 3 December 1850, Campbell Family Papers.

42. Virginia Shelton to her sister Fannie, 17 March 1851. Campbell Family Papers.

43. Virginia Shelton to her aunt and uncle, 3 December 1850, Campbell Family Papers.

44. Goffman, *Presentation of Self*, 106–40, on "Regions and Region Behavior."

45. Virginia Shelton to her uncle, 26 May 1851, Campbell Family Papers.

46. Virginia Shelton to her uncle, 28 September 1851, Campbell Family Papers.

47. Virginia Shelton to her aunt, 2 November 1851, Campbell Family Papers.

48. David Dickinson to his cousin, 12 April 1844, Douglas-Maney Family Papers, TSLA.

49. David Dickinson to his cousin, 12 April 1844, Douglas-Maney Family Papers.

50. *Maury Press*, 7 March 1860, emphasis mine.

51. See C. Clark, "Domestic Architecture as an Index to Social History"; and Herman, *Architecture and Rural Life in Central Delaware*. C. E. Clark, *American Family Home*, 15.

52. See especially John Kasson's chapter "Reading the City: The Semiotics of Everyday Life," in Kasson, *Rudeness and Civility*, 70–111. Kasson evaluates the ways

that nineteenth-century observers attempt to overcome "the enormous difficulty of reading the city at large and its inhabitants" (70). See also Upton "Another City." Upton identifies three "sublandscapes" composed of both artifactual and metaphorical elements through which urbanites made sense of the "conflicted and confusing . . . changes wrought by commerce and commercialism in the cultural landscape of the largest early republican cities" (62).

53. Feldberg, *Turbulent Era.*

54. These subjects are explored in greater depth in Part II, "Walking the Townscape."

55. McBride, "Oaklands"; Hughes, *Hearthstones,* 9–10.

56. Virginia Shelton to her aunt and uncle, 3 December 1850, Campbell Family Papers.

57. Virginia Shelton to her sister Fannie, 17 March 1851. Campbell Family Papers.

58. Virginia Shelton to her aunt and uncle, 6 June and 20 June 1855, Campbell Family Papers.

59. In 1854, Sarah, William, and D. H. Spence, "once trading under the name and style of Spence & Co.," sold town lot no. 69 to William Shelton. The 150-foot-square lot was on Vine Street beside the old city cemetery. The deed does not describe any structures that may have stood on the lot. It is difficult to determine whether this was the location of the Sheltons' "cottage"; there are no nineteenth-century structures remaining on this lot. Rutherford County Deed Book 7, p. 42.

60. Downing, *Cottage Residences, Rural Architecture and Landscape Gardening,* 31, 134. The term was not precise; in fact, Downing included plans for a "cottage villa" (89). An 1856 book of plans, addressed particularly to "mechanics and tradesmen of moderate circumstances, the small farmer, and the laboring man generally," focused on designs for a "humbler class of structures" than Downing's (Cleaveland, Backus, and Backus, *Village and Farm Cottages,* preface).

61. Virginia Shelton to her sister Margaret, 3 December 1850; and to her aunt and uncle, 3 December 1850, Campbell Family Papers.

62. Virginia Shelton to her uncle, 20 June 1855, Campbell Family Papers.

63. *Columbia Beacon,* 7 January 1848. During this period, wealthy Nashvillians built the fifth ward of the city into a segregated, elite neighborhood, " 'now decidedly the most beautiful and agreeable part of the city for private residences' " (Goodstein, *Nashville,* 122).

64. Virginia Shelton to her aunt and uncle, 3 December 1850, Campbell Family Papers. According to Anita Goodstein, turnpikes leading into Nashville became prominent residential sites. "As the city center grew more crowded, they began to build along the turnpikes elaborate homes that no longer aped town houses but were suited to more spacious lots" (Goodstein, *Nashville,* 122).

65. Virginia Shelton to her aunt and uncle, 3 December 1850, Campbell Family Papers.

66. Quoted in Tinker, "Nathan Vaught, Master Builder," 113–14.

67. Spence, *Annals of Rutherford County,* 2:114.

68. Ibid., 2:126.

69. Quoted in Tinker, "Nathan Vaught, Master Builder," 118. On 11 April 1860, the

Maury Press noted that "a beautiful block of three large stores is just completed on the square near Nelson's Hotel"—a reference to Vaught's project for William Dale.

70. In the 2 May 1860 issue of the *Maury Press*, an advertisement for new a furniture store in the corner building of W. J. Dale's new block on the north side of the public square includes a list of furniture for sale and advertises a related undertaking business.

71. *Maury Press*, 4 April 1860, contains a description of two new dry goods establishments on Main Street, "commenced sometime during the last fall."

72. My interpretation of the public square as a marketplace has been strongly influenced by the definition of medieval market squares as cultural intersections, as interpreted by Stallybrass and White (*Politics and Poetics of Transgression*, 27–28): "A marketplace is the epitome of local identity (often indeed it is what defined a place as more significant than surrounding communities) and the unsettling of that identity by the trade and traffic of goods from elsewhere." For public squares in Middle Tennessee, that "elsewhere" might be as nearby as a local county farm or as distant as Philadelphia or New Orleans, the two main sources of dry goods and groceries offered for sale by small-town merchants. At first glance, the public square appears to be the unambiguous heart of local identity. This, however, is deceiving because, as Stallybrass and White put it, the public square ultimately remained an intersection structurally dependent upon

remote processes of production and consumption, networks of communication, lines of economic force. As much a process of commercial convergence as an open space, the marketplace gives the illusion of independent identity, of being a self-sustaining totality, and this illusion is one of separateness and enclosure. . . . Thus in the marketplace "inside" and "outside" (and hence identity itself) are persistently mystified. It is a place where limit, centre and boundary are confirmed and yet also put in jeopardy. (27–28)

73. *Maury Press*, 20 June 1860.

74. Downing, *Cottage Residences*, 12–13.

75. Excerpt from the diary of Elvira Moore, 9–10 September 1854, published in the *Bedford County Historical Quarterly* 8, no. 2 (Summer 1982): 54–55.

76. Ibid. Four years earlier, the *Shelbyville Expositor* (10 December 1850) offered the following description of the courthouse site:

The Court House is a tolerable good building, but look at that old cedar fence that surrounds it, and which serves neither to ornament or protect, let us have that old fence taken down, and save it further trouble of falling, and surround it with a neat enclosure that will both serve to ornament and protect—then the Court House will look better—the town will look better, and the cows will be kept out of the yard—the trees will have an opportunity to grow, and the grass will flourish making it much more pleasant on a hot summer day."

Chapter Four

1. Virginia Shelton to her aunt, 15 May 1856, Campbell Family Papers. The house no longer stands. For a description and photograph, see Hughes, *Hearthstones*, 59.

2. Kate turned seventeen on 27 July 1859 (Carney Diary, SHC).

3. Carney Diary, 12 January 1859. Christie Anne Farnham found that walking became formalized as "a central part of the daily routine" in mid-nineteenth-century female colleges (*Education of the Southern Belle*, 126).

4. Carney Diary, 21 February 1859.

5. Ibid.

6. See *Murfreesboro News*, 2 February 1859, in which Neilson & Crichelow advertised their new partnership. Jordan & Elliot's dry goods store is also advertised in that issue of the *News*. Kate's father, Legrand Carney, had recently built a new building for his dry goods store on the Square. He had previously been a partner in one of the town's first drugstores. See *Murfreesborough Telegraph*, 13 November 1845.

7. Crockett's dry goods store is advertised in *Murfreesboro News*, 2 February 1859.

8. According to the *Murfreesboro News*, 2 February 1859 and 26 September 1860, Reed's Bookstore was on the south side of the public square. Reed described himself as a bookseller, stationer, and dealer in wallpapers, and sold everything from music and musical instruments—including violins, "accordeons," flutinas, guitars, banjoes, flutes, and "zitheras"—to chess and backgammon sets, dice, gold pens, inkstands, paperweights, razors, and "R. D. Reed's Superior Steel Pen."

9. Carney Diary, 19 March 1859.

10. The issue was originally defined in the classic article by Welter, "Cult of True Womanhood." Numerous subsequent studies have analyzed the mid-nineteenth-century redefinition of domesticity and femininity from diverse points of view; see Sklar, *Catharine Beecher*; and Douglas, *Feminization of American Culture*.

11. *Maury Press*, 26 September 1860.

12. Pope, "Preparation for Pedestals"; and Hickson, "Development of Higher Education for Women in the Antebellum South."

13. Carney Diary, 3 January 1859.

14. Population statistics in this chapter were calculated from 1850 manuscript census returns. In Shelbyville, women made up 51 percent of the total population, and 57 percent of women were younger than twenty. In Murfreesboro, women made up 49 percent of the population, and 53 percent of women were younger than twenty. In Columbia, women made up 52 percent of town population, and 59 percent of women were younger than twenty. In Franklin, women made up 52 percent of total town population, and 56 percent of women were younger than twenty.

15. In Shelbyville, 41 percent of all town women were slaves, and 59 percent of slave women were younger than twenty. In Murfreesboro, 48 percent of women were slaves, and 50 percent of slave women were younger than twenty. In Columbia, 40 percent of women were slaves, and 54 percent of slave women were younger than twenty. In Franklin, 45 percent of women were slaves, and 58 percent of slave women were younger than twenty.

16. The 1850 manuscript census returns for Murfreesboro list only one Bumpass family.

17. Carney Diary, 8 January, 21 April, 19 February 1859.

18. Carney Diary, 27 July 1859.

19. Virginia Shelton to her aunt, 9 January and 4 October 1851, Campbell Family Papers, Duke University.

20. Virginia Shelton to her sister Margaret, 3 December 1850, Campbell Family Papers.

21. Virginia Shelton to her aunt, 9 February 1851, Campbell Family Papers.

22. Virginia Shelton to her uncle, 29 May 1854, Campbell Family Papers.

23. Elizabeth Fox-Genovese analyses this household division of labor between managers and workers and the effect of life cycle on white women's responsibilities in *Within the Plantation Household*, 100–145. This division of labor between manager and servant was not necessarily unique to the South. Joan Hedrick examines the complex relationships between Harriet Beecher Stowe and the female servants she hired to help with housework—particularly in Cincinnati where some of these women were former or escaped slaves. See Hedrick, *Harriet Beecher Stowe*, 110–21.

24. Virginia Shelton to her uncle, 29 May 1854, Campbell Family Papers.

25. Virginia Shelton to her aunt, 22 February 1851, Campbell Family Papers.

26. Virginia Shelton to her aunt, 16 June 1853, Campbell Family Papers.

27. Virginia Shelton to her aunt, 4 October 1851, Campbell Family Papers.

28. John Shofner to Michael Shofner, 28 August 1834, original spelling, Shofner Papers.

29. John Shofner to Michael Shofner, 28 August 1834, original spelling, Shofner Papers, SHC.

30. *Western Freeman*, 4 June 1833.

31. Spence, *Annals of Rutherford County*, 1:240.

32. Edmund Cooper to William F. Cooper, 16 October 1842. Cooper Family Papers, TSLA.

33. Henry Cooper to Matthew Delamere Cooper, 26 April 1854, Cooper Family Papers.

34. *Murfreesboro News*, 2 February 1859.

35. Spence, *Annals of Rutherford County*, 2:107.

36. Alfred Hamilton to his father John Hamilton, 28 November 1858, Alfred Hamilton Letters, TSLA. Along the same theme, Leiper and Menefee, commission merchants near the railroad depot in Murfreesboro, offered fifty spinning wheels for sale in 1859 (*Murfreesboro News*, 2 February 1859).

37. Virginia Shelton to her aunt and uncle, 16 December 1850, Campbell Family Papers.

38. Virginia Shelton to her aunt, 23 December 1850, Campbell Family Papers.

39. Virginia Shelton to her sister Fannie, 17 March 1851, Campbell Family Papers.

40. Stansell, *City of Women*, 159.

41. Virginia Shelton to her aunt and uncle, 3 November 1850, Campbell Family Papers.

42. Virginia Shelton to her aunt, 2 November 1851, Campbell Family Papers.

43. Virginia Shelton to her uncle and aunt, 30 November 1851, Campbell Family Papers.

44. Virginia Shelton to her uncle, 24 November 1853, Campbell Family Papers.

45. Virginia Shelton to her uncle, 5 December 1853, Campbell Family Papers.

46. *Tennessee Herald*, 8 March 1823.

47. Kolodny, *Land Before Her*, 48.

48. Virginia Shelton to her sister Fannie, 17 March 1851, Campbell Family Papers.

49. Virginia Shelton to her uncle and aunt, 30 March 1852, Campbell Family Papers.

50. Virginia Shelton to her uncle, 22 March 1852, Campbell Family Papers.

51. Carney Diary, 3 March 1859.

52. Virginia Shelton to her uncle and aunt, 30 March 1852, Campbell Family Papers.

53. Ibid.

54. Carney Diary, 24 April 1859.

55. See, for example, Hale, *Flora's Interpreter, and Fortuna Flora*; and Ingram, *Flora Symbolica, or The Language & Sentiment of Flowers*.

56. Virginia Shelton to her uncle, 24 May 1856, Campbell Family Papers.

57. Carney Diary, 29 June 1859. Kate used her bouquets to make political statements when Union troops occupied Murfreesboro during the Civil War. She and a friend threw bouquets they had made to a group of Confederate prisoners marching under guard past her house. "An officer, ordered us to the house, but, contrary to military rules and regulations, we did not go until we got ready," she claimed. "Good many cursed us, when we hurrahed for Jeff Davis, John Morgan, and Beaureguard, but we heard very little of it until an old man that wanted to pick up our flowers that we had thrown to our soldiers and when we said he must not have them, because they were confederate flowers he cursed me, and kicked them." She added parenthetically, "An Officer, rode up and offered to buy one of my bouquets, (I suppose, as an insult). I told him, he could never get one for any consideration but, if he had been a Confederate soldier, he would be welcome. So the chap rode off." The language of flowers held powerful meanings for bouquet makers and recipients alike. Kate claimed that the soldiers threatened to burn down their house and she stayed up late, just in case, "but, seeing no prospect of a fire, went to bed, and slept very comfortably." Carney Diary, 7 May 1862.

58. Carney Diary, 15 August 1859. Hale, *Flora's Interpreter*, 25.

59. Virginia Shelton to her uncle and aunt, 7 December 1851, Campbell Family Papers.

60. Virginia Shelton to uncle and aunt, 30 March 1852, Campbell Family Papers.

61. Virginia Shelton to her uncle and aunt, 7 December 1851, Campbell Family Papers.

62. Virginia Shelton to uncle and aunt, 30 March 1852, Campbell Family Papers.

63. Carney Diary, 22 February 1859.

64. *Shelbyville Expositor*, 10 December 1850, emphasis in original.

65. Virginia Shelton to her uncle, 28 December 1851, Campbell Family Papers.

66. Edmund Cooper to William F. Cooper, 19 November 1843, Cooper Family Papers.

67. Ibid.

68. Matthew Delamere Cooper to William F. Cooper, 12 December 1835, Cooper Family Papers.

69. Duncan Brown Frierson to William F. Cooper, 12 January 1836, Cooper Family Papers.

70. From the "Reminiscences of Nathan Vaught" in Tinker, "Nathan Vaught, Master Builder," 111.

71. Horowitz, *Alma Mater*, 11.

72. Pope, "Preparation for Pedestals," 13.

73. Matthew Delamere Cooper to William F. Cooper, 12 December 1835, Cooper Family Papers.

74. Carney Diary; see entries for September 1859. While Kate was at school in Philadelphia, she took music lessons from a sister of her former music teacher at Soule (Carney Diary, 16 May 1860).

75. Pope, "Preparation for Pedestals," 30. For additional information about the mid-nineteenth-century trend toward higher education for women in the South, see Green, "Higher Education of Women in the South"; Hickson, "Development of Higher Education for Women in the Antebellum South"; and Clinton, *Plantation Mistress*, especially the chapter titled "Equally Their Due," 123–38.

76. *Western Freeman*, 6 March 1832.

77. Ibid.

78. Residents in all four county seats built female colleges during the 1850s: the Athenaeum and the Methodist Female College in Columbia; Soule College and Eaton Female College in Murfreesboro; the Franklin Female Institute; and the Shelbyville Female College, built in 1858 at a cost of $15,000 (*Goodspeed Histories*).

79. *Columbia Beacon*, 15 January 1847.

80. Tinker, "Nathan Vaught, Master Builder," 118.

81. *Murfreesboro News*, 2 February 1859.

82. Ibid. Eaton Female College in Murfreesboro also made "ample arrangements . . . for boarding in the Institution" (*Murfreesboro News*, 26 September 1860). By contrast, the Murfreesboro Military Academy, located in a building opposite the Methodist Female College in Murfreesboro, informed potential male students that boarding "can be had with private families on reasonable terms" (*Murfreesboro News*, 2 February 1859).

83. Manuscript census for Columbia, 1850.

84. *Maury Press*, 9 May 1860.

85. *Columbia Mirror*, 12 November 1857.

86. *Murfreesboro News*, 2 February 1859.

87. *Columbia Beacon*, 15 January 1847.

88. Hickson, "Development of Higher Education for Women in the Antebellum South," 79. Hickson discovered that the time and effort trustees spend on property management was second only to their responsibilities for managing school finances, but she simply interprets this as part of the evidence that female colleges were intended to be permanent institutions. On the other hand, Helen Lefkowitz Horowitz, in her book *Alma Mater*, offers thorough and insightful architectural analysis but considers female colleges in isolation rather than in the context of a townscape.

89. *Columbia Beacon*, 15 January 1847.

90. *Maury Intelligencer*, 4 January 1849.

91. *Maury Press*, 7 March 1860.

92. Tolbert, "Commercial Blocks and Female Colleges."

93. *Maury Press*, 7 March 1860.

94. The classic and controversial evaluation of this process is presented in Douglas, *Feminization of American Culture*. More recently, Carolyn Brucken explains "how gender was essential to the production of middle-class public space in antebellum America" in her analysis of the American luxury hotel (Brucken, "In the Public Eye," 203).

1. Edmund stopped clerking in 1837. See Edmund Cooper to William Cooper, 20 March 1837, Cooper Family Papers, TSLA.

2. See Berlin and Gutman, "Natives and Immigrants, Free Men and Slaves," 1192: "As expanding centers of commerce, every Southern city housed a small army of clerks—young, generally unmarried men who boarded together and aspired to counting houses of their own. In overwhelming proportions, these young men had been born in the South [rather than in the North or Europe], and (given the growth of Southern cities) probably in the countryside. . . . Thus, differences between those who labored in clerical, commercial occupations and manual, industrial ones were compounded by distinctions of nationality throughout the urban South." They argue that most immigrants were skilled laborers, and most menial work was performed by slaves. Hierarchies of labor were based on color, status, and nativity.

3. Matthew Delamere Cooper to William F. Cooper, 22 November 1842, Cooper Family Papers.

4. Edmund Cooper to William F. Cooper, 24 July 1837, Cooper Family Papers.

5. Edmund Cooper to William F. Cooper, 12 October 1836, Cooper Family Papers.

6. Spence, *Annals of Rutherford County*, 1:157.

7. Queensware was a popular, mass-produced earthenware.

8. Spence, *Annals of Rutherford County*, 1:157, 241.

9. Matthew Delamere Cooper to William F. Cooper, 17 January 1844, Cooper Family Papers.

10. Duncan Brown Frierson to William F. Cooper, 31 December 1834, Cooper Family Papers. John Spence also makes much of the indignities of shoe fitting before the development of standard sizing (Spence, *Annals of Rutherford County*, 1:158–59, 249).

11. Matthew Delamere Cooper to William F. Cooper, 1 November 1836, Cooper Family Papers.

12. His uncle left town to fight in the Indian wars in Florida.

13. Edmund Cooper to William F. Cooper, 14 November 1835, Cooper Family Papers.

14. Edmund Cooper to William F. Cooper, 16 January 1836, Cooper Family Papers.

15. Edmund Cooper to William F. Cooper, 20 March 1836, Cooper Family Papers. John Spence describes comparable uniforms—"blue cloth coat and pants, eagle buttons, white vest and black stock, white plume, red top, white pants for summer"—worn by the Murfreesboro Sentinels about 1825 (*Annals of Rutherford County*, 1:230).

16. Population statistics in this chapter were calculated from 1850 manuscript census returns. In Shelbyville, 74 percent of residents were under thirty, and 49 percent were male (790 men). In Franklin, 75 percent of residents were under thirty. In Murfreesboro, 72 percent of residents were under thirty. In Columbia, 74 percent of residents were under thirty.

17. The following calculations show the total male population for each town, including slaves and free men: Shelbyville, 790 men (49 percent of the population), 222 between the ages of ten and twenty-one (28 percent of male residents); Franklin, 744 men (48 percent of the population), 211 between the ages of ten and twenty-one (28 percent of men); Murfreesboro, 1,097 men (51 percent of the population), 128 between

the ages of ten and twenty-one (30 percent of men); Columbia, 1,197 men (48 percent of the population), 349 between the ages of ten and twenty-one (29 percent of men).

18. Joseph F. Kett uses the term "semidependence" to describe "the status of youth aged 10 to 21 in the early part of the nineteenth century" (*Rites of Passage*, 29). The age boundaries of this life stage were acknowledged by contemporaries like Silas Felton of Massachusetts, who said he spent his evenings either reading or "roving about . . . which is generally the case with boys 10 to 21 years old" (ibid., 40–41). More recently, E. Anthony Rotundo has examined middle-class boyhood as "a distinct cultural world with its own rituals and its own symbols and values. As a social sphere, it was separate both from the domestic world of women, girls, and small children and from the public world of men and commerce. In this social space of their own, boys were able to play outside the rules of the home and the marketplace" ("Boy Culture: Middle-Class Boyhood in Nineteenth-Century America," in Carnes, *Meanings for Manhood*, 15).

19. Nicholson, "Reminiscences of an Octogenarian," 16.

20. In Shelbyville, 33 percent of male residents were slaves, and 62 percent of male slaves were younger than twenty (54 percent of white males were younger than twenty). In Franklin, 40 percent of male residents were slaves, and 59 percent of male slaves were younger than twenty (53 percent of white males were younger than twenty). In Murfreesboro, 42 percent of male residents were slaves, and 54 percent of male slaves were younger than twenty (45 percent of white males were younger than twenty). In Columbia, 36 percent of male residents were slaves, and 58 percent of male slaves were younger than twenty (49 percent of white males were younger than twenty).

21. Number of male slaves between the ages of ten and twenty-one: Shelbyville, 86 (33 percent of slave men); Franklin, 89 (30 percent of slave men); Murfreesboro, 128 (28 percent of slave men); Columbia, 130 (30 percent of slave men).

22. Edmund Cooper to William Cooper, 16 December 1836, Cooper Family Papers.

23. See Chapter 6, "Small-Town Slaves," for a deeper examination of the distinctive experience of both male and female slaves in a small-town context.

24. E. C. to William F. Cooper, 5 March 1838, Cooper Family Papers.

25. From the reminiscences of Nathan Vaught, transcribed in Tinker, "Nathan Vaught, Master Builder," 96.

26. Quoted in Tinker, "Nathan Vaught, Master Builder," 97.

27. Tinker, "Nathan Vaught, Master Builder," 99.

28. Quoted in Tinker, "Nathan Vaught, Master Builder," 101–2.

29. *Tennessee Democrat*, 4 August, 9 December, 23 December 1841.

30. Daniel Walker Howe points out the significance of political oration during the Whig-Jacksonian period, describing the oratory as "a species of oral literature" and "a form of entertainment in the courthouse-centered county seats." Beyond literature and entertainment, rhetorical ability was crucial in a republic where free men had to be persuaded rather than coerced. See *Political Culture of the American Whigs*, 25–27.

31. Edmund Cooper to William F. Cooper, 12 October 1836, Cooper Family Papers.

32. Edmund Cooper to William F. Cooper, 14 August 1842, Cooper Family Papers.

33. Phillip P. Nelson to Mr. William N. Beals, 20 September 1849, Phillip P. Nelson Papers, TSLA. Unfortunately, Nelson was not living in Murfreesboro when the 1850 census was taken.

34. Virginia Shelton to her aunt, 26 May 1851, Campbell Family Papers, Duke University.

35. Virginia Shelton to her aunt, 2 November 1851, Campbell Family Papers.

36. Virginia Shelton to her aunt and uncle, 8 January and 18 January 1852, Campbell Family Papers. Probably the young women were boarding with the Sheltons because the rooms at the local female college were not yet finished. Soule Female College opened in 1853.

37. Virginia Shelton to her aunt and uncle, 14 October 1853, Campbell Family Papers.

38. John B. McEwen to David Campbell, 3 February 1822, Pope Family Papers, TSLA.

39. Laurie, " 'Nothing on Compulsion,' " 343. Laurie describes this as "the syncopated rhythm of the economy" in antebellum Philadelphia.

40. In her reminiscences, Caroline Nicholson describes an exhilarating bustle of activity in Columbia as renters, including herself, changed households around New Year's Day, "when the usual changes took place among renters" ("Reminiscences of an Octogenarian," 22). New Year's Day held different meanings for slaves. It was typically considered the major hiring and auction day by slaveowners, who negotiated yearly work contracts. Harriet Jacobs emphasized the trauma the holiday presented for slave families who became separated as members were sold or hired away (*Incidents in the Life of a Slave Girl*, 15–16).

41. Quoted in Tinker, "Nathan Vaught, Master Builder," 100.

42. In North Carolina, artisans routinely ranged over two or three counties seeking work, and town artisans frequently turned to rural jobs. This artisans' circuit expanded with the railroad. In fact, Jacob Holt, housebuilding counterpart to Nathan Vaught, had business across a nine-county region. See Bishir, Brown, Lounsbury, and Wood, *Architects and Builders in North Carolina*, 103, 147–48; Bishir, "Jacob W. Holt."

43. Quoted in Tinker, "Nathan Vaught, Master Builder," 107.

44. Quoted in ibid., 112.

45. M. D. Cooper to his brother Robert M. Cooper, 22 April 1833, Cooper Family Papers.

46. Ibid.

47. *Daily Republican Banner*, 25 April 1838.

48. Vance, *Merchant's World*.

49. Nicholson, "Reminiscences of an Octogenarian," 6, SHC.

50. Spence, *Annals of Rutherford County*, 1:236.

51. Nicholson, "Reminiscences of an Octogenarian," 24.

52. Edmund Cooper to William F. Cooper, 1 August 1842, Cooper Family Papers.

53. Edmund Cooper to William F. Cooper, 14 August 1842, Cooper Family Papers.

54. *The Agriculturist*, 146.

55. Rorabaugh, *Craft Apprentice*.

56. Temperance was the most popular reform movement in the South between the 1820s and the 1860s. The Sons of Temperance was one of the largest, most popular fraternal organizations in the region during the 1840s and 1850s. See Schultz, "Temperance Reform in the Antebellum South," 332.

57. *Western Freeman*, 12 June 1835.

58. Carney Diary, 14 January 1859, SHC.

59. Carney Diary, 28 January 1859.

60. Carney Diary, 11 February 1859.

61. Carney Diary, 11 May 1859.

62. On 18 January 1859, Kate described her sister's wedding, "the parlor is pretty well filled, and I think before the night was [over] many had taken *to much* [*sic*] to drink. . . . Good many of them remained all night here." The next day Kate continued her account of the celebration. "Today is Sister Mary's reception, and nearly all of the girls have some complaint. Fannie Wilson and I were very sick, and when we got up had to return to bed again and remain in there until about one o'clock, when we dressed and went down in the parlor." Serenaders performed in the hall that evening. Carney Diary, 18–19 January 1859.

63. For a discussion of drinking as a male custom, see Wyatt-Brown, *Southern Honor*, 278–81.

64. Edmund Cooper to William F. Cooper, 16 January 1836, Cooper Family Papers.

65. Edmund Cooper to William F. Cooper, 1 August 1842, Cooper Family Papers.

66. Spence, *Annals of Rutherford County*, 1:57.

67. This transformation is efficiently summarized in P. E. Johnson, *Shopkeeper's Millineum*, 55–61, quote on 56.

68. Stanley Schultz found scattered evidence of black temperance societies, including the Richmond African Society and a temperance society among slaves in Raleigh, North Carolina. In a few cases temperance societies were apparently integrated. See Schultz, "Temperance Reform in the Antebellum South," 335–36. This pattern may have been more common in antebellum southern cities with larger free black populations. See Chapter 6, "Small-Town Slaves," for further exploration of the distinctions between small-town and urban slavery.

69. 1850 manuscript census of Columbia.

70. *Maury Intelligencer*, 26 April 1849. According to the *Columbia Beacon*, 7 January 1847, the Sons of Temperance had a "hall" in the courthouse.

71. In northern cities, temperance reform was heavily imbued with class and ethnic concerns. Ultimately, temperance reform was also part of a broad national effort to constrain young men in changing economic and educational systems. See P. E. Johnson, *Shopkeeper's Millennium*; Allmendinger, *Paupers and Scholars*; Horlick, *Country Boys and Merchant Princes*.

72. Virginia Shelton to her uncle, 28 September 1851, Campbell Family Papers.

73. Carney Diary, 3 August 1859.

74. Duncan Brown Frierson to William F. Cooper, 12 January 1836, Cooper Family Papers.

75. *Maury Press*, 7 March 1860.

76. Matthew Delamere Cooper to William, 18 January 1837, Cooper Family Papers.

77. Nathan Vaught did "a quantity of work for the Jackson College Building" in 1859, but he did not specify whether this work chiefly involved repairs to an aging building or enlargements. Quoted in Tinker, "Nathan Vaught, Master Builder," 118.

78. Carney Diary, 9 March 1859.

79. Garrett, "The Burning of Jackson College," in *"Hither and Yon"*, 7–8.

80. Virginia Shelton to her aunt, 23 December 1850, Campbell Family Papers.

81. The Masons declared that the college was certainly "not a shanty." On the contrary, it was "a magnificent edifice,—about 140 feet in length, 40 in breadth, and three stories high. It is furnished with an excellent apparatus, and a library of about 2,000 volumes, independent of the libraries belonging, to the respective literary societies" (*Maury Intelligencer*, 4 January 1849).

82. *Maury Intelligencer*, 7 June 1849.

83. Pittard, "Union: Murfreesboro's Other University," 39–40. See Novak, *Rights of Youth*, for a discussion of student-faculty conflicts in early-nineteenth-century colleges.

84. *Maury Press*, 2 May 1860.

85. *Maury Press*, 30 May 1860.

Chapter Six

1. Henry's routine has been reconstructed from testimony given in the Middle Tennessee Supreme Court trial, *Henry, A Slave v. State of Tennessee*.

2. Henry's murder trial is analyzed in greater depth in the section titled "Murder, Theft, Arson, and Suspicion: Law and Order in the Townscape of Slavery." See also Tolbert, "Murder in Franklin."

3. For a history and provenance of the Doyle house, see Bowman, *Historic Williamson County*, 140–41.

4. According to the 1850 census, there were two Ragsdales in Franklin: Robert, a thirty-two-year-old shoemaker who owned nine slaves, and William, a twenty-one-year-old cabinetmaker who owned one slave. It is not clear which shop served as venue for the card game.

5. Middle Tennesseans often referred to members of the Church of Christ as Campbellites after the founder of the group, Alexander Campbell.

6. This was the testimony of J. L. Littleton at Henry's murder trial. See *Henry, A Slave v. State of Tennessee*.

7. Jacobs, *Incidents in the Life of a Slave Girl*, 35.

8. Ibid., 29.

9. Ibid.

10. Ibid., 97.

11. Vlach, *Back of the Big House*. Genovese, *Roll Jordan, Roll*. Rhys Isaac argues that the communal ethos of the slave quarter presented a sharp contrast by the end of the eighteenth century to the increasingly privatized dwellings of slave owners. See Isaac, *Transformation of Virginia, 1740–1790*.

12. Brown and Kimball, "Mapping the Terrain of Black Richmond"; David R. Goldfield, "Black Life in Old South Cities," in Campbell, *Before Freedom Came*, 123–53; Tyler-McGraw and Kimball, *In Bondage and Freedom*; Berlin, *Slaves Without Masters*; Wade, *Slavery in the Cities*; Starobin, *Industrial Slavery in the Old South*.

13. Goodstein, *Nashville*, 72.

14. Lamon, *Blacks in Tennessee*, 116, table. In 1800, there were 8,074 slaves, in a population that totaled 32,183. The slave population rose steadily, so that by 1850 there were 133,159 slaves in a total population of 483,179. By the mid-nineteenth century, one third of the population in Bedford County were slaves. Rutherford and Maury Counties

were more than 40 percent slave; and more than half the population of Williamson County was in bondage. See Ash, *Middle Tennessee Society Transformed*.

15. The population and wealth of Middle Tennessee were concentrated in the Central Basin counties around Nashville. In 1860, the population of Bedford County was 30 to 39 percent slave; Maury and Rutherford counties were 40 to 49 percent slave; and Williamson was 50 to 64 percent slave. See Ash, *Middle Tennessee Society Transformed*, 8, map.

16. County seats typically built shed-like market houses on the public square, which many residents complained were in disrepair at the time of the Civil War. Slaves and other property were sold at public auction in local market houses, but these dilapidated structures could not compare to the urban markets of Memphis, Richmond, or New Orleans, designed exclusively for the slave trade. In Murfreesboro, the market house was built on the north side of the Square near the public well in 1815 and enlarged in 1830. It was the "common place of auction sales by constables, sheriffs, etc., of negroes and other property" (*Goodspeed Histories of Maury, Williamson, Rutherford, Wilson, Bedford, & Marshall Counties of Tennessee*, 818).

17. From the reminiscences of Nathan Vaught, transcribed in Tinker, "Nathan Vaught, Master Builder," 129–30.

18. 1830 census. Total population in Franklin was 1,318.

19. Calculated from 1850 manuscript census. Thirty-nine percent of Columbia residents were slaves; 37 percent of Shelbyville residents were slaves.

20. Richard Wade found that slave women far outnumbered slave men in antebellum cities (*Slavery in the Cities*, 23–25). Ira Berlin discovered a similar pattern among free blacks; in nineteenth-century southern cities, African American women outnumbered African American men by a widening margin (*Slaves Without Masters*, 151, 177). In Middle Tennessee, Anita Goodstein found relative sexual equilibrium in antebellum Nashville: "Although black women outnumbered black men in every census tally from 1830 to 1860, the imbalance was not great, and it was physically easier in the city to contract marriages across slave owners' property lines" (*Nashville*, 139).

21. Calculated from the 1850 manuscript census. In Columbia, 56 percent of slaves were younger than twenty; in Murfreesboro, 52 percent; in Shelbyville, 60 percent. By comparison, most household servants in America before 1870 were in their teens and twenties, and those younger than fifteen may have represented as much as 15 percent of the total servant force. See Sutherland, *Americans and Their Servants*, 53.

22. Carney Diary, 15 February 1859, SHC.

23. Carney Diary, 3 January 1859.

24. According to Berlin and Gutman ("Natives and Immigrants, Free Men and Slaves," 1185): "As a general rule, urban slaves appear to have toiled in either the most backward sector of the economy as domestic servants and day laborers or in the most advanced sector of the economy as factory hands."

25. Population statistics were calculated from the 1850 manuscript census returns for Murfreesboro, Franklin, Shelbyville and Columbia. Free blacks in Franklin included twelve women and sixteen men. Free blacks also constituted only 1 percent of the total population in the other three county seats. Twenty free blacks lived in Murfreesboro, fourteen women and six men; twenty-two in Shelbyville, nine women and thirteen men;

and twenty-six in Columbia, sixteen women and ten men. The small free black presence in Middle Tennessee county seats is consistent with population patterns described by Ira Berlin (*Slaves Without Masters*, 181). He found that in the Lower South free blacks gravitated toward cities, while in the Upper South free blacks remained primarily rural peasants.

26. In 1860, as much as 18 percent of the total black population of Nashville was free (Goodstein, *Nashville*, 137).

27. Richard Wade has argued that racially mixed residence patterns were common throughout slavery and that "the purpose of this residential mixture was not, of course, to integrate the community but rather to prevent the growth of a cohesive Negro society. Local authorities used every available weapon to keep the blacks divided; housing was simply the physical expression of this racial policy" (*Slavery in the Cities*, 75). According to Ira Berlin, class was a greater determinant of residence than race, but segregation was creating black ghettos on the eve of the Civil War, particularly among free blacks: "Even within the context of the limited residential segregation of Southern cities, free Negroes were living farther apart from whites than were slaves." Though residential segregation was more pronounced in northern cities, the total degree of racial segregation in southern cities was obscured by varying degrees of intraward segregation. See Berlin, *Slaves Without Masters*, 252–57 (quote on 257). For analysis of the trend toward racial segregation in a northern city during the mid-nineteenth century, see Nash, *Forging Freedom*.

28. Goodstein, *Nashville*, 141. Ira Berlin notes that southern cities lagged far behind northern cities in the development of residential segregation. Although free blacks increasingly chose, or were compelled, to live in racially segregated districts within cities, there were few urban counterparts in the South to Boston's "Nigger Hill," Pittsburgh's "Hayti," and Cincinnati's "Little Africa" (*Slaves Without Masters*, 255).

29. See Schweninger, *From Tennessee Slave to St. Louis Entrepreneur*, for a free black's perspective on antebellum Nashville.

30. See Nash, *Forging Freedom*. Gregg D. Kimball found that skilled free blacks used architecture to distinguish themselves from unskilled blacks. The former lived in better neighborhoods and nicer houses. See "African-Virginians and the Vernacular Building Tradition," 125.

31. Edmund Cooper to William F. Cooper, 16 October 1842, Cooper Family Papers, TSLA1.

32. Changes in the legal status of slaves in Tennessee during this period are explained in Howington, " 'Not in the Condition of a Horse or an Ox.' " Howington emphasizes "the erratic quality of Tennessee manumission legislation," which was produced by "tension between the demands of the law and the demands of social control" (261). In 1842, the legislature modified their 1831 position somewhat by giving the county courts power to decide on a case-by-case basis whether to admit newly freed slaves as residents. In 1849, the legislature returned to the 1831 restrictions. In 1854, they required newly freed slaves to emigrate to Liberia.

33. Spence, *Annals of Rutherford County*, 2:46–47.

34. Goodstein, *Nashville*, 137–38.

35. Calculated from 1850 manuscript census. The complete figures are as follows: in Murfreesboro, 77 percent of households owned slaves (163 total households, 125 slave-

holding); in Columbia, 52 percent (297 total households, 155 slaveholding); in Shelby-ville, 51 percent (174 total households, 89 slaveholding); in Franklin: 68 percent (176 total households; 119 slaveholding). In *Middle Tennessee Society Transformed*, Stephen Ash estimated only 24 percent of "town families" in Middle Tennessee owned slaves in 1860 (see Table 2, "Residence by Slaveholding, 1860"). During the 1850s, the slave population increased, although at a slower rate than that of the white population. In Murfreesboro, slaves had dropped to 41 percent of the population by 1860. Neverthe-less, it seems unlikely that the proportion of slaveowners should have declined as dramatically as Ash's figures suggest. Ash's calculations were based on a random sample that included residents of towns other than county seats. He used a quantitative definition of town population with no reference to the landscape or actual town bound-aries. It is possible that slaveholding was more widespread in these four towns because the counties surrounding Nashville were the wealthiest in the region.

36. Under Tennessee law, freed slaves had to agree to leave the state for their new status to take effect. Families who did not wish to be split up often found it safer to hold members as slaves rather than to free them.

37. Calculated from the 1850 manuscript census: in Murfreesboro, 28 percent of slaveholders owned only 1 or 2 slaves; in Columbia, 31 percent; in Shelbyville, 33 percent; in Franklin, 42 percent.

38. Vlach, *Back of the Big House*, 12; John Michael Vlach, "Plantation Landscapes of the Antebellum South," in Campbell, *Before Freedom Came*, 25.

39. Westview is described in Ash, *Middle Tennessee Society Transformed*, 19; and Bowman, *Historic Williamson County*, 6–8. For descriptions of Middle Tennessee plantation houses, see also Patrick, *Architecture in Tennessee*; R. Smith, *Majestic Middle Tennessee*; and J. F. Smith, *White Pillars*. These sources provide little information about the slave world on these plantations.

40. Rural slave communities had a set of limitations different from their urban and small-town counterparts. Peter Kolchin has identified several factors that constrained the formation of slave communities in the countryside: the presence of most slaveown-ers on farms and plantations; the relatively small size of most farms, which curtailed interactions among slaves; slaves' lack of economic self-sufficiency and consequent dependence on owners; and the lack of newly imported Africans. See "Reevaluating the Antebellum Slave Community," 579–601.

41. By 1860, only 12 percent of Middle Tennessee farms grew cotton, mostly on a small scale for cash or home use (Ash, *Middle Tennessee Society Transformed*, 18). See also Gray, *History of Agriculture in the Southern United States*; B. H. Clark, *Tennessee Yeomen*; and Hilliard, *Hog Meat and Hoecake*.

42. Ash, *Middle Tennessee Society Transformed*, 10, 14–15.

43. B. H. Clark, *Tennessee Yeomen*, 28, Table I. Clark found that 57 percent of farming heads of household in the Central Basin owned no slaves, based on calculations from the 1850 and 1860 census schedules (41). These results are substantiated in Ash, *Middle Tennessee Society Transformed*, 15, Table II.

44. See the Chapter 2 section entitled "Main Streets and Turnpikes: The Ambiguous Borders of Town and Countryside" for further discussion of this six-mile radius of town influence.

45. Jacobs, *Incidents in the Life of a Slave Girl*, 87.

46. Ibid., 89.

47. Nicholson, "Memoirs," 245–46.

48. Carney Diary, 12 January 1859.

49. "An Ordinance in Relation to Slaves," published in the Shelbyville newspaper, *Western Freeman*, 17 December 1833, suggests that some slaves may have been living in separate households, unsupervised by whites. According to section 2 of the ordinance:

"It shall not, hereafter, be lawful for any slave or slaves to occupy or reside in any house or houses within said corporation, unless he, she or they shall have been actually hired by and be then in the bona fide employ of some white person or persons within the corporation aforesaid."

50. In Berlin's view, segregation grew "anywhere they [whites] felt the need to substitute physical space for social distance as a means of maintaining their racial hegemony" (*Slaves Without Masters*, 326). Segregation was most common where racial roles had become confused. Throughout the antebellum period, social distance was an effective means of maintaining racial hegemony for white small-town residents.

51. Carney Diary, 25 May 1859.

52. Carney Diary, 29 April 1859.

53. Carney Diary, 3 May 1859.

54. Spence, *Annals of Rutherford County*, 1:193.

55. Ibid., 2:1.

56. Quoted in Fowler, "Stories and Legends of Maury County," 118.

57. Nicholson, "Reminiscences of an Octogenarian," 16, SHC.

58. Spence, *Annals of Rutherford County*, 1:99.

59. Virginia Shelton to her aunt and uncle, 8 January 1852, Campbell Family Papers, Duke University.

60. Virginia Shelton to her uncle and aunt, 30 March 1852, Campbell Family Papers.

61. Carney Diary, 22 February 1859.

62. Virginia Shelton to her aunt, 9 February 1851, Campbell Family Papers.

63. The close intertwining of slave and free lives is powerfully documented by a wedding that took place in the Carney household in Union-occupied Murfreesboro. Kate's father was on his way home after spending a month in a Nashville jail as a prisoner of war, and the family was celebrating—but not simply his return. As her mother went to the depot to meet her father's train, Kate stayed at home, "very busy preparing the table for Nicies wedding supper (she is an old family servant that is to be married)." Indeed, Nicie was married by her own preacher in the same house where Kate's sister had wed a prosperous physician and plantation owner before the war. "The table was set in our dining room, and quite a pretty one too it was. She was married in the front hall, by Uncle Brack, their colored preacher. Every thing passed off very nicely." Slave and free guests participated together in a double celebration—the return of the master and the wedding of the servant. Carney Diary, 10 May 1862.

64. The anthropologist Susan Kent interprets spatial segmentation as an expression of power relationships and cultural complexity; see "A Cross-Cultural Study of Segmentation, Architecture, and the Use of Space," in *Domestic Architecture and the Use of Space*, 127–52. John Brinckerhoff Jackson notes that the segmentation of domestic space is still based largely on social class: "The working-class house has been largely immune to the appeal of the monofunctional space." In Jackson's view, the most striking

difference between elite and working-class houses is the elaborate, formalized apparatus for hospitality in the former ("The House in the Vernacular Landscape," in Conzen, *Making of the American Landscape*, 367–68). See also Lefebvre, *Production of Space*.

65. Gregg Kimball describes the kitchen as an integration of slave housing and work space in southern cities, "African-Virginians and the Vernacular Building Tradition," 126.

66. Virginia Shelton to her uncle, 6 June 1855, Campbell Family Papers.

67. Elizabeth Fox-Genovese argues that house girls grew up removed from the slave community, especially when white families lived much of year in towns (*Within the Plantation Household*, 153). This point of view overlooks the existence of a small-town slave community.

68. Quoted in Fowler, "Stories and Legends of Maury County," 118.

69. Carney Diary, 11 February 1859.

70. Carney Diary, 12 June 1859.

71. *Western Weekly Review*, 14 March 1851.

72. Virginia Shelton to her aunt and uncle, 18 November 1850, Campbell Family Papers.

73. Virginia Shelton to her uncle and aunt, 21 December 1851, Campbell Family Papers.

74. Virginia Shelton to her aunt and uncle, 18 November, 3 December, and 23 December 1850, Campbell Family Papers.

75. Virginia Shelton to her aunt and uncle, 7 December 1851, Campbell Family Papers. It is interesting to note that the Sheltons began soliciting new servants in December. Traditionally, yearly hiring took place on New Year's Day.

76. Virginia Shelton to her uncle and aunt, 21 December 1851, Campbell Family Papers.

77. Ibid.

78. This pattern of slave families working together in the same small-town households is also supported by Harriet Jacobs's experience in Edenton, North Carolina. Jacobs lived in the Norcum household with members of her own family, including her brother John and her aunt Betty, who "supplied the place of both housekeeper and waiting maid to her mistress" (Jacobs, *Incidents in the Life of a Slave Girl*, 12).

79. Virginia Shelton to her aunt and uncle, 18 November 1850, Campbell Family Papers. Perhaps adolescent African Americans used small-town hiring practices to gain some independence from their parents.

80. *Henry, A Slave v. State of Tennessee.*

81. Virginia Shelton to her uncle and aunt, 8 January 1852, Campbell Family Papers.

82. Gary Nash argues that carting—movement of commodities—was critically important to the antebellum urban economy. Furthermore, carters gained knowledge of streets and neighborhoods, and connections with local merchants; see *Forging Freedom*, 150. See also Hodges, *New York City Cartmen*.

83. Marie Tyler-McGraw and Gregg D. Kimball have said it well: "To think of segregation and integration in terms of physical separation is to miss much of the reality of the antebellum South" (*In Bondage and Freedom*, 10).

84. See also *Western Weekly Review*, 2 January 1852, for a description of a seemingly impromptu gathering of slaves at the Franklin Market House:

The "niggers" had a grand time of it Tuesday afternoon in our market house. It was raining hard, and about one hundred of them, in the full enjoyment of all the Christmas holiday, assembled in that public place, and such a shooting of squibs, such yells of delight, such hearty guffaus, and such uproarious jolity has rarely been witnessed upon our public square. The holidays are now past, and they will have no opportunity—so many of them—to show their handsome ivories for another twelve months. Let 'em glide.

85. *National Vidette*, 10 January 1828.

86. Quote is from trial transcript, *Henry, A Slave vs. State of Tennessee*. A Nashville newspaper described Barham as a member of the Odd Fellows and Eelbeck as "a Mason and a Son of Temperance" (*Daily Centre-State American*, 2 March 1850).

87. This reconstruction of events is based on testimony contained in the transcript, *Henry, A Slave v. State of Tennessee*. Henry was specifically tried for Eelbeck's murder. It is unclear whether Barham's murder was tried separately or not. The Eelbecks were more prominent residents than the Barhams. The coach maker Henry Eelbeck employed four skilled laborers and owned five slaves. By comparison, the grocer Levi N. Barham owned no slaves. An ad in the *Western Weekly Review*, 21 December 1849, described L. N. Barham & Co. as a "family grocery," selling pecans, lead and shot, castor oil, ground pepper, mackerel, rice, and loaf sugar—rather than liquor. The store also housed the business of a free black barber, Martin Scott. Scott announced the opening of his barber shop "in the frame house on Indigo street, immediately in the rear of L. N. Barham's Grocery" (*Western Weekly Review*, 25 October 1850). Like other "respectable" young small-town men (see Chapter 5), Barham and Eelbeck were apparently living in the store and may have clerked there. According to an early report of the murders in the *Daily Republican Banner and Nashville Whig* (26 February 1850), "It is supposed that the store in which they [Barham and Eelbeck] slept, belonging to young Barham, was attacked by robbers, and that the young men pursuing them, were killed."

88. News from the Franklin *Western Weekly Review* quoted in the Nashville *Daily Centre-State American*, 2 March 1850; also *Daily Republican Banner and Nashville Whig*, 4 March 1850.

89. The following newspapers contain articles about Henry's trial and execution: (Nashville) *Daily American*, 21 February, 22 February 1851; *Nashville Daily True Whig*, 13 January, 21 February, 22 February 1851; *Daily Republican Banner and Nashville Whig*, 26 February, 4 March 1850, 22 February 1851; *Nashville True Whig and Weekly Commercial Register*, 6 December 1850, 28 February 1851; (Franklin) *Western Weekly Review*, 15 November, 29 November 1850, 10 January, 21 February, 28 February 1851.

90. For example, Harriet Jacobs reports that in response to the Turner rebellion, whites rioted in Edenton, North Carolina (hundreds of miles from Southampton, Virginia); black residents were indiscriminately whipped and beaten, their property destroyed, and a black church was demolished (*Incidents in the Life of a Slave Girl*, 63–68).

91. *Western Weekly Review*, 29 November 1950.

92. Henry was executed in Nashville, along with another slave named Moses who had been convicted of murdering his master. The *Daily American*, 22 February 1851, reported that "the gallows [were] erected upon the Murfreesboro turnpike, about two

miles from the square. . . . An immense concourse had gathered to witness the execution." The two condemned men received last rites from a Catholic priest. "After the cords were adjusted, one of the negroes (we could not learn which) addressed the crowd as follows: 'Gentlemen, I am innocent. Gentlemen, you are hanging an innocent man. In all my life and fights dis hand never had any blood in it.'" For descriptions of the execution and identification of Henry as the man who addressed the crowd, see also *Nashville Daily True Whig*, 22 February 1851:

> [from the gallows] Henry spoke a few words to the crowd, declaring his innocence of the crime for which he had been convicted, and for which he was about to suffer death. The clergyman of the Catholic denomination, who had attended the prisoners in their last days of earthly probation, spoke in behalf of Moses, who also declared himself innocent. The boy Henry maintained a cheerful and indifferent appearance during the arrangement of the preliminaries, and mounted the scaffold with a smile upon his countenance. The countenance of Moses, however, indicated a state of mind more in unison with the circumstances that surrounded him, and seemed to indicate an appreciation of the awful and sudden transition from lusty life to cold inanimate clay, and from time to eternity, which awaited him.

See also *Nashville True Whig and Weekly Commercial Register*, 28 February 1851, for a similar description and assertion that Henry was the one who gave the speech at the gallows. According to the *Nashville Daily True Whig*, 21 February 1851, there were many residents from Franklin among the crowd: "The city yesterday indicated the presence of an unusual number of strangers, notwithstanding the inclement weather, principally from the country. It was suggested to us that the execution today had drawn them in, but for the sake of humanity we hope this was not the case." Listed as "Arrivals at the Principal Hotels" were E. M. Eelbeck of Franklin, registered at the City Hotel, and J. Bennett (Henry's owner) of Franklin at Union Hall.

93. *By-Laws of the Town of Franklin*.
94. *Henry, A Slave v. State of Tennessee*.
95. *By-Laws of the Town of Franklin*.
96. *Henry, A Slave v. State of Tennessee*.
97. *Western Freeman*, 17 December 1833; *By-Laws of the Town of Franklin*.
98. Fears of insurrection intensified in Middle Tennessee in the days leading up to secession and produced numerous rumors of slave plots in Nashville, Clarksville, and other towns. Maury County revived its slave patrol. See Ash, *Middle Tennessee Society Transformed*, 66–71.
99. *Western Weekly Review*, 8 March 1850.
100. *By-Laws of the Town of Franklin*.
101. Spence, *Annals of Rutherford County*, 2:126.
102. Schweninger, *From Tennessee Slave to St. Louis Entrepreneur*, 32.
103. *Bedford Weekly Yeoman*, 17 May 1854.
104. Carney Diary, 1 April 1859.
105. Raboteau, *Slave Religion*, 138–39, 142–43; E. D. Smith, *Climbing Jacob's Ladder*.
106. Jacobs, *Incidents in the Life of a Slave Girl*, 67.
107. Garrett, *"Hither and Yon" II*, 331.

108. Sobel, " 'They Can Never Both Prosper Together.' "

109. Berlin, *Slaves Without Masters*, 296.

110. *Maury Press*, 6 June 1860.

111. Berlin, *Slaves Without Masters*, 344–45.

112. This process occurred elsewhere in the South during the same period. Marie Tyler-McGraw and Gregg D. Kimball note that "in the period from 1790 to 1830, blacks in Richmond appear too have had more individual freedoms and less opportunity to earn money than they did in the three decades before 1860 when Richmond's business and industry expanded and diversified" (*In Bondage and Freedom*, 63).

113. Garrett, *"Hither and Yon,"* 29–30; and Garrett, *"Hither and Yon II,"* 333.

114. 1850 manuscript census for the town of Columbia.

115. John T. O'Brien, "Factory, Church and Community."

Epilogue

1. According to the 1850 manuscript census, William F. Lytle (son of town founding father) listed his occupation as farmer and owned seventy-six slaves.

2. Hughes, *Hearthstones*, 65. The plantation office was eventually moved to the site of the house museum, Oaklands, an antebellum home built by the Maney family.

3. Bowman, *Historic Williamson County*, 61–63.

4. Trimble, "Behind the Lines in Middle Tennessee," 70–71.

5. *Freedom's Watchman*, 16 October 1867.

6. *Freedom's Watchman*, 5 February 1868.

7. Local historian C. B. Arnette explains that his father's meat market, just off the Square in Murfreesboro, was next-door to the grocery store operated by Eugene Minor Woodson: "Slightly less than ebony in skin color, Eugene Woodson was tall, broad-shouldered and well respected by the colored community as well as by his fellow shop owners . . . on the Square" (*From Mink Slide to Main Street*, 14).

8. *Columbia Herald*, 29 October 1869, 25 February 1870.

9. *Columbia Herald*, 21 January 1870.

10. Spence, *Annals of Rutherford County*, 2:291–92.

11. Ibid., 2:265.

12. *Monitor*, 9 September 1865.

13. This attack, which took place 6 July 1867, is well documented by extensive eyewitness testimony found in the Freedmen's Bureau Quarterly Reports.

Primary Sources

Manuscripts

Chapel Hill, N.C.
    Southern Historical Collection (SHC), Wilson Library, University of North Carolina at Chapel Hill
        Hamilton Brown Papers
        Kate Carney Diary
        Gale-Polk Family Papers
        Caroline Nicholson, "Reminiscences of an Octogenarian," typescript
        George Polk Papers
        Nimrod Porter Papers
        Alice Ready Diary
        Michael Shofner Papers
Columbia, Tenn.
    Maury County Public Library
        Nathan Vaught, "Youth and Old Age," manuscript
Durham, N.C.
    Special Collections Department, William R. Perkins Library, Duke University
        Campbell Family Papers
Nashville, Tenn.
    Tennessee State Library and Archives (TSLA)
        Claybrook Collection
        Isaac Conger Diary
        Cooper Family Papers
        Douglas-Maney Family Papers
        Alfred Hamilton Letters
        Samuel Henderson Diary
        Walter King Hoover Papers
        Evander McIver Memoirs
        James Washington Matthews Journal
        Phillip P. Nelson Papers
        James H. Otey Diary
        James Knox Polk Papers

Pope Family Papers
Pounds Family Papers
John Sumner Russwurm Papers
James Norman Smith Memoirs
Samuel Escue Tillman Memoirs
Whiteside Family Papers, 1862–65, Small Collections
James Winchester Papers
Yeatman-Polk Family Papers

Public Documents

By-Laws of the Town of Franklin. Together with the Acts of Incorporation. Franklin, Tenn.: Printed by Henry Van Pelt, 1838.
Census, 1850 manuscript: Towns of Columbia, Franklin, Murfreesboro, Shelbyville.
County Court Minutes: Bedford, Maury, Rutherford, Williamson Counties
Deed Books: Bedford, Maury, Rutherford, and Williamson Counties
Freedmen's Bureau Quarterly Reports, Records of the Bureau of Refugees, Freedmen, and Abandoned Lands, Record Group 105, Reel 34, National Archives.
Henry, A Slave v. State of Tennessee, 1850, Middle Tennessee Supreme Court, Box 92A, TSLA.
The Mayor & Aldermen of The Town of Franklin vs. Job Mayberry, 11 October 1844. Circuit Court. TSLA.
Petition to form Rutherford County, 10 August 1803, Legislative Papers, TSLA.
Public Acts. General Assembly. State of Tennessee.

Newspapers

Bedford Yeoman
Central Monitor
Columbia Beacon
Columbia Herald
Columbia Mirror
Columbia Observer
Daily American
Daily Centre-State American
Daily Republican Banner
Daily Republican Banner and Nashville Whig
Democratic Clarion and Tennessee Gazette
Freedom's Watchman
Impartial Review and Cumberland Repository
Maury Intelligencer
Maury Press
The Monitor
Murfreesboro News
Murfreesborough Telegraph
Nashville Daily True Whig
Nashville Republican Banner

Nashville True Whig and Weekly Commercial Register
Nashville Whig
National Vidette
Rutherford Telegraph
Shelbyville Expositor
Tennessee Democrat
Tennessee Herald
The Monitor
Western Freeman
Western Weekly Review

Published Materials

The Agriculturist, and Journal of the State and County Societies. Edited by J. Shelby, G. Troost, and T. Fanning, vol. 2, no. 7 (July 1841).

Blackmore, Bettie Ridley. "Behind the Lines in Middle Tennessee, 1863–1865: The Journal of Bettie Ridley Blackmore." Edited by Sarah Ridley Trimble. *Tennessee Historical Quarterly* 12, no. 1 (March 1953): 48–80.

Cleaveland, Henry W., William Backus, and Samuel D. Backus. *Village and Farm Cottages.* Watkins Glen, N.Y.: American Life Foundation, 1982; originally published by D. Appleton and Co., 1856.

Downing, Andrew Jackson. *Cottage Residences, Rural Architecture and Landscape Gardening.* Watkins Glen, N.Y.: Century House/Library of Victorian Culture, 1967; originally published 1842.

First Annual Catalogue and General Advertisement of the Female Institute. Columbia, Tenn.: J. H. Thompson, printer, 1838.

Hale, Mrs. Sarah Josepha. *Flora's Interpreter, and Fortuna Flora.* Boston: Sanborn, Carter and Bazin, 1856.

Ingram, J. H. *Flora Symbolica, or The Language & Sentiment of Flowers.* London: Frederick Warnes & Co., [1869].

Jacobs, Harriet. *Incidents in the Life of a Slave Girl: Written By Herself.* Edited by Jean Fagan Yellin. Cambridge: Harvard University Press, 1987.

Morris, Eastin. *Eastin Morris' Tennessee Gazetteer 1834 and Matthew Rhea's Map of the State of Tennessee 1832.* Edited by Robert M. McBride and Owen Meredith. Nashville, Tenn.: Gazetteer Press, 1971.

Nicholson, Caroline. "Memoirs of Caroline Nicholson." Edited by Jill K. Garrett. *Maury County, Tennessee: Historical Sketches* (July 1967): 245–46.

Schweninger, Loren, ed. *From Tennessee Slave to St. Louis Entrepreneur: The Autobiography of James Thomas.* Columbia: University of Missouri Press, 1984.

Spence, John C. *Annals of Rutherford County.* 2 vols. (Vol. 1, *1799–1828*, Vol 2, *1829–1870*). Murfreesboro, Tenn.: Rutherford County Historical Society, 1991.

Secondary Sources

Allmendinger, David F., Jr. *Paupers and Scholars: The Transformation of Student Life in Nineteenth-Century New England.* New York: St. Martin's, 1975.

Annable, Edward C., Jr. "A History of the Roads of Rutherford County, Tennessee, 1804–1878: Historic Road Research, and Its Applications for Historic Resource Surveys and Local History." M.A. thesis, Middle Tennessee State University, 1982.

Arensberg, Conrad M. "American Communities." *American Anthropologist* 57 (December 1955): 1143–62.

Arnette, Charles Byron. *From Mink Slide to Main Street.* Murfreesboro, Tenn.: Williams Printing Co., 1991.

Arnow, Harriet Simpson. *Flowering of the Cumberland.* New York: Macmillan, 1963.

———. *Seedtime on the Cumberland.* New York: Macmillan, 1960.

Ash, Stephen V. *Middle Tennessee Society Transformed, 1860–1870.* Baton Rouge: Louisiana State University Press, 1988.

Bellamy, Donnie D. "Macon, Georgia, 1823–1860: A Study in Urban Slavery." *Phylon* 45 (1984): 298–310.

Berlin, Ira. *Slaves Without Masters: The Free Negro in the Antebellum South.* New York: Pantheon, 1974.

Berlin, Ira, and Herbert G. Gutman. "Natives and Immigrants, Free Men and Slaves: Urban Workingmen in the Antebellum American South." *American Historical Review* 88 (December 1983): 1175–1200.

Bishir, Catherine. "Jacob W. Holt: An American Builder." *Winterthur Portfolio* 16 (Spring 1981): 1–31.

Bishir, Catherine, Charlotte V. Brown, Carl R. Lounsbury, and Ernest H. Wood III. *Architects and Builders in North Carolina: A History of the Practice of Building.* Chapel Hill: University of North Carolina Press, 1990.

Blackmar, Betsy. "Re-walking the 'Walking City': Housing and Property Relations in New York City, 1780–1840." *Radical History Review* 21 (Fall 1979): 131–48.

Blumin, Stuart. *The Emergence of the Middle Class: Social Experience in the American City, 1760–1900.* Cambridge: Cambridge University Press, 1989.

Boniol, John Dawson, Jr. "The Walton Road." *Tennessee Historical Quarterly* 30 (Winter 1971): 402–12.

Bonner, James C. "Plantation Architecture of the Lower South on the Eve of the Civil War." *Journal of Southern History* 11 (1945): 370–81.

Bowman, Virginia McDaniel. *Historic Williamson County: Old Homes and Sites.* Franklin, Tenn.: Territorial Press, 1971; republished 1989.

Bracegirdle, Brian. *The Archaeology of the Industrial Revolution.* London: Heinemann Educational Books, 1973.

Brown, Elsa Barkley, and Gregg D. Kimball. "Mapping the Terrain of Black Richmond." *Journal of Urban History* 21 (March 1995): 296–346.

Brown, Roberta Lee. "A Historic Preservation Plan for Murfreesboro, Tennessee." M.A. thesis, Middle Tennessee State University, 1985.

Brownell, Blaine A. "Urbanization in the South: A Unique Experience?" *Mississippi Quarterly* 26, no. 2 (Spring 1973): 105–20.

Brownell, Blaine A., and David R. Goldfield, eds. *The City in Southern History: The Growth of Urban Civilization in the South.* Port Washington, N.Y.: National University Publications, Kennikat Press, 1977.

Brucken, Carolyn. "In the Public Eye: Women and the American Luxury Hotel." *Winterthur Portfolio* 31 (Winter 1996): 203–20.

Burdette, Benjamin L., and Jerry Wayne Cook. "The Original Town Lots of Shelbyville." *Bedford County Historical Quarterly* 1 (Winter 1975): 146–50.

Burton, Orville Vernon. *In My Father's House Are Many Mansions: Family and Community in Edgefield, South Carolina*. Chapel Hill: University of North Carolina Press, 1985.

Bushman, Richard L. *The Refinement of America: Persons, Houses, Cities*. New York: Alfred A. Knopf, 1992.

Campbell, Edward D. C., Jr., with Kym S. Rice, eds. *Before Freedom Came: African-American Life in the Antebellum South*. Richmond: Museum of the Confederacy, 1991.

Carnes, Mark C. *Secret Ritual and Manhood in Victorian America*. New Haven: Yale University Press, 1989.

Carnes, Mark C., and Clyde Griffen, eds. *Meanings for Manhood: Constructions of Masculinity in Victorian America*. Chicago: University of Chicago Press, 1990.

Cash, William J. *The Mind of the South*. New York: Alfred A. Knopf, 1941.

Celik, Zeynep, Diane Favro, and Richard Ingersoll, eds. *Streets: Critical Perspectives on Public Space*. Berkeley: University of California Press, 1994.

Clark, Blanche Henry. *The Tennessee Yeomen, 1840–1860*. Nashville, Tenn.: Vanderbilt University Press, 1942.

Clark, Clifford. "Domestic Architecture as an Index to Social History: The Romantic Revival and the Cult of Domesticity in America, 1840–1870." *Journal of Interdisciplinary History* 7 (Summer 1976): 33–56.

Clark, Clifford Edward, Jr. *The American Family Home, 1800–1960*. Chapel Hill: University of North Carolina Press, 1986.

Clinton, Catherine. *The Plantation Mistress: Woman's World in the Old South*. New York: Pantheon, 1982.

Conzen, Michael P., ed. *The Making of the American Landscape*. Boston: Unwin Hyman, 1990.

Corlew, Robert E. *Tennessee: A Short History*. Knoxville: University of Tennessee Press, 1981.

Coulter, E. Merton. "The Ante-Bellum Academy Movement in Georgia." *Georgia Historical Quarterly* 5 (December 1921): 11–42.

Cross, Robert Paul. "Bedford County Tennessee: Settlement to Secession, 1785–1861." M.A. thesis, Middle Tennessee State University, 1974.

Curry, Leonard P. "Urbanization and Urbanism in the Old South: A Comparative View," *Journal of Southern History* 40, no. 1 (February 1974): 43–60.

Darby, Elva M., and William J. Darby. "Maury-Darby Building: The Oldest Building on Franklin's Public Square." *Williamson County Historical Society Publication* 16 (Spring 1985): 105–18.

Davis, Natalie Z. "The Reasons of Misrule: Youth Groups and Charivaries in Sixteenth-Century France." *Past and Present* 50 (1979): 41–75.

Davis, Susan G. " 'Making Night Hideous': Christmas Revelry and Public Order in Nineteenth-Century Philadelphia." *American Quarterly* 34 (1982): 185–99.

——. *Parades and Power: Street Theatre in Nineteenth-Century Philadelphia*. Philadelphia: Temple University Press, 1986.

de Certeau, Michel. *The Practice of Everyday Life*. Berkeley: University of California Press, 1984.

Doerflinger, Thomas M. "Farmers and Dry Goods in the Philadelphia Market Area, 1750–1800." In *The Economy of Early America: The Revolutionary Period, 1763–1790*, edited by Ronald Hoffman, John J. McCusker, Russell R. Menard, and Peter J. Albert, 166–95. Charlottesville: University of Virginia Press, 1988.

Dorsett, Lyle W., and Arthur H. Shaffer. "Was the Antebellum South Antiurban? A Suggestion," *Journal of Southern History* 38, no. 1 (February 1972): 93–100.

Douglas, Ann. *The Feminization of American Culture*. New York: Alfred A. Knopf, 1977.

Earle, Carville, and Ronald Hoffman. "Staple Crops and Urban Development in the Eighteenth-Century South." *Perspectives in American History* 10 (1976): 7–77.

Ernst, Joseph A., and J. Roy Merrens. " 'Camden's Turrets Pierce the Skies!': The Urban Process in the Southern Colonies During the Eighteenth Century," *William and Mary Quarterly* 30, no. 4 (October 1973): 549–74.

Ernst, Joseph W. "With Compass and Chain: Federal Land Surveyors in the Old Northwest, 1785–1816." Ph.D. dissertation, Columbia University, 1958.

Farnham, Christie Anne. *The Education of the Southern Belle: Higher Education and Student Socialization in the Antebellum South*. New York: New York University Press, 1994.

Feldberg, Michael. *The Turbulent Era: Riot and Disorder in Jacksonian America*. New York: Oxford University Press, 1980.

Folmsbee, Stanley John. *Sectionalism and Internal Improvements in Tennessee, 1796–1845*. Knoxville: East Tennessee Historical Society, 1939.

Foner, Eric. *Reconstruction: America's Unfinished Revolution*. New York: Harper & Row, Publishers, 1988.

Fowler, William Ewing. "Stories and Legends of Maury County, Tennessee." M.A. thesis, George Peabody College for Teachers, 1937.

Fox-Genovese, Elizabeth. *Within the Plantation Household: Black and White Women of the Old South*. Chapel Hill: University of North Carolina Press, 1988.

Garrett, Jill K. *"Hither and Yon": The Best of the Writings of Jill K. Garrett*. Columbia, Tenn.: Daily Herald, 1986.

——. *"Hither and Yon" II: More of the Writings of Jill K. Garrett*. Edited by Carese Parker. Columbia, Tenn.: Polk Memorial Association, 1992.

Genovese, Eugene D. *Roll, Jordan, Roll: The World the Slaves Made*. New York: Vintage, 1971.

Gilchrist, Agnes Addison. *William Strickland: Architect and Engineer, 1788–1854*. Philadelphia: University of Pennsylvania Press, 1950.

Glassie, Henry. *Pattern in the Material Folk Culture of the Eastern United States*. Philadelphia: University of Pennsylvania Press, 1968.

Goffman, Erving. *Presentation of Self in Everyday Life*. Garden City, N.Y.: Doubleday Anchor, 1959.

Goldfield, David R. *Cotton Fields and Skyscrapers: Southern City and Regions, 1607–1980*. Baton Rouge: Louisiana State University Press, 1982.

——. *Urban Growth in the Age of Sectionalism: Virginia, 1847–1861*. Baton Rouge: Louisiana State University Press, 1977.

Goldin, Claudia Dale. *Urban Slavery in the American South, 1820–1860: A Quantitative History.* Chicago: University of Chicago Press, 1976.

The Goodspeed Histories of Maury, Williamson, Rutherford, Wilson, Bedford, & Marshall Counties of Tennessee, reprinted from *Goodspeed's History of Tennessee.* Columbia, Tenn.: Woodward & Stinson Printing Co., 1971; originally published 1886.

Goodstein, Anita Shafer. *Nashville, 1780–1860: From Frontier to City.* Gainesville: University of Florida Press, 1989.

Gottdiener, M. *The Social Production of Urban Space.* Austin: University of Texas Press, 1985.

Gowans, Alan. *Images of American Living: Four Centuries of Architecture and Furniture as Cultural Expression.* New York: Harper & Row, 1964.

Gravely, Will B. "The Rise of African Churches in America (1786–1822): Reexamining the Contexts." *Journal of Religious Thought* 41 (1984): 58–73.

Gray, Lewis C. *History of Agriculture in the Southern United States to 1860.* Reprint, New York: Peter Smith, 1941; originally published 1933.

Green, Fletcher M. "Higher Education of Women in the South Prior to 1860." In *Democracy in the Old South and Other Essays by Fletcher Melvin Green,* edited by J. Isaac Copeland, 199–219. Nashville, Tenn.: Vanderbilt University Press, 1969.

Grier, Katherine C. *Culture and Comfort: People, Parlors, and Upholstery, 1850–1930.* Rochester, N.Y.: Strong Museum, 1988; distributed by University of Massachusetts Press, Amherst.

Groth, Paul. "Streetgrids as Frameworks for Urban Variety." *Harvard Architecture Review* 2 (Spring 1981): 68–75.

Habakkuk, H. J. "Fluctuations in House-Building in Britain and the United States in the Nineteenth Century." *Journal of Economic History* 22 (June 1962): 198–230.

Hanawalt, Barbara A., and Kathryn L. Reyerson, eds. *City and Spectacle in Medieval Europe.* Minneapolis: University of Minnesota Press, 1994.

Harper, Herbert L. "The Antebellum Courthouses of Tennessee." *Tennessee Historical Quarterly* 30 (Spring 1971): 3–25.

——. "The Courthouses of Williamson County," *Williamson County Historical Society Publication* 1 (Fall 1970): 5–20.

Hasselbring, Jeri McLeland. *National Register Properties, Williamson County, Tennessee.* Franklin, Tenn.: Hillsboro Press, 1995.

Hedrick, Joan D. *Harriet Beecher Stowe: A Life.* New York: Oxford University Press, 1994.

Herman, Bernard. *Architecture and Rural Life in Central Delaware, 1700–1900.* Knoxville: University of Tennessee Press, 1987.

——. "Time and Performance: Folk Houses in Delaware." In *American Material Culture and Folklife: A Prologue and Dialogue,* edited by Simon J. Bronner, 155–86. Ann Arbor, Mich.: UMI Research Press, 1985.

Hickson, Shirley Ann. "The Development of Higher Education for Women in the Antebellum South." Ph.D. dissertation, University of South Carolina, 1985.

Hilliard, Sam B. *Hog Meat and Hoecake: Food Supply in the Old South, 1840–1860.* Carbondale: Southern Illinois University Press, 1972.

Hodges, Graham Russell. *New York City Cartmen, 1667–1850.* New York: New York University Press, 1986.

Hofstra, Warren R., and Robert D. Mitchell. "Town and Country in Backcountry Virginia: Winchester and the Shenandoah Valley, 1730–1800." *Journal of Southern History* 59 (November 1993): 619–46.

Horlick, Allan Stanley. *Country Boys and Merchant Princes: The Social Control of Young Men in New York*. Lewisburg, Pa.: Bucknell University Press, 1975.

Horowitz, Helen Lefkowitz. *Alma Mater: Design and Experience in the Women's Colleges from Their Nineteenth-Century Beginnings to the 1930s*. New York: Alfred A. Knopf, 1985.

Howe, Daniel Walker. *The Political Culture of the American Whigs*. Chicago: University of Chicago Press, 1979.

Howington, Arthur F. " 'Not in the Condition of a Horse or an Ox': *Ford v. Ford*, the Law of Testamentary Manumission, and the Tennessee Courts's Recognition of Slave Humanity." *Tennessee Historical Quarterly* 34 (1975): 249–63.

Huffman, Frank J. "Town and Country in the South, 1850–1880: A Comparison of Urban and Rural Social Structures." *South Atlantic Quarterly* 76 (Summer 1977): 366–81.

Hughes, Mary B. *Hearthstones: The Story of Historic Rutherford County Homes*. Murfreesboro, Tenn.: Mid-South Publishing Co., 1942.

Hutchins, Catherine E., ed. *Shaping a National Culture: The Philadelphia Experience, 1750–1800*. Winterthur, Del.: Henry Francis du Pont Winterthur Museum, 1994.

Isaac, Rhys. *The Transformation of Virginia, 1740–1790*. Chapel Hill: University of North Carolina Press, 1982.

Johnson, Hildegard Binder. *Order Upon the Land: The U.S. Rectangular Land Survey and the Upper Mississippi Country*. New York: Oxford University Press, 1976.

Johnson, Paul E. *A Shopkeeper's Millennium: Society and Revivals in Rochester, New York, 1815–1837*. New York: Hill and Wang, 1978.

Kasson, John. *Rudeness and Civility: Manners in Nineteenth-Century Urban America*. New York: Hill and Wang, 1990.

Kent, Susan, ed. *Domestic Architecture and the Use of Space: An Interdisciplinary Cross-Cultural Study*. Cambridge: Cambridge University Press, 1990.

Kenzer, Robert C. *Kinship and Neighborhood in a Southern Community: Orange County, North Carolina, 1849–1881*. Knoxville: University of Tennessee Press, 1987.

Kett, Joseph F. *Rites of Passage: Adolescence in America, 1790 to the Present*. New York: Basic, 1977.

Kimball, Gregg D. "African-Virginians and the Vernacular Building Tradition in Richmond City, 1790–1860." In *Perspectives in Vernacular Architecture IV*, edited by Thomas Carter and Bernard L. Herman, 121–29. Columbia: University of Missouri Press, 1991.

Kniffen, Fred B. "Folk Housing: Key to Diffusion." In *Common Places: Readings in American Vernacular Architecture*, edited by Dell Upton and John Michael Vlach, 3–26. Athens: University of Georgia Press, 1986.

Kolchin, Peter. "Reevaluating the Antebellum Slave Community: A Comparative Perspective." *Journal of American History* 70 (December 1983): 579–601.

Kolodny, Annette. *The Land Before Her: Fantasy and Experience of the American Frontiers, 1630–1860*. Chapel Hill: University of North Carolina Press, 1984.

Lamon, Lester C. *Blacks in Tennessee, 1791–1970*. Knoxville: University of Tennessee Press, 1981.

Lang, Marvel. "The Development of Small Towns as a Settlement Process in Mississippi." *Mississippi Geographer* 9 (Spring 1981): 5–14.

Lapsansky, Emma Jones. " 'Since They Got Those Separate Churches': Afro-Americans and Racism in Jacksonian Philadelphia." *American Quarterly* 32 (Spring 1980): 54–78.

Laurie, Bruce. " 'Nothing on Compulsion': Life Styles of Philadelphia Artisans, 1820–1850." *Labor History* 15, no. 3 (Summer 1974): 337–66.

Lefebvre, Henri. *The Production of Space*. Translated by Donald Nicholson-Smith. Oxford: Blackwell, 1974.

Longstreth, Richard. "Compositional Types in American Commercial Architecture." In *Perspectives in Vernacular Architecture II*, edited by Camille Wells, 12–23. Columbia: University of Missouri Press, 1986.

Lounsbury, Carl. "The Structure of Justice: The Courthouses of Colonial Virginia." In *Perspectives in Vernacular Architecture III*, edited by Thomas Carter and Bernard Herman, 214–26. Columbia: University of Missouri Press, 1989.

Lounsbury, Carl R. *An Illustrated Glossary of Early Southern Architecture and Landscape*. New York: Oxford University Press, 1994.

McBride, Robert M. "Oaklands: A Venerable Host, A Renewed Welcome." *Tennessee Historical Quarterly* 22 (December 1963): 303–22.

Machin, R. "The Great Rebuilding: A Reassessment." *Past and Present* 77 (November 1977): 33–56.

Meinig, D. W. *Continental America, 1800–1867*, vol. 2 of *The Shaping of America: A Geographical Perspective on 500 Years of History*. New Haven: Yale University Press, 1993.

Mrozowski, Stephen A., and Mary C. Beaudry. "Archaeology and the Landscape of Corporate Ideology." In *Earth Patterns: Essays in Landscape Archaeology*, edited by William M. Kelso and Rachel Most, 189–208. Charlottesville: University Press of Virginia, 1990.

Nash, Gary B. *Forging Freedom: The Formation of Philadelphia's Black Community, 1720–1840*. Cambridge: Harvard University Press, 1988.

Novak, Steven J. *The Rights of Youth: American Colleges and Student Revolt, 1798–1815*. Cambridge: Harvard University Press, 1977.

Oakes, James. *The Ruling Race: A History of American Slaveholders*. New York: Vintage, 1982.

O'Brien, John T. "Factory, Church and Community: Blacks in Antebellum Richmond." *Journal of Southern History* 44 (November 1978): 509–36.

Patrick, James. *Architecture in Tennessee, 1768–1897*. Knoxville: University of Tennessee Press, 1981.

Perry, Lewis. *Boats Against the Stream: American Culture Between Revolution and Modernity, 1820–1860*. New York: Oxford University Press, 1993.

Pillsbury, Richard. "The Morphology of the Piedmont Georgia County Seat Before 1860." *Southeastern Geographer* 28 (November 1978): 115–24.

———. "The Urban Street Pattern as a Culture Indicator: Pennsylvania, 1682–1815." *Annals of the Association of American Geographers* 60 (1970): 428–46.

Pittard, Homer. "Union: Murfreesboro's Other University." *Rutherford County Historical Society Publication* 1 (June 1973).

Pocious, Gerald L. *A Place to Belong: Community Order and Everyday Space in Calvert, Newfoundland.* Athens: University of Georgia Press, 1991.

Pope, Christie Farnham. "Preparation for Pedestals: North Carolina Antebellum Female Seminaries." Ph.D. dissertation, University of Chicago, 1977.

Price, Edward T. "The Central Courthouse Square in the American County Seat." In *Common Places: Readings in American Vernacular Architecture*, edited by Dell Upton and John Michael Vlach, 124–45. Athens: University of Georgia Press, 1986.

Raboteau, Albert J. *Slave Religion: The "Invisible Institution" in the Antebellum South.* New York: Oxford University Press, 1978.

Reader, W. J. *Macadam: The McAdam Family and the Turnpike Roads, 1798–1861.* London: Heinemann, 1980.

Reps, John. *Town Planning in Frontier America.* Princeton, N.J.: Princeton University Press, 1969.

Roberts, Warren E. "The Tools Used in Building Log Houses in Indiana." In *Common Places: Readings in American Vernacular Architecture*, edited by Dell Upton and John Michael Vlach, 182–203. Athens: University of Georgia Press, 1986.

Rorabaugh, W. J. *The Craft Apprentice: From Franklin to the Machine Age in America.* New York: Oxford University Press, 1986.

Rutman, Darrett B., with Anita H. Rutman. "The Village South." In *Small Worlds, Large Questions: Explorations in Early American Social History, 1600–1850*, 231–72. Charlottesville: University Press of Virginia, 1994.

Ryan, Mary P. *Women in Public: Between Banners and Ballots, 1825–1880.* Baltimore: Johns Hopkins University Press, 1990.

St. George, Robert Blair. " 'Set Thine House in Order': The Domestication of the Yeomanry in Seventeenth-Century New England." In *Common Places: Readings in American Vernacular Architecture*, edited by Dell Upton and John Michael Vlach, 292–314. Athens: University of Georgia Press, 1986.

Schultz, Stanley K. "Temperance Reform in the Antebellum South: Social Control and Urban Order." *South Atlantic Quarterly* 83 (1984): 323–39.

Seip, Terry L. "Slaves and Free Negroes in Alexandria, 1850–1860." *Louisiana History* 10 (Spring 1969): 147–65.

Shepard, E. Lee. " 'This Being Court Day': Courthouses and Community Life in Rural Virginia." *Virginia Magazine of History and Biography* 103 (October 1995): 461–70.

Shirley, Michael. *From Congregation Town to Industrial City: Culture and Social Change in a Southern Community.* New York: New York University Press, 1994.

Sklar, Kathryn Kish. *Catharine Beecher: A Study in American Domesticity.* New York: W. W. Norton, 1973.

Smith, Edward D. *Climbing Jacob's Ladder: The Rise of Black Churches in Eastern American Cities, 1740–1877.* Washington, D.C.: Smithsonian Institution Press, 1988.

Smith, J. Frazer. *White Pillars: The Architecture of the South.* New York: Bramhall House, 1941.

Smith, Reid. *Majestic Middle Tennessee.* Prattville, Ala.: Paddle Wheel Publications, 1975.

Sobel, Mechal. "'They Can Never Both Prosper Together': Black and White Baptists in Antebellum Nashville, Tennessee." *Tennessee Historical Quarterly* 38 (Fall 1979): 296–307.

Spera, Elizabeth Gray Kogen. "Building for Business: The Impact of Commerce on the City Plan and Architecture of the City of Philadelphia, 1750–1800." Ph.D. dissertation, University of Pennsylvania, 1980.

Stallybrass, Peter, and Allon White. *Politics and Poetics of Transgression*. London: Methuen, 1986.

Stansell, Christine. *City of Women: Sex and Class in New York, 1789–1860*. New York: Alfred A. Knopf, 1986.

Starobin, Robert S. *Industrial Slavery in the Old South*. New York: Oxford University Press, 1970.

Stilgoe, John R. *Common Landscape of America, 1580–1845*. New Haven: Yale University Press, 1982.

Sutherland, Daniel E. *Americans and Their Servants: Domestic Service in the United States from 1800 to 1920*. Baton Rouge: Louisiana State University Press, 1981.

Taylor, George R. *The Transportation Revolution, 1815–1860*. New York: Rinehart, 1951.

Taylor, William R. *Cavalier and Yankee: The Old South and American National Character*. Cambridge: Harvard University Press, 1979.

Tinker, Nancy C. "Nathan Vaught, Master Builder of Maury County: A Study of Middle Tennessee Greek Revival Architecture." M.A. thesis, Middle Tennessee State University, 1983.

Tolbert, Lisa C. "Commercial Blocks and Female Colleges: The Small-Town Business of Educating Ladies." In *Shaping Communities: Perspectives in Vernacular Architecture VI*, edited by Carter L. Hudgins and Elizabeth Collins Cromley, 204–15. Knoxville: University of Tennessee Press, 1997.

——. "Murder in Franklin: The Mysteries of Small-Town Slavery." *Tennessee Historical Quarterly* 57, no. 4 (December 1998).

Tuan, Yi Fu. *Segmented Worlds and Self: Group Life and Individual Consciousness*. Minneapolis: University of Minnesota Press, 1982.

Turner, Victor, ed. *Celebration: Studies in Festivity and Ritual*. Washington, D.C.: Smithsonian Institution Press, 1982.

Turner, William Bruce. *History of Maury County, Tennessee*. Nashville, Tenn.: Parthenon Press, 1955.

Twiss-Garrity, Beth A. "Double Vision: The Philadelphia Cityscape and Perceptions of It." In *Shaping a National Culture: The Philadelphia Experience, 1750–1800*, edited by Catherine E. Hutchins, 1–14. Winterthur, Del.: Henry Francis du Pont Winterthur Museum, 1994.

Tyler-McGraw, Marie, and Gregg D. Kimball. *In Bondage and Freedom: Antebellum Black Life in Richmond, Virginia*. Richmond: Valentine Museum, 1988.

Upton, Dell. "Another City: The Urban Cultural Landscape in the Early Republic." In *Everyday Life in the Early Republic*, edited by Catherine E. Hutchins, 61–117. Winterthur, Del.: Henry Francis du Pont Winterthur Museum, 1994.

——. "Imagining the Early Virginia Landscape." In *Earth Patterns: Essays in Landscape Archaeology*, edited by William M. Kelso and Rachel Most, 71–86. Charlottesville: University Press of Virginia, 1990.

——. "Pattern Books and Professionalism: Aspects of the Transformation of Domestic Architecture in America, 1800–1860." *Winterthur Portfolio* 19 (Summer/Autumn 1984): 107–50.

——. "The Southern Cultural Landscape as Meeting Ground and Debating Ground." Paper delivered at African American Landscapes Symposium, North Carolina Agricultural and Technical State University, Greensboro, March 1995.

——. "White and Black Landscapes in Eighteenth-Century Virginia." *Places* 2 (1985): 59–72.

Vance, James E., Jr. *The Merchant's World: The Geography of Wholesaling.* Englewood Cliffs, N.J.: Prentice-Hall, 1970.

Vlach, John Michael. *Back of the Big House: The Architecture of Plantation Slavery.* Chapel Hill: University of North Carolina Press, 1993.

——. "Plantation Landscapes of the Antebellum South." In *Before Freedom Came: African-American Life in the Antebellum South,* edited by Edward D. C. Campbell Jr., with Kym S. Rice, 21–49. Richmond: Museum of the Confederacy, 1991.

Wade, Richard. *The Urban Frontier: The Rise of Western Cities, 1790–1830.* Cambridge: Harvard University Press, 1959.

Wade, Richard C. *Slavery in the Cities: The South, 1820–1860.* New York: Oxford University Press, 1964.

Wakelyn, Jon L. "Antebellum College Life and the Relations between Fathers and Sons." In *The Web of Southern Social Relations: Women, Family, and Education,* edited by Walter J. Fraser Jr., R. Frank Saunders Jr., and Jon L. Wakelyn, 107–26. Athens: University of Georgia Press, 1985.

Walston, Mark L. "'Uncle Tom's Cabin' Revisited: Origins and Interpretations of Slave Housing in the American South." *Southern Studies* 24 (Winter 1985): 357–73.

Ward, James A. "A New Look at Antebellum Southern Railroad Development." *Journal of Southern History* 39 (August 1973): 409–20.

Warner, Sam Bass, Jr. *The Private City: Philadelphia in Three Periods of its Growth.* Philadelphia: University of Pennsylvania Press, 1968.

Weaver, Herbert, and William G. Eidson. "The James K. Polk Home." *Tennessee Historical Quarterly* 24 (Spring 1965): 3–19.

Welter, Barbara. "The Cult of True Womanhood, 1820–1860." *American Quarterly* 18 (1966): 151–74.

West, Carroll Van. "The Democratic and Whig Political Activists of Middle Tennessee." *Tennessee Historical Quarterly* 42 (1983): 3–17.

Wilentz, Sean. *Chants Democratic: New York City and the Rise of the American Working Class, 1788–1850.* New York: Oxford University Press, 1984.

Wood, Joseph S. "The New England Village as an American Vernacular Form." In *Perspectives in Vernacular Architecture II,* edited by Camille Wells, 54–63. Columbia: University of Missouri Press, 1986.

Wyatt-Brown, Bertram. *Southern Honor: Ethics and Behavior in the Old South.* New York: Oxford University Press, 1982.

Page references in italics refer to illustrations.

Blackmar, Betsy, 240 (n. 10), 243 (n. 60)

Blacks, free, 5; urban, 120, 233 (n. 9); male, 159; of Nashville, 198; restrictions on, 200; building of African churches, 222–23, 229–31; social institutions of, 223–24; segregation of, 224, 260 (nn. 27–28); stores for, 229; censuses of, 259 (n. 25); skilled, 260 (n. 30)

Block square plan, 25–29, 234 (n. 18), 237 (n. 25); in the Midwest, 237 (n. 26); in Virginia, 237 (n. 27). *See also* Grids

Blumin, Stuart, 247 (n. 38)

Boarders: young men as, 119, 161, 162–64, 184; female, 137, 163, 253 (n. 82)

Bookkeeping, 156, 252 (n. 57)

Bowman, Elizabeth, 71

Brickmasons, 35, 85–86, 87; slaves as, 197, 244 (n. 86)

Brittain, James, 64

Brucken, Carolyn, 253 (n. 94)

Building boom (1850s), 9, 89, 115; railroads' effect on, 91, 246 (n. 15); causes of, 94; female colleges in, 101; slave churches in, 222. *See also* Architectural transformation

Building materials: hierarchy of, 8, 51; of temporary townscapes, 35

Buildings: relationships among, 52–53; urban models for, 63–71. *See also* Architecture; Commercial blocks; Courthouses; Dwellings; Houses

Bumpass, Sarah, 130

Bumpass family, 250 (n. 16)

Burn's Spring church (Columbia), 222

Cadets of Tennessee, 175, 177

Calhoun, John C., 241 (n. 28)

Calliopean Society (Union University), 180

Campbell, David, 131

Campbell, William Bowen, 131

Campbellites, 8, 258 (n. 5)

Canebrakes, clearing of, 18, 95, 133, 226

Cannon, Rachel Adeline, 104

Carney, Amanda, 210

Carney, John, 210

Carney, Kate, 120, 123–25, 204, 250 (n. 2); diary of, 124, 130, 172–73; walks of, 124–25, 127, 128, 129, 157, 158, 187; social calls of, 130; on marriage, 131; use of flowers, 140–41, 252 (n. 57); at Soule Female College, 149; on serenades, 172–73, 178; male visitors of, 173–74; on slaves, 196; on visiting, 207; on arson, 220; during Union occupation, 252 (n. 57), 262 (n. 63); in Philadelphia, 253 (n. 74)

Carney, Katherine, 135; on Kate's walks, 124–25; on gardening, 140

Carney, Legrand, 123, 173, 250 (n. 6); college trusteeship of, 144; as prisoner of war, 262 (n. 63)

Carney, Mary, 174, 203, 257 (n. 62)

Carney family: dwelling of, 123, *124*, 125, 228; slaves of, 196, 204, 220; water supply of, 207

Carnton (Franklin), 226, 227

Carpenters, slave, 197, 203

Carriages, 58

Carter, Tod, 226

Carter house (Franklin), *202*, *203*

Carter's Grove (Franklin), 226

Carting, 263 (n. 82)

Censuses, 5, 6, 234 (nn. 12–13), 246 (n. 24); slaves in, 210, 250 (n. 15), 259 (nn. 19–21); women in, 250 (n. 14); age in, 254 (nn. 16–17); free blacks in, 259 (n. 25); slaveholders in, 261 (n. 37)

Central square plan. *See* Block square plan

Ceremonies: town-centered, 72–81, 83–88; hierarchies in, 75, 81; rural, 81; cornerstone-laying, 84–85, 88, 180, 245 (n. 3). *See also* Rituals

Charlotte (Tenn.), courthouse of, *41*, 239 (n. 56)

Cherry, George, 222–23

Chickasaw Treaty of 1830, 70

Childress, Jake, 191

Childress, John W., 57

Christian Church (Campbellites), 8, 258 (n. 5)

Churches: African, 14, 101, 120, 220–23, 229–30; in shanty townscapes, 38; of Murfreesboro, 48; Methodist Episcopal, 73, 150, 177; Gothic, 235 (n. 2); role in community, 238 (n. 49)

Circuit riders, 49, 228

Cities, antebellum, 6, 240 (n. 3); spatial organization of, 63; neighborhoods of, 100–101, 260 (nn. 27–28); slavery in, 192, 194, 197, 200, 204, 259 (n. 24); cultural landscape of, 248 (n. 52); clerks in, 254 (n. 2)

Civic groups, 75, 81. *See also* Freemasons; Oddfellows, Independent Order of; Sons of Temperance

Civil War, 231; Murfreesboro during, *109*, 252 (n. 57); plantations during, 226–27

Clark, Blanche Henry, 261 (n. 43)

Clark, Clifford, 234 (n. 2)

Class: in town space, 14, 63, 107, 260 (n. 27); in female activities, 130, 135; in male activities, 159–60

Clay, Henry, 76, 79

Clerks, 119, 156, 161; conduct of, 158, 165; in antebellum cities, 254 (n. 2)

Clothing: and social status, 58, 241 (n. 41); fashion in, 71, 127; homespun, 134; standard sizing in, 254 (n. 10)

Colleges. *See* Female colleges; Male colleges

Columbia (Tenn.): architectural transformation of, 1–2, 95; establishment of, 4, 19; size of, 6; developmental phases of, 10; courthouse square of, 25; grid of, 28; land clearing in, 34; incorporation of, 43, 239 (n. 65); population of, 48, 240 (n. 4), 250 (n. 14), 255 (n. 17); ferry house of, 50–51; Polk home, 51, *52*, 53, 175; State Bank in, *68*, *69*, 70,

243 (n. 73); ladies' fairs of, 73, 74; Methodist Episcopal Church of, 73, 150; militia companies of, 74; women of, 74; illuminations in, 79, 80; in election of 1848, 79–80; expansion of, 93; residential neighborhoods of, 107; commercial blocks of, 109, 111, *112*; courthouses of, 112–13, 238 (n. 55); commercial establishments of, *128*; businessmen of, 154; Polk law office, *164*; temperance rally (1849), 175, 177; map of, *176*; female colleges of, 179; railroad depot of, 179–80; Masonic hall of, 181, 237 (n. 34); Embargo Street, 195; slave population of, 196, 255 (nn. 20–21), 259 (nn. 19, 21); African churches in, 222, 230; Dyer Johnson house, *223*; turnpikes to, 239 (n. 1); universities of, 246 (n. 6); free blacks of, 259 (n. 25); slaveholders of, 261 (nn. 35, 37)

Columbia Athenaeum, 146–47, *147*, *148*, 253 (n. 78); soirees of, 150

Columbia Blues (militia), 161

Columbia Female Institute, 143–46, *145*; principal of, 146; student body of, 148; founding of, 178; location of, 179

Columbia Junto, 161, 174, 181

Columbia Observer, 63

Commerce: in public squares, 31, 32, 50, 166, 249 (n. 72); urban models for, 96; specialization in, 101, 111–12, 247 (nn. 30, 38); in renovated townscapes, 112–14, 151; and domesticity, 151; mobility in, 165–69; slave participation in, 213; segregation in, 229

Commercial blocks, 9, 14, 108–12, 228; specialized, 101, 111–12; of Murfreesboro, 108–9; of Columbia, 109, 111, 112; partnerships in, 166

Commercial buildings, 156; on courthouse squares, 36, 227; of townscapes, 38, 50; of Franklin, 53; double-house form of, 55–56

Conger, Isaac, 49

Consumption: and architectural transformation, 92; conspicuous, 100; revolution in, 236 (n. 21)

Cooper, Edmund, 120, 134; on railroads, 90–91; on Shelbyville, 142–43; as clerk, 153–58, 159, 166, 254 (n. 1); education of, 154; leisure time of, 157–58; on racial distinctions, 159, 199; legal career of, 169–70, 174; in militia, 187

Cooper, Mary Agnes Frierson, 153

Cooper, Matthew Delamere, 143, 153–54; business success of, 167–68; on Jackson College, 179

Cooper, William F., 143, 153, 157

Cornerstone-laying ceremonies, 84–85, 88, 180, 245 (n. 3)

Cottages, 14, 101, 105; domestic ideal of, 106; in renovated townscape, 107; of Murfreesboro, 107, 108

Cotton crop, 261 (n. 41)

Counties: censuses of, 5, 6; political importance of, 21; social importance of, 235 (n. 8)

County seats: development of, 2, 23, 133, 228, 234 (n. 18); role in cultural change, 4, 7; architectural renovation of, 4, 24, 81, 100–101, 228; spatial patterns of, 4, 46, 199; grid designs of, 7; immigration to, 7; establishment of, 17–23, 235 (n. 6); planning for, 21; failure of, 21–22; governmental functions of, 23; commercial importance of, 23, 59–60, 62, 91, 151; expansion of, 24, 92–93, 226; role in community life, 31; ceremonial use of, 32, 75; social life of, 32, 101; social patterns of, 46; incorporation of, 47–48; turnpikes between, 62; party politics in, 80; population of, 158–65, 218, 250 (nn. 14–15), 254 (nn. 16–17); lawyers of, 169; serenades in, 171; temperance movement in, 174–75; slave population of, 194, 196, 197, 200, 250 (n. 15), 255 (nn. 20–21), 259 (nn. 19, 21), 261 (n. 35); racial segregation in, 204; characteristics of, 227–28;

female colleges in, 253 (n. 78); market houses of, 259 (n. 16); free blacks of, 259 (n. 25)

Courthouses, 227; as "houses," 14; "shanty," 19, 40; placement of, 24; brick, 41, 238 (n. 55); multiple uses of, 49–50; renovated, 112–14; first Mondays at, 165; of Virginia, 239 (n. 61)

Courthouse squares. See Public squares

Crafts, 135, 136

Credit, 168

Creek War, 156

Crichelow & Rice (firm), 129

Crockett & Co. (firm), 166, 250 (n. 7)

Cumberland Gap, 20

Cumberland Presbyterians, 8

Cumberland River, 17

Dale, William, 249 (nn. 69–70)

Debating clubs, 153, 161, 171, 181; at Union University, 180

Democrats, 8, 245 (n. 110); in election of 1848, 76, 77–79

Depressions, economic, 48, 89, 178

Dickinson, David, 99–100

Disorderly conduct, 47; of young men, 120, 165, 170, 171, 181, 184; of slaves, 215. See also Violence, racial

Distillery, 97

Ditches, J. M., 238 (n. 56)

Doggeries, 170, 171, 174; of Murfreesboro, 51

Dog trot houses, 36, 236 (n. 22), 237 (n. 24)

Domesticity: standards of, 92; in renovated townscape, 112–16, 127, 129, 136–37, 151, 164, 171; and commerce, 151; privatized, 164, 208; redefinition of, 250 (n. 10)

Double houses, 54–55, 55, 56, 238 (n. 63)

Downing, Andrew Jackson, 100, 106

Doyle, Catherine, 190, 258 (n. 3)

Dresser, Amos, 218

Drummond and Lutterloh (architects), 144

Immigration, trans-Appalachian, 7, 20, 237 (n. 25); speed of, 18–19
Industrial zones, 97, *98*
Insurrection, fear of, 215, 218–20, 264 (n. 90), 265 (n. 98)
Isaac, Rhys, 258 (n. 11)
Italianate architecture, 104, 105, *106*, 113, 226; in colleges, 146

Jackson, Andrew, 4, 70, 84, 228
Jackson, John Brinckerhoff, 262 (n. 64)
Jackson College (Columbia), 143, 178, 257 (n. 77); location of, 179–80; debates at, 181
Jacksonian era, 46; politics of, 75–76
Jacobs, Harriet, 4, 263 (n. 78); on small-town slavery, 192–93, 203; as fugitive, 193; on town intimacy, 206, 213, 223; on slave churches, 221; on New Year's Day, 256 (n. 40); on Turner rebellion, 264 (n. 90)
Jefferson (Tenn.), 21–22
Johnson, Andrew, 154
Johnson, Dyer, 198, 222; house of, *223*
Johnson, Elizabeth C., 175, 177, 222
Jones, James C., 79
Jordan & Elliott (firm), 125, 127, 166, 250 (n. 6)

Kasson, John, 247 (n. 52)
Kent, Susan, 262 (n. 64)
Ketchum, Levi, 35
Kett, Joseph F., 255 (n. 18)
Kimball, Gregg D., 238 (n. 43), 260 (n. 30), 263 (n. 65), 266 (n. 112)
King, James, 191
Kitchens, 263 (n. 65); detached, 208–9
Kolodny, Annette, 139
Ku Klux Klan, 231

Labor, 210–11; division of, 92, 251 (n. 23); female, 134–35, 136, 251 (n. 23); of boys, 158–59; hierarchies of, 254 (n. 2). *See also* Household production
Ladies' fairs, 70, 73–74

Lafayette, Marquis de, 161
Land clearing, 18–19, 95, 133, 226; in Columbia, 34
Land grants, 7
Landscape, southern, 2, 239 (n. 3); small towns in, 5; of Middle Tennessee, 13
Laurie, Bruce, 165, 256 (n. 39)
Lawyers, circuits of, 169, 228
Lebanon (Tenn.), 131; Sons of Temperance in, 176
Lebanon Pike, 125
Lefebvre, Henri, 235 (n. 2)
Leiper and Menefee (firm), 251 (n. 36)
Liquor: availability of, 156, 174; for serenaders, 173; male consumption of, 257 (n. 63)
Littleton, Joseph L., 198, 258 (n. 6)
Log dwellings, 36–37, 238 (n. 44); replacement of, 42
Lots, price of, 31–32
Lowell (Mass.), 244 (n. 85)
Lyon, Mary, 144
Lytle, John, 35–36, 235 (n. 1)
Lytle, Judy, 203
Lytle, William: and establishment of Murfreesboro, 17, 18, 21, 22; home of, 225, 226
Lytle, William F., 266 (n. 1)

Maberry and Faircloth (masons), 53
Macadamized roads, 61–62
McConnell, Peter, 190, 217
McFadden & McKnight (firm), 166
McPhail's office (Franklin), *163*
Main streets, 31, 227; extension of, 59, 80
Male colleges, 120, 178–84; spatial strategies of, 179–80, 181, 184
Maney, Sally, 102, 104
Maney house (Oaklands), Murfreesboro, 102–4, *102–6*; location of, 108; Jefferson Davis at, 226; office of, 266 (n. 2)
Markets: county seats as, 62, 91, 151; slave, 194; in towns, 235 (n. 6), 240 (n. 3), 248 (n. 72)
Marrs, John A., 64

Masonic halls, 63; of Franklin, 42, 65–67, *66*, *67*; of Philadelphia, 64, *65*; architecture of, 64–65; of Murfreesboro, 67; function of, 70; church services in, 143; of Columbia, 181, 237 (n. 34); of Nashville, 238 (n. 49). *See also* Freemasons

Maury, Abram, 25

Maury County (Tenn.): establishment of county seat, 19; brick courthouse of, 40; in election of 1848, 79; Episcopalians of, 143; slave population of, 202, 258 (n. 14), 259 (n. 15); racial violence in, 231; slave patrol of, 265 (n. 98)

Maury Intelligencer, 175

Maury Press, 127

Mayes and Frierson (firm), 154–56, 159, 166

Mechanic's Union Society of Columbia, 161

Meinig, D. W., 238 (nn. 49, 54)

Merchants: of Murfreesboro, 38–39, 125, 127; circuits of, 63–64, 168–69; role in architectural transformation, 88; specialized, 96, 111; female clientele of, 138; investment in female colleges, 147, 151, 228; partnerships of, 166, 168; capital for, 168

Methodist Episcopal Churches, 48, 73; female colleges of, 146, 150, 253 (n. 78); of Murfreesboro, 177

Middle Tennessee: slavery in, 2, 201–2, 221–23; map of, *3*; entrepreneurs of, 4; architectural transformation of, 4, 81, 87; slaveholders of, 5, 6, 261 (nn. 35, 37); cultural hearths of, 6–7, 237 (n. 24); town building in, 10, 17, 19, 21; migration into, 20; settlement system of, 20–21; town commissioners of, 24; cultural experimentation in, 25; commercial center of, 45; economic cycles of, 48, 89, 178; commercial structures of, 53, 108–12; spatial organization in, 60, 127; party politics in,

80; female colleges of, 144, 146, 147, 178; demographics of, 158; road building in, 168; legal landscape of, 169; seasonal work in, 170; agricultural landscape of, 201; culture of, 228; urban population of, 233 (n. 9); slave population of, 258 (n. 14), 259 (n. 15); plantations of, 261 (n. 39)

Militia companies, 74, 75, 77, 153, 171; regalia of, 157–58, 254 (n. 15)

Mills, 51, 94, 97. *See also* Factories; Sawmills

Mitchell, Robert D., 235 (n. 7)

Mobility: in town economy, 165–70; of professionals, 169

Moore, Elvira, 114–15

Morris, Eastin, 48, 49, 69, 92, 240 (n. 4)

Morrison, David, 243 (n. 73)

Mt. Lebanon Baptist Church, 222

Murder trials. *See* Henry (slave in Franklin): murder trial of

Murfree, Col. Hardy, 102

Murfree, William L., 202

Murfreesboro (Tenn.): building boom in, 1, 96; establishment of, 4, 8, 17–20; political rivalries in, 8; developmental phases of, 10, 48; grid of, 18; public square of, 29, 31, 38–39, *230*, 231; town plan of, 29, *30*, 31; Main Street of, 31, 39, 62; brick buildings of, 32, 35, 96; businessmen of, 34–35, 38–39, 125, 127; shanty townscape of, 34–39; industry in, 35; storehouses of, 38; commerce in, 39, *129*; brick courthouse of, 40, 41–43, *110*, 238 (nn. 55–56); incorporation of, 43, 239 (n. 65); as state capital, 45; population of, 48, 240 (n. 4), 250 (n. 14), 254 (nn. 16–17); "Dogerys" of, 51; double houses of, 54–55, *55*; Spence house, *57*; Masonic hall of, 67; parades in, 83–84; communal unity of, 84–85; architectural transformation of, 87, 88; rail service to, 89–90, 247 (n. 37); expansion of, 92; Depot Hill, *98*, 247 (n. 37); map

of, *98, 126, 182–83*; cottages of, 106;
renovated townscape of, 107–8, 127;
commercial blocks of, 108–9, 111;
Union occupation of, *109*, 252 (n. 57);
renovated courthouse of, *110*, 113–14;
College Street, 125; women residents
of, 130; Methodist Episcopal Church
of, 177; slave population of, 196,
200, 250 (n. 15), 255 (nn. 20–21), 259
(n. 21), 261 (n. 35); free blacks of,
200, 259 (n. 25); fires in, 219; African
American churches of, 230; racial violence in, 230; platting of, 240 (n. 11);
elections in, 244 (n. 97); Whig rally
in, 245 (n. 107); market house of,
259 (n. 16); slaveholders of, 260
(nn. 27, 35)
Murfreesboro Sentinels, 254 (n. 15)
Myerhoff, Barbara, 245 (n. 5)

Nash, Gary, 263 (n. 82)
Nashville (Tenn.): shanty townscape of,
17; centrality of, 45, 239 (n. 1); rail
service to, 89, 90, 96; African Americans of, 197, 200, 222, 260 (n. 26); free
blacks of, 198; Masonic hall of, 238
(n. 49); Whigs of, 246 (n. 16); elite
neighborhoods of, 248 (n. 63)
Nashville Basin, 2, *3*, 45; architectural
renovation in, 4; slave population of,
194, 259 (n. 15)
Nashville-Shelbyville turnpike, 61, 62,
133, 242 (n. 54)
Nashville Whig, 40
Nazareth (Columbia suburb), 93
Neatrophian Society (Jackson College),
181
Neely, George, 192
Neely, Phil P., 150
Neighborhoods: class-based, 14, 63, 107,
260 (n. 27); working-class, 174. *See
also* Spatial organization
Neilson & Crichelow (firm), 125, 127,
166, 250 (n. 6)
Nelson, Phillip P., 162, 255 (n. 33)

Networks: between towns, 59–63; of
women, 135–36, 152; trading, 168–69
New England, towns of, 235 (n. 8)
News, communication of, 205–6, 210
New Year's Day, 165, 256 (n. 40); slave
hiring on, 263 (n. 75)
New York City: construction in, 240
(n. 10); social differences in, 243
(n. 60)
Nicholson, A. O. P., 161–62, 235 (n. 4);
legal practice of, 169
Nicholson, Caroline O'Reilly, 18, 36,
168–69, 206; marriage of, 235 (n. 4);
on New Year's Day, 256 (n. 40)
North Carolina: building boom in, 246
(n. 20); artisans of, 256 (n. 42)
Northeast, urban grown in, 59

Oakes, James, 23
Oaklands. *See* Maney house
O'Brien, Fannie Blount, 62
Odd Fellows, Independent Order of, 74,
75; rituals of, 79; in cornerstone-laying
ceremonies, 83, 87; regalia of, 158
O'Neill, Peggy, 241 (n. 28)
Orange County (N.C.), 233 (n. 4)
Oratory: in town life, 161, 162; role in
republic, 255 (n. 30)
Otey, James H., 143
Outbuildings, 57. *See also* Kitchens

Paint: cost of, 8, 37; colors of, 37–38, 94,
238 (n. 46)
Panic of 1819, 48
Panics, financial, 165
Parades, 75, 76–78; urban, 78; in
Murfreesboro, 83–84; militia compa-
nies in, 158; temperance, 175
Partnerships: business, 166, 168; of pro-
fessional men, 169
Patriarchy, 195, 199
Pennsylvania: cultural hearths of, 6–7,
236 (n. 21); street plans of, 7, 234
(n. 18)
Perkins, Peter A., 202

Ready, Charles, 23

Reconstruction: small-town life during, 229–31

Reed's Bookstore (Murfreesboro), 125, 250 (n. 8)

Richmond (Virginia): domestic architecture of, 238 (n. 43); black population of, 266 (n. 112)

Richmond African Society, 257 (n. 68)

Rites of passage, 245 (n. 5); communal, 86, 87

Rituals: town-centered, 15, 20, 67, 72; fraternal, 79, 171, 181; Masonic, 85; of construction, 88; of visiting, 141–43. *See also* Ceremonies

River transportation, 60, 133

Roads: of Bedford County, 60, 61; John Spence on, 60, 242 (n. 52); macadamized, 61–62; of Middle Tennessee, 168; of Rutherford County, 242 (n. 48); impact of country, 242 (n. 51). *See also* Turnpikes

Roberts, Warren E., 238 (n. 44)

Roberts and Green (firm), 64

Robertson, James, 194

Robinson, Hugh, 18, 29, 240 (n. 11)

Romantic Revival, 234 (n. 2)

Rotundo, E. Anthony, 255 (n. 18)

Rucker, Joanna, 67, 70–71, 243 (n. 82); on fraternal organizations, 74; on illuminations, 245 (n. 107)

Rucker, Sarah, 71

Rutherford, Griffith, 21

Rutherford County (Tenn.): establishment of county seat, 17–20; creation of, 21; brick courthouse of, 40; road system of, 242 (n. 48); slave population of, 258 (n. 14), 259 (n. 15)

Rutman, Darrett, 5, 234 (n. 14)

Saloons, 101, 171

Sawmills, 35

Schultz, Stanley, 257 (n. 68)

Scott, Martin, 198

Seamstresses, 135; itinerant, 130

Seasonal festivals, 245 (n. 5)

Second Bank of the United States, 68, 68–69

Segregation, 231; in townscapes, 149, 260 (n. 27); in county seats, 204; and social distance, 214, 262 (n. 50), 263 (n. 83); in commerce, 229; in antebellum cities, 260 (n. 28). *See also* Race; Spatial organization

Semidependence: of young men, 158–65; of slaves, 159

Serenaders, 171–74, 178, 185, 257 (n. 62)

Shelbyville (Tenn.): establishment of, 4; developmental phases of, 10; courthouse square of, 25; central block plan of, 29, 31, 234 (n. 18); Main Street of, 31; courthouse of, 41, 114, 238 (n. 55), 249 (n. 76); incorporation of, 43, 59; population of, 47, 49, 240 (n. 4), 254 (nn. 16–17); turnpike to, 61, 62, 133, 242 (n. 54); merchants of, 64; 1848 Whig rally in, 76, 77–79, 80; as commercial center, 90–91; rail service to, 91–92; prosperity of, 94; townscape of, 94, 114, 138–39; Belmont Street, 107; weaving factory of, 134; female residents of, 138, 142–43; serenades in, 172; slave population of, 196, 200, 250 (n. 15), 255 (nn. 20–21), 259 (nn. 19, 21); slave ordinances of, 218; fires in, 219–20; universities of, 246 (n. 6); free blacks of, 259 (n. 25); slaveholders of, 261 (nn. 35, 37)

Shelbyville Expositor, 91, 142, 249 (n. 76)

Shelbyville Female Academy, 115, 146, 253 (n. 78)

Shelbyville plan, 25, 29, 234 (n. 18), 237 (n. 25)

Shelton, David, 54–55, 131, 132

Shelton, Virginia, 1, 243 (n. 65); on double houses, 54–55; on turnpikes, 62; arrival in Murfreesboro, 89; piano of, 90, 137, 246 (n. 13); on railroads, 90, 91; domestic renovation by, 99, 104–5, 106–7, 209; and Maney family, 103;

household management of, 131–32, 136; garden of, 136, 139–40; on visiting, 141, 142, 207, 208; boarders of, 162–64, 256 (n. 36); on temperance movement, 177–78; on Union University, 180–81; water supply of, 207; hiring of slaves by, 211–12

Shelton, William: at Union University, 89, 131; domestic renovations by, 104–5; at Appollonian Society, 140; boarders of, 162–64, 256 (n. 36); on temperance, 177; hiring of slaves by, 211–12; property of, 248 (n. 59)

Shenandoah Valley: plantation economy of, 20; towns of, 25; settlement system of, 235 (n. 7); trade with Philadelphia, 236 (n. 21)

Shofner, John, 46–47, 133; on transportation, 60; on ladies' fairs, 73–74; on Whig rallies, 76, 77–79

Slave families, 212–13, 221, 224, 263 (n. 78)

Slaveholders, 5, 6, 120; urban, 192, 194, 197, 200, 204, 259 (n. 24); use of child slaves by, 196; privacy of, 208, 258 (n. 11); authority of, 218–19; of Murfreesboro, 260 (n. 35); rural, 261 (nn. 40, 43)

Slave legislation, 200, 218, 220, 260 (n. 32), 261 (n. 36)

Slave markets, 194

Slaveowning, 218; patterns of, 197, 200; in Maury County, 202

Slaves: of Middle Tennessee, 2, 201–2, 221–23, 258 (n. 14), 259 (n. 15); in small towns, 5, 72, 120, 121, 187–224, 263 (n. 67); influence on townscapes, 9–10, 116; churches for, 14, 101, 120, 220–23, 229–30; role in town building, 17, 19, 34; in town ceremonies, 72, 243 (n. 82), 244 (n. 86); as brickmasons, 86; artisans among, 88; role in architectural transformation, 88; autonomy of, 120, 214–15, 219, 223; female, 130, 196–97, 250 (n. 15), 251 (n. 23), 259 (n. 20), 263 (n. 67); domestic, 131, 132,

206; drunkenness of, 174–75; prayer meetings of, 187, 190, 198, 213, 214, 215, 217, 222, 228; curfew for, 187, 217, 218, 220; in cities, 192, 194, 197, 204; hiring of, 192, 201, 208–14, 218, 263 (n. 75); on plantations, 193–94, 197, 201, 202; in county seats, 194, 196, 197; spatial integration of, 195, 204–20, 224, 229, 260 (n. 27), 262 (n. 63); dwellings of, 195, 258 (n. 11), 262 (n. 49); in censuses, 196, 200, 210, 250 (n. 15), 255 (nn. 20–21), 259 (nn. 19, 21), 261 (n. 35); rural, 197, 202–3, 261 (n. 40); manumission of, 200, 260 (n. 30), 261 (n. 36); accessibility of towns to, 202–3; communication of news, 205–6, 210; domestic space for, 208–9; community among, 210, 220–23; negotiating by, 213; privacy for, 214; testimony by, 216–17; clothing of, 241 (n. 41); male, 255 (nn. 20–21); in temperance movement, 257 (n. 68); auction of, 259 (n. 16); weddings of, 262 (n. 63); meetings of, 263 (n. 84). *See also* Race; Segregation

Smith, Franklin Gillette, 146

Smith, James Norman, 237 (n. 34)

Social reform movements, 234 (n. 2). *See also* Temperance movement

Sommerhill, William, 86

Sons of Temperance, 75, 83, 185, 256 (n. 56), 257 (n. 70); celebrations of, 171, 175; of Lebanon, 176

Soule Female College (Murfreesboro), 123, 125, 128–29, *149*, *182*, 253 (n. 78); teachers of, 130, 144; businessmen's interest in, 147; cost of, 150; buildings of, 180; opening of, 256 (n. 36)

South, antebellum: racial geography of, 2; society of, 2, 233 (n. 4); renovations of 1850s, 4, 87, 89; culture of, 10, 45, 236 (n. 21); town building in, 234 (n. 17); county seat plans of, 234 (n. 18); women's education in, 253 (n. 75); free blacks in, 260 (n. 25)

Tools, construction, 238 (n. 44)

Town and country, 240 (n. 3); distinctions between, 5, 234 (n. 12); architectural borders between, 58–59, 107; effect of turnpikes on, 59–63; party politics in, 80; in renovated townscape, 115; social distance between, 133; women's roles in, 133, 152; in South Carolina, 233 (n. 4); settlement system of, 235 (n. 7); political activism in, 245 (n. 110)

Town building: slaves' role in, 17, 19, 34; participants in, 19–20; and county formation, 21, 22, 235 (n. 8); grid plans for, 23–24; "houses" in, 46–59; in 1850s, 137; in the South, 234 (n. 17)

Town plats. *See* Grids

Towns, antebellum: rural aspects of, 2, 5; spatial intimacy of, 4, 197, 204–20; urban models for, 4, 10, 15, 45, 46, 63–71; as vernacular forms, 4; free blacks of, 5, 198; slaves' experience of, 5, 72, 187–224; versus cities, 5–6; measurement of size, 5–6, 234 (n. 12); boundaries of, 6, 246 (n. 24); cultural interpretation of, 6; economic function of, 7; cultural influence of, 7, 10, 148, 231; social structure of, 8, 133–43, 152, 165–78, 228–29; measures of development for, 8–9; relocation of, 9; developmental phases of, 9, 13–14; identity of, 10, 15, 72–81, 115, 119, 244 (n. 85); racial distinctions in, 15, 81, 130, 159, 193, 199, 262 (n. 50); social hierarchies of, 15, 63, 81; colonial era of, 20; street patterns of, 23–32; oral traditions of, 33; color schemes of, 37–38, 94; incorporation of, 43; aldermen of, 47; neighborhoods in, 50–51; networks between, 59–63; social life of, 70–71; fashion in, 71; warehouse districts of, 97, *98*, 247 (n. 37); demographics of, 120, 250 (nn. 14–15), 254 (nn. 16–17); slave population of, 120,

250 (n. 15); women's activities in, 130–33; factories of, 134; street improvement in, 142; value of female colleges to, 148–51; cultural goals of, 150–51; effect of economic cycles on, 165–66, 228; law and order in, 187–89, 214–20; white supremacy in, 195; accessibility to slaves, 202–3; churches of, 227; destruction of buildings in, 227; market function of, 235 (n. 6), 240 (n. 3); female population of, 250 (nn. 14–15)

Townscapes: urban models for, 4, 10, 15, 45, 46, 63–71; spatial organization of, 9, 14–15, 43, 47, 49, 50, 51, 70, 96; slaves' influence on, 9–10, 116; women's influence on, 9–10, 73–74, 115–16, 244 (n. 104); survival of, 10, 14; architectural vocabulary of, 14, 51, 56, 63, 101; of "houses," 14, 46–59, 95; commercial structures of, 38, 50; place of courthouse in, 42; permanent, 45; social context of, 46, 119; ceremonial aspects of, 72–81; spatial specialization in, 95–101, 111, 115; commercialization of, 133–34, 135, 151; cultural influence of, 147; spatial segregation in, 149, 260 (n. 27); feminization of, 151; privacy in, 164, 207, 208; spatial integration in, 195, 204–20, 229; control mechanisms in, 196; temporal boundaries in, 204–5; communal intimacy in, 204–8, 220; water supply of, 205, 206–7; labor relationships in, 210–11; post-emancipation, 229–31. *See also* Grids; Space

Townscapes, renovated, 14, 95; gentrification of, 100, 151; architectural vocabulary of, 101–12; dwellings of, 102–8; of Murfreesboro, 107–8; domesticity of, 112–16, 127, 129, 151, 164, 171; of Shelbyville, 114, 138–39; women's role in, 136–43, 151–52; young men in, 158–65; educational reform in, 170; temperance in, 176; female colleges in, 179, 180, 184; male colleges in, 179–

Williamson County (Tenn.): slave population of, 259 (n. 15); brick courthouse of, 40

Winchester (Tenn.), 234 (n. 18)

Women: influence on townscapes, 9–10, 73–74, 115–16, 244 (n. 104); role in town building, 17; in political rallies, 77, 78–79; role in renovated townscapes, 88, 136–43, 151–52; genteel, 119, 127, 141, 142–43, 151; school teachers, 130; transient, 130; as slaves, 130, 196–97, 250 (n. 15), 251 (n. 23), 259 (n. 20), 263 (n. 67); activities in town life, 130–33; household management of, 132–33, 135; leisure activities of, 135; networks of, 135–36, 152; as consumers, 138; gardening by, 138–41; visiting rituals of, 141–43; education for, 143–51, 253 (n. 75). *See also* Female colleges; Young women

Woodbury Turnpike, 62

Woodson, Eugene Minor, 266 (n. 7)

Yancey, Philip, 243 (n. 75)

Young men, 254 (nn. 16–17); role in townscape, 9, 115, 120, 158–65; access to streets, 119, 153; as college students, 119, 160, 181, 258 (n. 83); as boarders, 119, 161, 162–64; disorderly conduct of, 120, 165, 170, 181, 184; in town life, 121; autonomy of, 158, 159, 162; semidependence of, 158–65; fraternal organizations of, 164; idleness of, 170, 181; visiting by, 173–74; in temperance movement, 175, 257 (n. 71); education of, 178–84; integration into civic authority, 185; social sphere of, 255 (n. 18)

Young women: in town life, 121, 127, 158; as boarders, 137, 163, 253 (n. 82); concerts by, 149; as slaves, 152